11654507

Renaissances Before the Renaissance

Renaissances Before the Renaissance

CULTURAL REVIVALS OF LATE ANTIQUITY AND THE MIDDLE AGES

EDITED BY WARREN TREADGOLD

STANFORD UNIVERSITY PRESS
Stanford, California   1984

Stanford University Press
Stanford, California

© 1984 by the Board of Trustees of the
Leland Stanford Junior University

Printed in the United States of America
ISBN 0-8047-1198-4   LC 83-42793

Preface

This book addresses the problem of what happened to Western culture between the first century A.D. and the Renaissance. Today nearly all scholars would agree that this period was not one of continuous decline or stagnation, but instead saw several revivals of culture. It is now common practice to speak of "renaissances" during this time, such as the "twelfth-century renaissance" and the "Carolingian renaissance." To my knowledge, however, no one has yet attempted a comprehensive survey of these cultural revivals. This book offers the first such attempt.

The book's seven chapters were originally papers read in a seminar held at Stanford University during the autumn of 1981. The sessions were attended by a group of interested faculty and graduate students from Stanford, the University of California at Berkeley, and other neighboring institutions. Professor Walter Horn, of Berkeley, introduced the series with a paper on "Survival, Revival, and Transformation." This paper, originally delivered in 1979 at a Harvard University symposium, has recently been published in R. L. Benson and Giles Constable, eds., *Renaissance and Renewal in the Twelfth Century* (Cambridge, Mass., and Los Angeles, 1982). In its place I have written an Introduction that sets the seven cultural revivals treated here in their cultural and historical contexts. I have also added a brief Conclusion. The choice of subjects and the views expressed in the Introduction and Conclusion are my own, but the views expressed in the other papers are those of their authors.

My special thanks go to the Stanford University Program for Faculty Renewal, and particularly to its director, Wayne Vucinich, for giving me the opportunity to organize the original seminar.

W.T.

Contents

Contributors

George Hardin Brown received his Ph.D. from Harvard University and is now Associate Professor of English at Stanford University. He has written articles on paleography and on Old English language, literature, and culture. He is completing a book on the Venerable Bede and preparing a study of Christ as a warrior-lord in Old English literature.

Alan Cameron is Anthon Professor of Latin Language and Literature at Columbia University. His publications include *Claudian: Poetry and Propaganda at the Court of Honorius* (1970), *Porphyrius the Charioteer* (1973), *Circus Factions: Blues and Greens at Rome and Byzantium* (1976), *The Greek Anthology: From Meleager to Planudes* (forthcoming), and numerous articles on Greek, Roman, and Byzantine literature and history.

John J. Contreni is Professor of History at Purdue University. His publications include a translation of Pierre Riché's *Education and Culture in the Barbarian West from the Sixth to Eighth Centuries* (1976), *The Cathedral School of Laon from 850 to 930: Its Manuscripts and Masters* (1978), and *Codex Laudunensis 468: A Ninth-Century Guide to Virgil, Sedulius, and the Liberal Arts* (1984). He is currently completing an edition of the biblical glosses of John Scottus.

Stephen C. Ferruolo, Assistant Professor of History at Stanford University, received his training as a medievalist from Oxford and Princeton. He is the author of a forthcoming book, *The Origins of the University: The Schools of Paris and Their Critics, 1100–1215*, and is currently studying religious leaders and movements of the late twelfth and early thirteenth centuries.

B. P. Reardon studied at Glasgow, Cambridge, and Nantes, and taught in Canada and Wales before becoming Professor of Classics at the University of California, Irvine. His principal interest lies in late Greek literature, especially the romance, and his publications include *Courants littéraires grecs des IIe et IIIe siècles après J.-C.* (1971). In 1976 he organized the first International Conference on the Ancient Novel.

Ihor Ševčenko has held research appointments at Dumbarton Oaks and the Institute for Advanced Study, and visiting appointments at the University of Munich, the Università di Studi di Bari, and All Souls College, Oxford. He is currently Dumbarton Oaks Professor of Byzantine History and Literature, and Associate Director of the Ukrainian Research Institute, at Harvard University. He has written on Byzantine intellectual and literary history, Byzantine-Slavic cultural relations, Greek paleography, and Byzantine epigraphy.

Warren Treadgold received his Ph.D. from Harvard University, has taught at UCLA and Stanford University, and is now Assistant Professor of History at Hillsdale College, Michigan. His publications include *The Nature of the 'Bibliotheca' of Photius* (1980), *The Byzantine State Finances in the Eighth and Ninth Centuries* (1982), and various articles on medieval history and literature. He is now preparing a general history of Byzantium from 780 to 842.

Renaissances Before the Renaissance

Introduction:
Renaissances and Dark Ages

WARREN TREADGOLD

In Late Antiquity and the Middle Ages, the otherwise fairly steady progress of Western civilization in accumulating knowledge was interrupted several times. As school curricula became more restricted and fewer people received any education at all, people wrote and read less, and some of the literary works of earlier times were permanently lost. Eventually, each of these periods of relative ignorance ended with a new expansion of knowledge. The cultural setbacks, of varying severity, may be called "dark ages"; the cultural revivals, of varying vigor, may be called "renaissances."[1]

Plain as it is that these cultural phenomena occurred, and conveniently as these terms describe them, the labels "renaissance" and "dark age" still come in for a good deal of criticism. Certain scholars accept one of them but not the other; some reject both. The usual criticism is that the labels are confusing or overly subjective. Some scholars contend that a period should not be stigmatized as a dark age simply because it was deficient in literacy or classical culture; they adduce such examples as the charm of Irish mythology and the beauty of Merovingian jewelry to refute the "myth" of the Dark Ages. Others argue that a revival of classical culture is not enough to qualify a period as a renaissance. Slavish copying of classical models, they may observe, does not necessarily represent cultural progress and certainly need not produce a spirit of humanism like that which characterized the Renaissance proper. If we simply abandon the association of "dark age" and "renaissance" with classical learning, however, the former can come to mean any cultural development a given scholar dislikes, and the latter any development he approves of. "Renaissances" will multiply uncontrollably and meaninglessly, as modern critical literature expands.

We can conclude either that the labels should never be used or else that they should be used carefully, with their original connotations. If we choose the latter course, to speak of a "renaissance" or a "dark age" does not necessarily imply any more approval or disapproval than to speak of knowledge or ignorance of the Greek and Latin Classics. Few consider such knowledge a bad thing in itself, however badly its possessors may employ it and however meritorious other sorts of achievement may be. The words "dark age" and "renaissance" might still be confusing if they were taken to denote a time of total ignorance of the Classics, and a time with the attitude toward the Classics that specifically characterized the Renaissance proper; but such definitions are so obviously inappropriate to any part of late ancient or medieval history that to warn against them seems superfluous. A greater danger is the unwarranted assumption that knowledge of classical literature entails an acceptance of the values of classical culture. This assumption, however, has no necessary connection with the words "renaissance" and "dark age." (It is, however, closely connected with the word "humanism," which has two distinct but often woefully confused meanings: the study of secular literature and the adoption of a secular view of the world.)[2] Although by using the word "renaissance" a scholar can exaggerate the activities of one or two men into a full-scale cultural movement, this tendency too is really independent of the word.

We can therefore avoid confusion and undue subjectivity by defining a "renaissance" as any revival of knowledge of Greek and Latin literature after a "dark age," which can be defined as a setback to such knowledge. By this definition, widespread knowledge of the Classics would not make for a renaissance if in the previous period such knowledge had been similarly widespread; a continuous existence is not a rebirth or revival. Admittedly, it can be difficult to decide when a cultural movement should no longer be called a renaissance but simply a continuation of an established trend—unless and until a clear-cut cultural decline set in. Still, to talk about a "renaissance" that lasted for five centuries—as did the higher level of Greek culture established by the Second Sophistic—seems to stretch the meaning of the word excessively. A reasonable place to draw the line is when the main rediscoveries of earlier literature ended, although writers may have continued to exploit these rediscoveries in new ways long thereafter.

Of course, the label "renaissance" has often been applied to revivals not only of secular Greek and Latin literature but also of vernacular literature, theology, and especially art. When vernacular literature existed and was influenced by literature in the classical languages, as it usually was, it should plainly be included in the definition of a "renaissance." For literary historians, however, it makes sense to exclude theology and art, simply because advances or declines in literary knowledge seem to have had no uniform or inevitable influence on theology or art. Such a lack of parallel development may seem strange in view of the debts that much Christian theology owed to classical philosophy and rhetoric and that much late ancient and medieval art owed to classical models. Sometimes a parallel is clear: the theologians of the Carolingian period did use their improved knowledge of Latin grammar and rhetoric when they wrote, and the classicizing tendencies of the fourth century in the Latin West were expressed in both literature and art.

Yet artistic and theological "renaissances" fall into rather different patterns from strictly literary ones. Major theologians such as Gregory the Great and John of Damascus lived in times that can only be called dark ages with respect to secular learning. The Second Sophistic, crucial though it was as a literary movement, cannot properly be called an artistic movement at all; and some artistic movements—the "Theodosian renaissance," for example—had no real parallel in literature. Consequently, even though theology and art sometimes do fit into the pattern set by secular literature, any effort to lump all three together into the same developmental scheme would frequently distort the history of each. Here, then, our primary

concern will be with Greek and Latin literature apart from theology.

By our definition of a renaissance, our story starts with the
Greek and Latin Classics that the renaissances rediscovered.
The period of the original development of ancient literature is
indicated fairly accurately by the selection of Greek and Latin
texts that are usually counted as Classics today. This literature
began with Homer in Greek, probably in the eighth century
B.C. The fifth century B.C. was the high point of Greek drama,
and to a lesser extent of Greek historiography, but the development of philosophy and oratory alone would be enough to
show that Greek literature retained great vitality during the
fourth century. Hellenistic literature—that written under Alexander the Great and especially under his successors as kings
of the Greek world—is less highly regarded by most modern
classicists, though Renaissance scholars had a higher opinion
of it; especially before much of it was lost, it was large in
bulk and often very learned. Greek literature remained the focus of classical civilization until rather later than it is represented in the modern canon, which closes roughly with the
death of Theocritus about 250 B.C. In the late second century,
Polybius wrote his great history in Greek; among early Latin
writers, Plautus and Terence were largely translators of Menander and other Greek comedists, and as late as the early first
century Lucretius was mainly an interpreter of Greek Epicure-
anism.

Latin did not become the more important literary language
until the first century B.C. It was then that authors like Cicero
and Catullus, although they were heavily influenced by Greek
literature and even translated it sometimes, created a substantially independent Latin literature, while Greek letters receded
into the cultural background of the Mediterranean world.
Rome's subsequent "Golden Age" of Virgil and Horace was a
high point for its literature, and its later "Silver Age" of Tacitus and Juvenal showed, as the name implies, only a slight falling off in achievement. After the middle of the second century
A.D., however, when the modern canon ends with the death of

Suetonius about 140, both the quality and the quantity of Latin literature fell off abruptly.

Such was the period of the original cultural life that in the Renaissance proper was supposedly reborn in its full vigor. There is at least one rather striking difference, however, between the cultural vitality of the Renaissance and that of classical times. Unlike the Renaissance, which led to increasingly spectacular progress in learning and literary production, classical culture peaked, declined, and was followed by those dark ages. After a series of brilliant innovations—including the virtual invention of tragedy, comedy, history, epic and lyric poetry, oratory, philosophy, and science as we know them— Greek literature began to lose its inventiveness. Later, the Roman genius for creative adaptation of Greek literature, after some impressive triumphs, also began to fail.

During the Hellenistic period, the major genres of Greek literature gradually gave way to minor genres: epic poetry to didactic poetry, lyric poetry to epigrams, comedy to mime, oratory to rhetoric, history to antiquarian collections, and living philosophy and science to compilations of earlier work. The pattern for Rome was not entirely dissimilar, in that from the Silver Age onward, rhetoric and compilations of earlier material gradually became the main genres of a diminished Latin literature. Though such later works and the surviving schools and libraries maintained Greek and Latin culture in their way, the spirit of Periclean Athens and Augustan Rome proved ephemeral. Even the scholarship of the early Hellenistic period progressed only so far, became codified, and ceased to make significant new discoveries. It was almost as if first Greek and then Latin literature had hit an invisible ceiling—a ceiling that was not, however, a barrier for the Renaissance.[3]

Current explanations for the decline of classical culture are not fully satisfactory. Even in ancient times, men understood that Athenian democracy and the Roman Republic had provided the law courts and festivals that supported oratory and drama, so that when these forms of government declined their corresponding forms of literature declined as well. Both ancients and moderns have often generalized this explanation to make the "loss of freedom" of the Greeks and Romans the cause of their literary decline. Unfortunately for this general theory, such authors as Pindar and Aristotle enjoyed the patronage of despots, and the courts of Ptolemy Philadelphus and Augustus proved congenial to the production of great literature, though perhaps not to the production of great oratory and drama.

Another cause of decline could have been that the great works of classical literature came to form such an intimidating legacy that successors despaired of writing anything comparable. Yet, as much as they respected the Classics, the authors of the Renaissance and of much of the Middle Ages were not so intimidated. Still another cause of decline might be that the ancients never developed what might be called an idea of progress; in particular, they showed little interest in technology, a field in which the Middle Ages were markedly more imaginative.[4] But this failure does not seem to be directly related to literary progress.

Probably the severest limitation on the development of ancient literature was the ancient system of education, which from the fifth-century Sophists on tended to be stereotyped and rhetorical. The study of literature was largely confined to secondary education, and there to a few authors who were much the same for all students and mostly chosen for their style. The private reading of the educated man seems to have continued more or less in the course set by his schooling. Quite early the number of standard authors was made up of the likes of Homer, Euripides, Demosthenes, and Menander, and later writers could neither hope to find room in the canon, nor have much chance of lasting importance if they did not. Accordingly, authors came to write only minor and ephemeral literature, which they did not expect to last, or scholarly compilations that might find some place as guides to earlier writers.

Higher education provided somewhat greater scope for literary endeavor in the places and for the subjects in which it was available. Thus the several advanced schools of philosophy in Athens provided philosophers with the opportunity to make original contributions as late as the first century B.C.; even later, various medical schools made advances in medical literature possible. Alexandria's comparatively large educational institutions fostered new writing in science and philology down to the end of the Ptolemaic period, and even sustained new creative literature throughout the third century B.C. But the few scholars at the specialized schools could themselves absorb only so much knowledge, and in any case formed a very small reading public. The Romans, in starting up a whole new literature in another language, made room for many new literary works. Soon, however, the roster of standard Latin authors was also filled up, probably somewhat sooner than in Greek because educated Romans devoted much of their time and interest to standard Greek authors. Of course, a lone bibliophile rummaging in the great Library at Alexandria could still discover and read texts far off the beaten track. But the nature of ancient education severely restricted the number of works that would be read at all widely.[5]

Greek culture had already begun to suffer from this limited capacity to absorb literature before the Roman conquest dealt it another blow. The last major Greek author before the break was perhaps Polybius, the historian of Rome's conquests who was himself deported to Rome after Macedon fell in 167 B.C. Though Greek culture took its captors captive in the sense that it provided much of the inspiration for Roman literature, annexation by Rome quickly diminished the cultural importance of the Greek cities. Coming after two centuries of pronounced decline, the first century A.D. was a particularly bleak time for Greek literature—unless we count Jewish and Christian writers outside the Greek mainstream, such as Philo, Josephus, and St. Paul. The fire that destroyed Alexandria's Library in 48 B.C. almost certainly caused the first substantial and permanent losses of Greek literature. After the transportation of Pergamum's smaller library to Alexandria as a partial replacement, Pergamum no longer counted as a major cultural center.[6] At Athens most of the philosophical schools became extinct, and the rest dormant.[7] The center of literary activity and patronage for the Mediterranean basin had plainly shifted to Rome, and though some Greeks went to Rome and wrote Greek there, they could hardly hope to compete with the Latin authors of the Golden and Silver ages.

Shortly after the close of the Silver Age, Rome ran into serious political and military trouble of its own. The difficulties
began in the reign of Marcus Aurelius with a plague and a German invasion in A.D. 166. The assassination of Marcus's in-
competent son Commodus, in 192, began almost a hundred
years of political instability. Military revolts and civil wars
were further aggravated by German and Persian invasions. The
fiscal collapse that followed severely damaged the Empire's administration, economy, and urban life. In the third century the
Empire, especially its Western part, came close to falling to the
invaders. Though all this did not have to lead to a decline in
literature, the general disruption of patronage and civilized life
did not do Latin literature any good; presumably, it deepened
the literary decline that was already evident. In that decline's
initial form, writers turned back to archaic Latin for their stylistic models, a trend that not only proved unproductive but
led Latin literature into a virtual dark age. Yet it corresponded
to a similar, slightly earlier trend in Greek letters, by means of
which, rather surprisingly, that literature resumed its place as
the leading literature of the Mediterranean world.

This second-century revival of Greek culture was, by the definition of "renaissance" proposed here, the first renaissance of
Western civilization. It proved a deep and durable one, but it is
often underrated today. It does not even have a satisfactory
name. Its usual name, the "Second Sophistic," refers strictly
speaking only to rhetorical works, whereas the whole movement included much more—notably the biographies of Plutarch, the satires of Lucian, and most of the extant Greek novels. In this movement, Greek writers seemed suddenly to have
freed themselves from the constraints that had been inhibiting
their predecessors for nearly four hundred years. Indeed, in
spite of the political problems of the third century A.D., which
affected the Greek East only a little less than the Latin West,
the continued expansion of Greek literature was not really
threatened again until the later sixth century. Greek literature
was still strong in the reign of Justinian (527–65), when Procopius wrote his masterly histories; but since no decline pre-

ceded Justinian, to speak as some do of a "Justinianic renaissance" seems inappropriate.

Several developments in the second century allowed Greek literature to make this partial escape from a closed literary canon and an inflexible educational system. First, the authors of the Second Sophistic felt that literature should be written only in the pure Attic dialect of ancient Athens. They rejected earlier authors who had written in other dialects, and thus made room for their own works, written in the revived Attic that now became and remained the approved form of Greek. This reexamination of the criterion for standard authors brought some flexibility to the whole idea of a literary canon and even made possible a new genre, the novel, as long as it was written in the right style. Second, higher education revived as new chairs were founded for professors of philosophy, rhetoric, and other subjects at Athens, Alexandria, and elsewhere; the result was a larger and more diverse cultural community. Finally, beginning in the third century, many Christian writers began to incorporate elements of Greek philosophy and rhetoric into their writing, bringing still more expansion and diversity. In one way or another, between the second and sixth centuries A.D. the ancient world became able to accommodate more Greek literature than before, and that literature expanded accordingly.[8]

The Latin dark age lasted from the middle of the second century to the middle of the fourth, but once the Empire's political and military crisis began to abate, a Latin renaissance set in as well. It too involved a rejection of some authors previously considered standard, but in this case it was the archaic Latin authors, so admired in the preceding period, who were devalued, while Silver Age writers became the new literary models. Like the Greek East, the Latin West now provided an audience for new literature—first in Gaul, where the schools were particularly numerous and lively, and then in Rome itself. The literary opportunities attracted not only Latin writers but Greeks who were willing and able to write in Latin, of whom the most important were the poet Claudian and the historian Ammianus Marcellinus. Christians were active in this Latin literary revival from the start; Sts. Jerome and Augustine must be counted as classical scholars and major contributors to Latin literature of the fifth century, as Sts. Gregory of Nazianzus and John Chrysostom had been to the Greek literature of the fourth century. The barbarian invasions notwithstanding, Italy in the early sixth century produced the philosopher and Hellenist Boethius, whose *Consolation of Philosophy* is sometimes considered the last Latin "Classic."[9]

The Second Sophistic and the fourth-century Latin revival, with their continuations that lasted into the sixth century, were complementary movements. The first influenced the second, and both took place within the same Roman Empire and shared many characteristics. The literature produced in them rounded out the canon of Greek and Latin Classics as these were known up to the end of the nineteenth century. Yet, the works of these first two renaissance movements differed somewhat from those of the original flowerings of Greek and Roman literature. Inevitably, they were more derivative. They largely lacked the old pagan or secular view of humanity, along with the traditional forms of drama, oratory, and lyric poetry. The oratory and poetry of the time were more public, and mostly centered on the imperial court; though their stylistic virtuosity was greatly admired at the time, most modern critics find them artificial.

By contrast, historical writing became more serious and impartial, as it paid less attention to personalities and more to public events. Thus Procopius's *Wars* and Ammianus's *Res Gestae* come closer to our modern idea of what history should be than do the works of Herodotus and Tacitus. In philosophy and theology, moreover, the third through fifth centuries saw the Golden Age of patristic literature and the highly sophisticated synthesis of Neoplatonism. By the sixth century, Christians had completed their takeover of all forms of classical culture; the literature they produced in the process was creative, personal, and learned, yet it seemed to have given up little or nothing of older achievements.

Then came the Dark Age par excellence. In the West an erosion of education set in not long after the Western Empire disintegrated completely in 480. The Western Empire's disappearance, however slowly its effects made themselves felt, proved in the end a very bad thing for Latin culture. The governmental machinery that had required a large, urban, and educated elite gradually ran down in the hands of barbarian rulers, who often wished to maintain it but could never do so completely. The old Roman elite slowly shrank and became barbarized, and finally secular education disappeared, along with the secular educated class it had served. The Church maintained some parish, episcopal, and monastic schools, but their total enrollment was smaller than that of the old secular schools and their curriculum generally excluded secular literature; it was often limited to the Psalter.

The demise of the Western imperial court also deprived Latin culture of its most important center. Though in some places, such as Spain, learning declined more gradually than in others, all eventually felt the loss of the literary patronage and central meeting place that the imperial court had provided. Justinian's reconquest of North Africa in 533 probably helped things there: Corippus was still writing Latin verse of a high standard about 570. But in a Greek-dominated Empire, Latin Africa, with Rome and the other scraps of reconquered Italy that the Empire was able to hold, soon became a cultural backwater. The measure of the disaster is that the great majority of the Latin literature that was ever lost disappeared between 550 and 750, when secular texts were left uncopied and were often even erased or discarded.[10]

In the East the Empire survived as what we now call the Byzantine Empire, but it too suffered a cultural decline. Although this decline was considerably briefer and less severe than the one the West experienced somewhat earlier, it still deserves to be called the "Byzantine Dark Ages." Some detect a decline in cultural vitality as early as 550, and nearly all agree that a decline accompanied the political and military disasters that began in 602; but the authors of the Empire continued writing secular poetry and history in correct classical Greek until about 650. Then for over a century, scarcely any secular literature was produced, and the copying of manuscripts fell off almost as drastically as in the West. The East, unlike the West,

maintained some secular schools and an educated civil service
of laymen, but this bureaucracy lost much of its power and
prestige to the army during the Empire's military tribulations
in the seventh and eighth centuries.

Theological literature survived these mostly contemporane-
ous Eastern and Western dark ages, but it too suffered notice-
ably from the general decline of education. Even the greatest
theologians of the time, Gregory the Great in the West and
Maximus Confessor in the East, wrote with much less sophistication of both thought and language than had their great patristic predecessors. Those earlier authors, like the readers for
whom they wrote, had studied classical philosophy and style at
secular schools. Once these schools no longer provided that
knowledge, most readers could not understand much of Augustine or Gregory of Nazianzus; still less could most writers em-
ulate them. Most of the remaining schools at last taught little
more than basic literacy with only the Bible as a text. Few students attained real competence in reading and writing classical
Greek and Latin—both complicated languages no longer spoken in their old forms. With such disadvantages, which applied
to the West far more than to the East, no literary culture of any
sort could thrive.

The first significant cultural improvement, which it might
be somewhat hyperbolic to call a "renaissance," appeared, curiously enough, in a place far away from the Mediterranean:
the British Isles. The Anglo-Saxon invaders almost eradicated
Christianity and Latin culture in Great Britain, but between
600 and 650 both were reintroduced by missionaries from
Rome and from Ireland, where an idiosyncratic form of monastic culture had flourished since about 450. The arrival from
Rome in 669 of the scholarly missionary Theodore of Tarsus (a
Byzantine by origin) proved a turning point in the development
of education in England. Over the following century, English
monastic and episcopal schools multiplied and produced several important scholars. The most distinguished of these, Bede,
wrote an ecclesiastical history that is still recognized as a masterpiece. This cultural revival, sometimes called the "North-

umbrian renaissance," did not extend beyond a small group of churchmen and scarcely touched upon secular literature. Nonetheless, it proves that church schools could maintain a moderately high level of culture.

In the early eighth century, Anglo-Saxon missionaries also founded monasteries on the Continent. These became leading cultural centers and soon participated in a broader-based, more substantial revival of learning: the Carolingian renaissance. This movement may be said to begin about 751 with the reign of Pepin the Short, the first Carolingian king of the Franks, and to end in the late ninth century with the decline of the Carolingian kingdoms. It was a revival largely planned by the Carolingian rulers, often with the help of Anglo-Saxon scholars. Their purpose was not specifically to promote literary study, but rather to educate priests and monks. In the process, however, the Carolingians greatly improved the educational system of the Western European Continent and brought about a surge of copying of manuscripts that preserved most of the earlier secular and Christian literature that has survived. The scholars of the Carolingian period distinguished themselves not only as educators but as authors; probably the best-known figures are the historian Paul the Deacon, the biographer Einhard, and the philosopher John Scottus Eriugena. The Carolingian renaissance never reestablished anything like the level of knowledge that had prevailed in Late Antiquity, but its system of schools did once again equip men to read and write standard classical Latin.

Not long after the beginning of the Carolingian renaissance, Byzantium staged its own cultural revival, commonly called the "Macedonian renaissance." The Macedonian dynasty of Byzantium, however, deserves far less credit for the revival of culture in the East than does the Carolingian dynasty for its revival in the West: in fact, the Byzantine cultural resurgence began in the late eighth century, whereas the first Macedonian emperor took power in 867 and the Macedonians who played the most important part in promoting scholarship reigned between 886 and 959. It was the old secular educated class, emerging from its temporary eclipse, that was primarily responsible for the revival. In a movement parallel to that in the West, Byzantine scholars now began to collect and copy earlier Greek literature—which was much more difficult to preserve than Latin literature because it had always been so much larger in bulk.

In Byzantium the task of rediscovery involved more editing, lexicography, and compiling than in the West, and this work tended to crowd out new writing. Some of the literary compilations of the Macedonian period, however, attained a certain distinction. Excerpts included in encyclopedic works such as the *Bibliotheca* of Photius and the anonymous *Suda* supply fundamental parts of our knowledge of Greek literature. By the eleventh and early twelfth centuries, the first phase of rediscovery was over; then Byzantine literature, reaching a stage of development comparable to that of Late Antiquity, produced the histories of Michael Psellus and Anna Comnena and other notable works of history, philosophy, and poetry. Some have spoken of a "Comnenian renaissance" in this period, since during most of it the Comnenian dynasty was in power. But brilliant though the time was, it followed no dark age; it was, rather, a continuation of the movement begun as the Macedonian renaissance.

Like the Second Sophistic and the fourth-century Latin revival, the Macedonian and Carolingian renaissances, with the latter's Anglo-Saxon prelude, were to some extent parallel developments, overlapping in time. The parallel is apt in that both movements brought major improvements in education and both included much rediscovery and copying of earlier literature, Christian and secular. Further, the writers of both movements, as if overpowered by the literature that they had rediscovered, tended to imitate the style and content of the Classics, among which they counted works of Late Antiquity. Their literary forms were therefore philology, epistolography, history, theology and philosophy of a generally conservative sort, and somewhat more original poetry.

Beyond this, however, the parallel between the Carolingian and Macedonian renaissances breaks down. The Carolingian renaissance was planned by crowned heads and carried out by churchmen trained at church schools; the Macedonian renaissance was primarily the spontaneous accomplishment of a lay elite trained at secular schools. The former began and ended at a substantially lower educational level than the latter. Scholars of the Carolingian period were intimidated by the seemingly unmatchable attainments of earlier writers; their Macedonian counterparts were much readier to criticize earlier Greek authors. Finally, despite Theodore of Tarsus's Byzantine origin and Eriugena's highly unusual knowledge of Greek, Byzantine influence on the Anglo-Saxon revival and Carolingian renaissance was inconsequential; and the West had virtually no influence on the Macedonian renaissance.

In fact, it was the Carolingian and Macedonian renaissances that first established the mutual independence of the cultures of Byzantium and the West. Before the eighth century, most of the culture that both East and West possessed had been inherited directly from the Mediterranean-wide Roman Empire, in which Greek literature had heavily influenced Latin and Latin literature had slightly influenced Greek. After the eighth century, although Byzantines and Latins often traded and sometimes fought with each other, they had no significant influence on each other's thinking or writing. The increasing estrangement between the Western and Byzantine churches that began in the ninth century is the measure of the change. After the Carolingian and Macedonian renaissances, the two sides could and did take pride in having developed new cultural traditions of their own.[11]

The second set of renaissance movements—the Anglo-Saxon revival, the Carolingian renaissance, and the Macedonian renaissance with its continuation into the eleventh and twelfth centuries—eventually ended in a new set of mainly military reverses. The Anglo-Saxon revival, which had partly spent itself in furthering the Carolingian renaissance, suffered from the effects of Viking raids and conquests through much of the ninth and tenth centuries. The Carolingian Empire disintegrated during the ninth century in a series of dynastic partitions and civil wars; and between the late ninth and the late tenth centuries, most of Western Europe was raided by Vikings, Saracens, or Magyars. The disruption caused by these raids and the general political disorganization of the times continued to hamper cultural progress until the middle of the eleventh century. In 1071 the Byzantines were severely defeated by the Seljuk Turks, and despite a temporary rally their Empire was in rapid decline by the later twelfth century. In 1204, in a catastrophe for the Byzantines, the Latins on the Fourth Crusade conquered and sacked Constantinople and set up various states of their own in parts of the old Empire. The Latin occupation of Constantinople lasted until 1261, when Greeks from a Byzantine successor state reoccupied the city.

Such military upheavals disrupted education and literature as they disrupted civilized life in general, so that at least the late ninth and the tenth centuries in the West are usually considered another dark age. Yet this age was much less dark than the one that had followed the dissolution of the Western Roman Empire. The number of schools did not shrink dramatically, and, apparently, little if any Latin literature was lost. Manuscripts were copied less frequently, but often enough to replace those that wore out or were destroyed. Literary study continued. Some have pointed out that the increased production of art at the court of the Ottonian emperors, often called the "Ottonian renaissance," had a counterpart in literary activity; they invariably cite the scholarship of Gerbert of Aurillac, whom Otto III made Pope Sylvester II (999–1003). This movement seems too narrowly based to be called a renaissance of general culture, however—unless perhaps we include in it the contemporary cultural activity in the monasteries, which had little to do with the Ottonian court.[12]

This dark age, therefore, resembled the decline that followed the great barbarian invasions less than it did the stagnation of Greek literature after the Roman conquest and of Latin literature after A.D. 150. The same is true of the cultural decline in Byzantium around the time of the Fourth Crusade. The destruction of Greek manuscripts in the sack of Constantinople does seem to have been serious, but the damage to the Byzantine educational system was less grave, because many scholars took refuge at the courts of the Greek successor states, especially at Nicaea. The Carolingian and Macedonian renaissances had evidently accomplished too much for these cultures to sink back to their prerenaissance levels. Before long, new recoveries began.

★

As before, the recovery of the West started in Anglo-Saxon England with a monastic revival, initiated this time by the embattled King Alfred. Between 871 and 899 Alfred not only patronized learning but also himself translated Latin works into Anglo-Saxon. In the tenth century the revival was institutionalized with the foundation of a number of reformed Benedictine monasteries and monastery schools. At the same time, Benedictine monastic reform was spreading on the Continent from the monastery of Cluny in Burgundy, founded in 910, and the monastery of Gorze in Lorraine, founded in 933. These monastic reforms continued their complicated course into the eleventh century. Taken together, the reformed Benedictine monasteries were the leading cultural centers of Western Europe at the time. Whether this fact makes the Benedictine reform movement in England or elsewhere a "renaissance" is debatable, however, since its literary production was not particularly large or outstanding. Still, like the first Anglo-Saxon cultural revival and its eighth-century missions on the Continent, the Benedictine reform of the tenth and early eleventh centuries created conditions in which a wider revival soon grew up.

This is known today as the twelfth-century renaissance, although many claim it actually began in the middle of the eleventh century. The most widely acknowledged of the pre-Renaissance renaissances, it was also the one that most resembled the Renaissance proper—not only in time and place but also in extent and originality. There were definitely more scholars working during the twelfth-century renaissance than in any period in either West or East since the barbarian invasions, and possibly even than in Greek or Roman Antiquity. They read and copied far more manuscripts than ever before, and rediscovered some Greek authors who were gradually being translated from Arabic versions. Twelfth-century scholars also wrote many new works, though still almost entirely in traditional genres. Nevertheless, the twelfth century saw new trends such as the increasingly critical-minded philology and theology of John of Salisbury and Peter Abelard and the increasingly secular-minded Latin Goliardic and courtly vernacular poetry. These works were something new, not because their authors had discovered new classical models but because they adapted earlier literature with a new freedom. Similarly momentous and new was the foundation in several places during the twelfth century of the first institutions in history that can strictly be called universities. Given that it was also a time of technological advance, commercial expansion, and foreign conquest, the twelfth-century renaissance was substantially different from and more vigorous than any previous cultural revival.

By contrast, as the Byzantines began to recover from the ravages of the Fourth Crusade, they staged a more traditional sort of cultural revival: the Palaeologan renaissance. Even after the twelfth century, Byzantine scholars in every field knew more of what had been known in Antiquity than did Western scholars, and under the Palaeologan dynasty (1261–1453), they produced the most advanced classical scholarship of medieval times. The understanding that some Palaeologan scholars showed of classical authors—Demetrius Triclinius of the dramatists George Gemistus Plethon of Plato—required an intellectual effort that was original in its way. Yet this immense knowledge of Antiquity was really too much for the tiny group of Palaeologan scholars to preserve and exploit properly, as certain of them complained themselves. They were hampered not only by their small numbers but also by the dwindling of their Empire's resources and by a rising anticlassical movement in their Church. From the fourteenth century on, many Palaeologan scholars migrated to Renaissance Italy, where they found more favor and greater rewards than at home. After Constantinople fell to the Ottoman Turks in 1453, Byzantine secular learning did not long survive the demise of the imperial court that had supported it. The Greek East quickly sank into the most profound dark age of its history, from which it was finally to emerge only with Western help.

Did the West enter anything like a dark age after the twelfth-century renaissance? The answer depends mostly on one's opinion of Scholasticism. To be sure, the Mongol invasion in the thirteenth century and the Black Death in the fourteenth did damage, but that damage did not affect culture directly. Knowledge of the Greek Classics was certainly spreading through the West in these centuries—first, knowledge of

Greek philosophy and science, translated from the Arabic, and later, knowledge of Greek literature in Greek, brought by Byzantine scholars. Scholasticism did not favor the study of classical works on their own terms or of classical poetry at all, but with its great debt to Aristotle, it was hardly anticlassical; and as a comprehensive, complex, and ingenious system of thought, it cannot fairly be called anti-intellectual. It was much more a continuation of the twelfth-century renaissance than a repudiation. The name of the Renaissance proper obviously does not imply that it was a rebirth of the spirit of the twelfth century after a thirteenth-century dark age but rather that it was a rebirth of the spirit of Antiquity after the relative darkness of the whole Middle Ages. This implication is largely correct. The scholars of the fourteenth- to early-sixteenth-century Renaissance did try harder than those of any earlier cultural revival to study the Classics without the influence of intermediaries—though they always included works of Late Antiquity among those Classics and showed considerable respect for many Byzantine literary productions.

Such were the ups and downs of cultural history during the long gap between classical Antiquity and the Renaissance. Plainly, not all the dark ages were equally dark, nor were all the revivals equally brilliant. Considering only the level of secular learning, and discounting certain variations among different fields of knowledge, we may estimate that the Second Sophistic and the fourth-century Latin revival essentially made up for the modest declines that had preceded them. By the fifth century A.D., the well-educated of the East or West knew about as much literature, philosophy, and science as had the well-educated of any earlier time; and though some earlier works were unavailable or neglected, some important new works had been written. After the sixth century, the level of knowledge in the East fell well below its high point in Antiquity. By the eleventh century, however, the Macedonian renaissance made up most of the difference and later the Palaeologan renaissance filled in most of the gaps that remained.

In the West, after the sixth century, secular learning was set back very far, although at different rates in different places, and the Carolingian renaissance and the Anglo-Saxon revivals, in the countries where they spread, recovered only part of the ground that had been lost. Then Western cultural history becomes harder to evaluate. It is difficult to compare twelfth-century scholarship with that of Antiquity or of the other revivals, because twelfth-century scholars, though ignorant of much literature, philosophy, and science that had been known before, made substantial original contributions of their own to these fields. Similarly, although it is safe to say that the learned men of the Renaissance proper knew more about most subjects than any of their predecessors, such a comparison ignores some important differences in the character of the knowledge involved and the use made of it.

The most striking of these differences was that the twelfth-century renaissance succeeded partly, and the Renaissance proper succeeded spectacularly, in passing beyond the limits that had confined cultural advances throughout Antiquity, Late Antiquity, and the Byzantine Middle Ages. The renaissances of Late Antiquity and at Byzantium revived, along with the earlier culture, its resistance to further progress. Some scholars, unable to discover some earlier works and finding others not to their taste, did produce new secular literature—in particular, they commented on and imitated earlier works and continued earlier historiography down to their own times. The rise of monasteries and other ecclesiastical institutions also provided an audience for new Christian literature, often bringing indirect benefits to secular learning as well. Even new and original literature occasionally slipped in, such as the novels of the Second Sophistic or the poetry of the continuation of the Macedonian renaissance.

Nonetheless, the secular learning of Late Antiquity and in Byzantium did not typically advance beyond the achievements of the ancients, except perhaps by doing the sort of thing that they had done but doing it better. Even Greek Christian literature became markedly less original after the fourth century, as the great patristic writings came to be considered to form a canon in their own right. Such restraint upon creativity recalls that which brought the spontaneous falling off of classical literature in the first place. The causes too seem similar: the prestige of the Classics, the absence of an idea of progress, and above all the restricted ability of a traditional system of education to create a reading public for more literature. When substantially more, or more original, works were written, they either pushed out earlier Classics or, more often, found few readers.

The scholars of the Carolingian renaissance and the Anglo-Saxon cultural revivals did not have to deal with such problems. The secular school system of the West had disappeared long before them, and with it a great deal of earlier literature—including virtually all Greek literature, which every well-educated reader of Latin had used to read as well. By the twelfth century, when more Western literature began to appear than the traditional schools could handle, a great expansion of learning was made possible by the foundation of the first universities. This institutional innovation came more naturally in the medieval West precisely because the West lacked well-established secular schools of the classical type. Such schools never developed into true universities, however much they expanded or multiplied at Athens, Alexandria, and Constantinople.

The later medieval West also had one unequivocal advantage over the other milieus that produced cultural revivals: much more than any of them, it was an expanding society, with a growing population and economy that tended to encourage innovation of all kinds. The Renaissance proper emerged in a society that, at least over the long run, shared the same advantage. By contrast, the cultural revivals of Late Antiquity occurred amid military and economic crises, the Palaeologan renaissance in an increasingly desperate political and military situation, the Anglo-Saxon revivals in times of poverty and invasion, and the Macedonian and Carolingian renaissances in periods of comparatively moderate economic expansion.

Whatever the attendant circumstances it should be stressed that all of these revivals were mainly the work of their own societies, not of outside influences. Western emperors patronized the Second Sophistic, Eastern authors joined in the fourth-century Latin revival, and Anglo-Saxon scholars taught during the Carolingian renaissance—but none of these influences was a determining cause. The first and principal audience of the Second Sophistic was Greek; the schools of Gaul were producing new Latin literature in the fourth century before Greek writers arrived at Rome; and Carolingian scholars came from Gaul, Germany, and Italy as well as England. The influence of East and West on each other's cultural revivals between Late Antiquity and the Renaissance was negligible. Outside forces in the form of invasions and conquests often contributed to the dark ages in the East and West, but when these cultures revived during the Middle Ages, each revived itself. Eventually by beginning a new cultural revival after each setback, and finally by receiving scholars and texts from the last Byzantine renaissance, the West emerged from its cycle of dark ages and renaissances into a Renaissance that no dark age would follow.

CHAPTER I

The Second Sophistic

B. P. REARDON

The phenomenon to be discussed in this chapter is the re-newed and extensive Greek literary activity that began with the Flavian emperors in the last decades of the first century A.D. and was at its height in the second century.[1] The term "Second Sophistic" is sometimes used, loosely, as a general label for that activity, of which strictly speaking it is one facet. Judgments have varied on the nature and quality of this literature. The topic will be discussed in the following pages, but for the present we may observe that there is reason enough to accept the term "renaissance" that has sometimes been used,[2] inasmuch as the period illustrates the central ideas of revival, survival, and transformation. I do not propose to discuss other aspects of the culture of the period, such as its art or architecture; the renaissance is primarily a literary phenomenon. It will be desirable, however, in due course, to glance briefly at some more general features of the age. The political fact of the Roman Empire, the psychological fact of religious ferment, the cultural fact of the development of the Greek language—these were part of the fabric of second-century Greek culture, and must be built into any analysis of it.

The term "Second Sophistic" was invented by the early third-century Greek writer Philostratus, the historian of the movement it denotes.[3] He used it in the sense not of a revival but of a second stage, a development of the original Sophistic movement of the late fifth century B.C. That movement had seen the spread of systematic rationalism, sceptical, relativist, destructive of conventional values. It engaged the interest of Euripides and Thucydides, and produced serious thinkers like Protagoras and Gorgias, whose doctrines Socrates and Plato were to challenge; it proclaimed that, in the phrase of Protagoras, "man is the measure of all things"; and some of its practitioners maintained that the supreme skill was skill in persuading, skill with words, the art of rhetoric. These men were philosophers, who employed the spoken word; that happens to be almost a literal translation of Philostratus's phrase for them in the opening words of his *Lives of the Sophists*. The rhetorical skills taught by the first Sophistic were of course put to practical use in the democratic politics of the fifth and fourth centuries. But in the latter part of the fourth century, says Philostratus, sophistic rhetoric changed its nature (*Lives* 481); it now occupied itself with, for instance, verbal sketches of human character-types—such as the rich man, the poor man, the warrior, the despot—and "particular topics based on history." In other words, "sophistic" orators dealt, now, no longer with real political or social issues, but with what we might call "occasional" topics, a kind of belles lettres; they became littérateurs of the spoken word. Philostratus attributes this change of direction to Aeschines, the political opponent of Demosthenes, when Aeschines was in exile in Rhodes. The movement should not be called the "new" Sophistic, he says, because it was old; "second" is a better term.

The historian of the movement thus anchors the second-century revival firmly in the classical age. In fact there are some major literary-historical problems connected with this genealogy. Their nature can be indicated briefly, though they cannot be examined in any detail here. One concerns the history of rhetoric in the period from the fourth century B.C. to the first century A.D.; we know a certain amount about it, but not enough, and one of the problems is that Philostratus almost totally ignores this whole Hellenistic period, four hundred years. He simply jumps from Aeschines to Nicetes of Smyrna, who lived under Vespasian and Domitian. We should like to know why. The art of rhetoric most certainly did not disappear; far from it. It would be understandable if Philostratus made the Second Sophistic *begin* with Nicetes; but as we have seen, he goes out of his way to set its beginnings in the classical period. We shall have reason to find that fact significant. He is by no means the only writer of his time who behaves in that manner; in fact there are very few who do not. The second problem lies in Philostratus's conception of what constitutes sophistic in the first place. For again he goes out of his way to say that philosophers are not really sophists at all (*Lives* 479, 492). Philosophers, it seems, are essentially people who ask questions; sophists are people who speak in public on similar matters as if they knew the answers (*Lives* 480). A reasonable distinction, one might think, until one observes that using that criterion Philostratus treats Dio Chrysostom, Dio the Golden-Mouthed, as a philosopher, and Protagoras as a sophist. Now Dio, intelligent as he is, is something less than a philosophical luminary, whereas Plato himself took Protagoras seriously enough to write a long dialogue disagreeing with him. Perhaps what one should conclude from this is that Philostratus himself was no great intellect. Again, we shall find that fact significant.

All of this is to say that the source is vitiated, as far as the Second Sophistic proper is concerned. Scholarship, one might say, is contaminated with literature; perhaps not for the first time, and certainly not for the last. Philostratus had no wish to be a scholar. We have to use him, as we have to use Plutarch, for purposes a certain distance from his own intentions.

Be these things as they may, what *was* the Second Sophistic? It was a literary movement whose staple diet consisted of rhetorical declamations on unreal themes—unreal in the sense that they had no connection with contemporary life. The practice is perhaps more familiar in Roman culture of the early Empire; this rhetorical tradition lies behind Seneca's tragedies, for instance. Its source is, of course, Hellenistic Greek rhetorical education. The standard fare is declamation on themes drawn from classical Greek history, or on fictitious and farfetched legal issues. To take an example of the first type, one of the stars of the movement, Polemo, is credited with a declamation maintaining that "Demosthenes swears that he did not take the bribe of fifty talents" (*Lives* 538). The topic is historical enough; it concerns a notorious accusation of political corruption in the fourth century B.C. But Demosthenes died more than four hundred years before Polemo was born. It is as if a speaker were to stand in front of a modern audience and assume the character of Cardinal Wolsey exculpating himself before Henry VIII. And if he did it well, the audience would positively enjoy it; better than a play, they would say. To do it well he would only have to imitate Polemo, as Philostratus describes his performances: "He used to rise to such a pitch of excitement that he would jump up from his chair"—Polemo had arthritis, and normally performed seated—"when he came to the most striking conclusions in his argument, and whenever he rounded off a period he would utter the final clause with a smile, as though to show clearly that he could deliver it without effort, and at certain places in the argument he would stamp the ground just like the horse in Homer" (*Lives* 537).

A sophistic performance par excellence was thus a dramatic vignette with a historical theme. Nowadays actors do something similar in historical plays. Of course, Polemo would write his own text, or better still improvise it; and he would perform solo. But readers may have seen Ruth Draper performing dramatically a text of her own. An important difference remains, however. Ruth Draper's dramatic sketches represented a Scottish immigrant on Ellis Island, or a duchess opening a garden party; not, normally, a scene from distant history. A Second Sophistical performance in this dramatic genre would concern itself invariably with distant Greek history: the Persian or Peloponnesian Wars, or fourth-century politics; nothing later than Alexander.

In another form of sophistic declamation the speaker addressed a fictitious legal question, such as the case of a wrongfully disinherited son, or a public benefactor paradoxically condemned by his beneficiaries. These speeches are the *controversiae* of the Latin tradition, as the political speeches are the *suasoriae*. In another vein, there were still real political occasions when a sophist could deploy political rhetoric, even under the authoritarian regime of the Empire—in addressing the restive population of a turbulent city, for example (there are such speeches by Dio Chrysostom and Aelius Aristides). The same Dio, and others such as Maximus of Tyre, would read-

ily deliver eloquent exhortations to virtue, or popular philosophical discourses—for all the world like elegant and fashionable eighteenth-century preachers—to audiences who clearly
expected stylish literary entertainment as much as strenuous
intellectual exercise. And there were not infrequent particular
social occasions when rhetoric found employment: a public
festival, or the arrival of a visiting emperor. For these latter, the
modern equivalent would no doubt be the ceremonial address
delivered at an academic gathering, or perhaps an after-dinner
speech. Here there was more possibility of saying something;
orators do sometimes succeed in saying something on such occasions.

For all that, this is all essentially epideictic rhetoric, display
rhetoric. In the democracies of the fifth and fourth centuries,
skill with words was an indispensable element in civic life.
Now, it is a decoration upon it. From performing a political
function, rhetoric had come in the Hellenistic world to consti-
tute a framework for education. In the revived Greek world—
revived after the economic chaos caused by Roman conquest
and Roman civil wars—rhetoric flourished as an art—for art's
sake, one might say.

To summarize: a revival of epideictic rhetoric as an art form
began to take place toward the end of the first century A.D.; it
reached its height in the second century, and lasted into the
third.[4] This movement is often thought of as dominating the
literary activity of the period, and as itself constituting a cultural revival. In fact, however, this rhetorical movement is
only one aspect, and a fairly limited one, of the literary activity
of the time. Other things were happening too, more important
things, which in their totality and coexistence do amount to
something that might reasonably be called a renaissance. I
shall discuss those other phenomena briefly, then consider
some characterizations that have been offered of this period
and its culture, which for convenience I shall refer to simply as
"the second century."

Philostratus does not purport to be writing a literary history
of the second century, and simply does not mention some major literary figures, such as Plutarch, about contemporary with

Nicetes, and Lucian, whose *floruit* one can put under Marcus Aurelius in the 160's. In the latter case the omission is a little surprising, since some of Lucian's activity was clearly sophistic in nature. Neither of these writers needs much comment here. Plutarch has since the Renaissance been one of the best known of all ancient writers, throughout Europe. Lucian's witty satirical dialogues, notably the *Dialogues of the Dead*, have repeatedly aroused interest and emulation, from Erasmus onward, and so have some other works such as the *True Story*—the earliest Baron Münchhausen tale, again satiric in intention, aimed at spinners of tall tales such as Homer and Herodotus. Plutarch's *Lives* and *Moralia*, and Lucian's works, can be fairly classed as belles lettres, occasional pieces of a miscellaneous kind, ranging from biography and essay to short story, satire, and pastiche. Philostratus himself, with his *Lives of the Sophists* and *Life of Apollonius of Tyana*, as well as with assorted other works—on a hero-cult, athletics, pictures at an exhibition—fits readily into the same group. These writers resemble the versatile professional writers of other ages, such as the eighteenth century, as distinct from *homines unius generis* like dramatists or historians.

And in some other cases Philostratus reports only part of the picture; he gives a quite misleading impression of Aelius Aristides, for instance, who became in later centuries *the* model of rhetorical art.[5] He does, it is true, mention in passing Aristides's *Sacred Tales*, or *Religious Diary*, a fascinating farrago of dreams and self-centered hypochondriac autobiography, totally devoid of rhetorical art. He might well have omitted that. But he concentrates on the standard declamations that Aristides performed, as did every other sophist; and in Aristides's case these must surely take second place to his ceremonial speeches, which Philostratus disregards, such as the massive encomium *To Rome*—exceptionally, a document of great historical importance, that describes in some detail the operation of the Roman Empire. He also ignores, with more reason, a number of nonsophistic writers. Several important historical works survive from the period, such as the numerous volumes of Arrian, including his *Anabasis* of Alexander, our major source for that topic. Dio Cassius's *History of Rome*, unsatisfactory as it is in some ways, is another important work, as are the histories of Appian, and, later, Herodian; and much more historical writing, though it has not survived, has left some traces. There are antiquarian works of considerable importance: Pausanias's *Guide to Greece,* still indispensable to archaeologists; the *Deipnosophistae,* or *Professors at Dinner,* of Athenaeus, a mine of quotations from lost literature and an inexhaustible if disordered collection of learning, on anything whatever in the Greek tradition; and Diogenes Laertius's *Lives and Opinions of the Famous Philosophers,* an uncritical but again valuable collection of material for the history of philosophy. And there is a mass of pietistic and superstitious literature purporting to see in natural phenomena indications of divine providence and care for the world.

A certain thematic unity runs through these names and works. Almost without exception they draw upon Greek tradition—exactly as sophistic declamations do. And *classical* Greek tradition at that: in enormous preponderance, the themes of these writers are taken from the fifth and fourth centuries, not even the Hellenistic age. Even the exceptions confirm this tendency. Plutarch's Roman *Lives* are paired with Greek lives, and part of his purpose is to demonstrate that even in the field of action, not just in the field of intellect, Greece could match Rome: for every Caesar there is an Alexander, for every Cicero a Demosthenes. Cultured Greeks, in short, are determined to preserve their long tradition.

But the most important of the literary products Philostratus does not discuss in his *Lives of the Sophists* is the romance, or novel.[6] There is certainly a theme running through the romance texts, and it is a very different one: the theme of ideal human love. One of these stories, Longus's *Daphnis and Chloe,* has been a favorite in all ages, and its subject is taken up in other arts—by Ravel, by Watteau. It is an idyllic pastoral story of two foundling children who, growing up together in the countryside, go through the pains of adolescence and nascent love, as well as more material and worldly trials, to emerge finally into the happy-ever-after of ideal adult love in the countryside. This is the world of Sidney's *Arcadia,* of *Paul et Virginie.* Another of these stories, Heliodorus's *Ethiopica,* was also familiar to the Renaissance. Translated early in the sixteenth century, it has an interesting history in France in particular, where it was sometimes most curiously adapted—for instance by Alexandre Hardy in 1623, in his *Les chastes et loyalles amours de Théagène et Cariclée réduites du grec d'Héliodore en huit poèmes dragmatiques* [sic] *ou théâtres consécutifs;* and Fontainebleau offers a series of paintings showing scenes from the story.

The romance is a major topic in literary history; yet it is not well known even among classicists, or among historians of prose fiction.[7] A century ago the great Erwin Rohde took over five hundred pages to express his contempt for these miserable, sentimental products of a decadent world.[8] It is true that his guess at the chronology of the genre was wildly wrong. Shortly after his own day papyrology began a process of discovery that pushed Rohde's whole sequence of texts backward some hundreds of years. Instead of stretching from the second to the fifth or sixth centuries A.D., the series began in the first century A.D., if not earlier, and was probably over by the third century—although Heliodorus perhaps wrote his novel-to-end-all-novels in the period of Julian the Apostate, in the late fourth century. With that possible exception, the half-dozen fully extant texts are for practical purposes contemporary with the Second Sophistic. Certainly the high tide of the genre was in the second century; almost every year new fragments confirm that. Although relatively few complete texts have survived, if we take into account the new fragments, notices in Byzantine lexicons, and other scattered items of information, we can count probably thirty or forty such fictional prose narratives; they range from comic stories, through novels of love and cliff-hanging adventure, to narratives informed by various ideological purposes.

And never a word in Philostratus. Or rather, we probably do have his comment on the genre—but not in his *Lives of the Sophists.* In an imaginary letter (another of his literary occupations) he anachronistically addresses one Chariton, who sounds like the author of the earliest fully extant romance, *Chaereas and Callirhoe* (probably first century A.D.). "Do you think," he asks, "that people are going to remember your stories when you are dead? If a man is a nobody when he is alive, what can he possibly be when he is dead?" Rohde was not the first establishment figure to despise early romance.

Little more need be said about romance here; it is a field in itself. But two observations should be made. First, it is true that the earliest examples of the form are sentimental, melodramatic, and apparently simplistic treatments of a crude enough story. Boy meets girl and the pair fall in love; they are separated, and travel around the Mediterranean in search of each other, facing death or a fate worse than death on every page, and surviving by the skin of their teeth; eventually a deity takes pity on them and they are ecstatically reunited. Later examples of the form, however, such as *Daphnis and Chloe,* are infinitely more sophisticated. And no doubt "sophisticated" is precisely the right word: romance writers have learned skill with words, in the hothouse of sophistic. Second, it is possible to view romance less contemptuously than did Philostratus and Rohde. The form was at least potentially of major importance, and already embodied, within its own conventions, something like a vision of human existence. Romance offers, if not allegory, perhaps a myth—a myth whose vitality and energy reflects not an old world but a new one.

So much by way of description of the literature. In turning to analysis, we may begin by observing some features of the society of the period that cannot be disregarded in such a discussion; they are perhaps more familiar, however, and thus need only brief mention. First, it is noteworthy that this whole renewal of literary activity appears to begin, or to gather enough strength to become apparent, at about the time when the Roman Empire emerges from its Julio-Claudian teething troubles and embarks, under thoroughly professional emperors, on what Gibbon could call the most felicitous period of human history (though we might not now agree with Gibbon in that). And it appears to die down, albeit temporarily, when in the first half of the third century that felicitous period is very seriously disturbed by invasion, economic crisis, and administrative disintegration. It would seem that social stability was a necessary condition for cultural revival. Secondly, the second century is the age of religion rampant, so to speak. Not only Christianity, but Gnosticism, Isis-worship, Mithraism, and other cults flourish. The phenomenon of religious fervor is notorious, and constitutes part of the psychological context in which this "renaissance" took place. In particular, the new form of romance displays, as we have just seen, a form of religious vision. Thirdly, a very striking feature of this literature and this age is its linguistic practice. Classical Greek language, in being diffused, had changed; it had become simplified, into the *koine dialektos*, the Basic Greek, of the New Testament. In the second century, the educated of the day make common cause in attempting to restore to the Greek language its former complexity, subtlety, and richness. The matter is of course not simple, but the Atticizing movement is a major feature of this period; it is of a piece with the sustained effort to keep alive or resuscitate other aspects of the Greek tradition.

We may now turn to some of the analyses that have been put forward of this whole period. The analysis of Philostratus, first of all. It is plain that he does regard his own age, or rather the age immediately preceding and leading to his own, as a literary reflowering. He is not concerned to describe *all* the flowers in the garden, but he goes to town on the orchids—which sprang unheralded and unbidden, it would seem, out of the blue, a century and a half before his own time. His only interest in the cultural archaeology of the matter is to attach the Second Sophistic willy-nilly to the first Sophistic. We can perhaps leave him at that.

Second, in our time it has been tempting to see this world as above all archaizing. The judgment has been expressed, quite recently, in the following way: "Reading the bulk of second century literature, that is to say such writings as reflect general tendencies, one is not transported into a real world, but into a sham one, in a museum of fossils."[9] No explication of this view is needed, but it may be glossed with a summary of subsequent remarks by the author, to the effect that this archaizing literature offers "a lifeless routine, destitute of push and energy"; man is content with what has been achieved, and feels impotent; his attitude is "possibly connected with the political situation, and certainly with religious developments"; he "just accepts what comes."

A third analysis, offered by the American scholar Ben Edwin Perry, is that this is a profoundly romantic age.[10] The demise of the city-state had been spiritually fatal; Hellenistic man "had had his soul blown into fragments, and scattered abroad into a vastly expanded world," where he himself is tiny—"the bigger the world, the smaller the man." Hence, the cultured take refuge in an ivory tower, renouncing the contemporary world, trying in a romantic gesture to write like Plato in the age of Hadrian, and surrendering to the irrational, the purely personal. The less cultured are mirrored in romance, which is "latter-day epic for Everyman"; man has become passive, a spiritual wanderer. "The upsurge of genuinely popular taste and feeling, which may be described as profoundly *romantic* in its outlook, is breaking through the upper crust of a traditional and intellectual formalism which had long kept it suppressed and concealed: and after the second century this secular romanticism passes more and more often into the form of religious mysticism, in which it was finally absorbed."

These assessments of the second century will serve as a basis for some comments. If the assessments appear to offer a rather negative view, for the present that should not be taken as implying either my agreement or my disagreement with them. First, on the "museum" interpretation. At this stage one might ask whether it is *possible* for people, on any large scale, to turn their faces toward the past. We may indeed think "Stop the world, I want to get off"; but the world won't stop. We have to stay on, and we know it. It is true that neurosis may result, and in fact neurosis and hypochondria flourish in the second century; Aelius Aristides, committing his chronic ill-health to the care of Asclepius, is typical of his age. But neurosis is not the same thing as refusal of the present. Secondly, Perry's "romantic" interpretation. It is broadly similar to Van Groningen's, of course, but in some ways more sympathetic to the second century. Reaction against a new age, suggests Perry, makes people turn about to look for what is familiar to them. But what they can find of the old world will be falsified by the conditions of the new world, and also by their own psychology; the way in which you look for things determines what you find. Perry dates the spiritual change to the passing of the autonomous city-state; but we may wonder how familiar, by now, that really was to people. If it was the autonomous city-state that people hankered after, why did they wait four centuries to do so? Four centuries is a very long time. Much had happened between Alexander and Vespasian, much Hellenistic water had passed under the bridge. Hellenistic, but still Greek: until relatively recently, the Greek world had remained Greek. Now it was Roman. I wonder whether it is not there that the problem lies: not so much in the transition from Athens to Alexandria as in the transition from Alexandria, the Great Leap Forward, to a new ideology.

I shall return to these points, and also to Philostratus's own not very profound view. At this point I shall offer some other comments, rather less negative than those discussed so far. First, there is an earlier sequence, in the Greek world, in which a legendary period of glory was followed first by some centuries of obscurity and then, relatively rapidly, by a reemergence into the light, accompanied by a consciousness of having a glorious past. That reemergence happened in the eighth century B.C., which has its blaze of literary light in the Homeric epics. The antecedents and the process of creation of these poems are very much a battleground for scholars, as indeed is the whole period, which is taking shape only now, as archaeology progresses. But this much seems clear, that the Homeric poems do look back to the Mycenaean or post-Mycenaean age, though they readily confuse it, in the fabric of their text, with elements from later and contemporary society. It would seem that they may be trying not just to preserve the older Greek tradition, but to "fix" it, almost as a photographer fixes a negative; to arrest it, establish it, determine what that tradition was, and was to be. Here a great deal depends on the actual process by which the monumental poems were themselves established— by the relationship of oral process, notably, to the written form that finally emerged as the "authorized version." But looking beyond that, there may have been, in the creation of the poems, an element of finding out what Greeks thought about themselves, about Greece: what they wanted to preserve, in the simplest terms. And there may be an analogy in the second century—although in the Second Sophistic proper the image appears almost in caricature.

Next, one feature of the literary activity of the second century is so obvious that people have sometimes not seen it, or having seen it have not really realized its significance. Quite simply, all of this activity is in prose. Traditionally, creative literature in Greek has been in verse. And much of what has been discussed here, sophistic as well as novel, must be called creative literature. The adoption of prose for creative literature is not a renaissance, nor a survival; it is a revolution. There is another arrow to add to this quiver of concepts. Perry, it is true, in his great book on the ancient romances, does indeed see that the use of prose for fiction is a novel state of things, and he discourses at great length and in a most enlightening way on the use of prose in Greek literature. But even Perry is not especially impressed by the phenomenon. I am. Prose as a vehicle of expression is entirely different from verse, and capable of major achievements. To stay for a moment in the same area, I am impressed also by what appears to me to be a new critical sensibility struggling to be born, and indeed being born in the treatise of "Longinus" *On the Sublime,* which could be dated at either end of our period but at any rate is within it. In "Longinus," for the first time in Greek critical thought, the idea is propounded that greatness in literature is a function and reflection of greatness in the mind that conceives it. The point is too specialized to discuss, but it is worth a mention here in passing to add some substance to the suggestion of literary *revolution.*

Next, in several aspects of second-century culture there is a similar phenomenon of a return to the old, a fidelity to tradition. The term "archaism" comes readily to mind. But we should note that it is usually thought of, by those who practice it, as a return not to the old, but to the good, a fidelity to the true. Alike in linguistic purism, in the preservation of historical knowledge of the Greek past, in the conscious emulation of earlier writers—*mimesis* in the secondary sense of that term,

inadequately translated by "imitation"—in all these facets of
the period, there is among other motives the desire to preserve
not what is merely old but what is good. Whether the true, the
good, are absolute things, whether they *can* be "preserved," is
another matter. They surely cannot be preserved in the way
onions can be pickled. But the second-century Greek cultural
establishment apparently thought they could.

A final point on these interpretations. Whatever the absolute
objective value of this cultural activity, if there can be objective value, there *is* an air of self-consciousness and—pace Van
Groningen and Perry—of confidence about the period. The second century was proud of its museum.

Before returning finally to the matter of interpretation, let us
turn to some problems and limitations affecting our approach
to the second century. First, the nature of the evidence. We
have seen that Philostratus is not the literary historian of the
period; but we have no other. We have to piece the literary history together as best we can from various sources, manuscript
tradition among them. That is a common enough literary-historical problem; for the second century we have to be positively careful not to allow ourselves to be blinded or misled by
Philostratus's own taste, and arbitrariness, and his own very elegance; for he follows no method in compiling his *Lives of the
Sophists*, except the method that in respect of style Fowler
calls "elegant variation." His aim, like that of the sophistic
preachers, is to entertain quite as much as to instruct. Second,
the incidence of survival of texts is as much a problem here as
elsewhere. The vagaries of ideological and cultural prejudice
operate, and distort the picture. Lucian hardly receives a mention from any contemporary or near-contemporary figure, but
his works are preserved in a relatively good tradition. The romance, as we have seen, has a bad press—in fact it hardly has
any press at all, but what it does have is bad—and only the
more sophisticated texts survive in fairly good shape. Some,
the more primitive, survived only in one thirteenth-century
manuscript, of poor quality. Many did not survive at all; they
have been appearing as papyrus fragments since 1893, and any
issue of *Zeitschrift für Papyrologie und Epigraphik*, these days,

may well contain a juicy morsel, which complicates yet further the evidence for the history of romance. We have already seen that the distortion of history has been very serious in this case.

Next, it should be observed that the Second Sophistic is geographically and culturally a limited phenomenon; it is limited to *Greek* literature. It is true that there is at the same time an archaizing movement in Latin, but it is nothing like as extensive or deep-rooted as in Greek.

Finally, a question of social level also arises.[11] Traditional, sophistic, cultivated literature is on the whole an upper-class phenomenon, as could be expected. Romance, the new form, appears, if only from Philostratus's snobbish view of it, to be aimed at a rather lower cultural level, at least initially, although it does have its ambitions, and it may have been the relaxation of the literate (perhaps as we read James Bond, or detective stories). It is true that as romance rises in esteem it rises in cultural specific gravity as well; to read Heliodorus, it pays to be educated. This *coexistence* of the old and the new, however, is not a matter of a simple dichotomy in cultural levels. It is a striking feature of the age that traditional and novel expression are often in contact and tension: in Aristides and Polemo themselves, sophists par excellence; in Lucian; in Philostratus; in romance itself. Furthermore, this is distinctly an age of popular culture, of popularization of literature and a certain degree of premastication of demanding authors; "the best of Plato" existed in second-century drugstores too. The question of the social mix of the readership, of the destination and audience of literature, is the more interesting in view of the linguistic phenomenon of Atticism, which has been touched on. For the quarrel between Atticists and *koine*-speakers can be seen as the origin of the dual forms of modern Greek, *demotike* and *katharevousa*, "demotic" and "purifying," although linguistic historians sometimes prefer to date the divergence to the twelfth century. In fact *koine* was well on the way to existence in Polybius, in the second century B.C., if not even in Menander and Xenophon in the fourth. So here at least there is a continuum; this linguistic dichotomy is not a new phenomenon. I do not know what the implications of this are for the concept of "renaissance"—whether, for instance, that term implies a substantial discontinuity in culture. Nor do I know how modern theories of language and what language is used for would treat this phenomenon of linguistic dichotomy in general—it occurs of course in other languages, perhaps in some degree in all languages. But certainly it flares up brightly in the second century, and in the Second Sophistic itself at times. The whole question of the development of the Greek language may serve as a framework, or a topic of reference, whereby to assess the cultural significance of the literary activities of the period.

My own assessment of the second century would lie, rather undramatically, somewhere in the middle of those I have been discussing. Philostratus is sympathetic to his period, but uncritical. Perry and Van Groningen are critical, but unsympathetic; both are themselves classicists, and paradoxical as it may seem, a classicizing approach is wrong for the second century.

Philostratus is right in observing that by the time the Roman Empire got its second wind, things started happening in Greece. But his account of what those things were is partial, in both senses of the word. We have noticed the inadequacy, for our purposes, of what should be called his social biography of the exotic sophistic movement. He does not attempt to justify the historical framework in which he sets it, and that very fact is eloquent. That he should wish to give it roots in classical Greece is normal enough in the second century, and it is also historically correct. As for his own times, it is plain that he simply *wanted* to begin again in the late first century, and for that he is probably a good witness. The renascence of rhetoric at that time looks like a simple social fact, which fits with other social facts, such as the entry of prominent Greeks into the upper ranks of Roman society. Indeed, the sophistic literary movement has been seen as *primarily* a reflection of this social movement. In 1969 G. W. Bowersock argued, with much cogent historical evidence to support his thesis, that the social and political importance of the figures who parade through Philostratus's *Lives of the Sophists* was greater than their cultural importance.[12] These are people from the top stratum of Greek society, wealthy and influential quite apart from their literary activities. They participate fully in and sometimes dominate the lives of their own cities; Dio Chrysostom—Dio of Prusa in Bithynia, that is—is a good example. They go on embassies to Rome on behalf of their cities, and their eloquence on such missions could be very effective, as Philostratus reports in several cases; they are benefactors of their cities, as the sophist Herodes Atticus built in Athens the theater of Herodes familiar to modern tourists. Bowersock's conclusion is that "the Second Sophistic has more importance in Roman History than it has in Greek Literature." This view is as sweeping as other of Bowersock's conclusions about the nature and the place in society of these second-century Bloomsbury groups. But to refute it needs equally hard historical evidence. The question is reexamined in a recent paper by E. L. Bowie; he concludes that "after all . . . the Second Sophistic has more importance in Greek literature than in Roman history."[13] That said, it remains true that sophists were socially prominent; that explains, among Philostratus's other distortions of literary history, the inordinate amount of space he gives to the literarily minor figure of the millionaire Herodes Atticus. Philostratus's enthusiasm, then, must be treated with caution.

As for the "museum" assessment: in a sense it is right, but I am inclined to think it myopic. People do not live in museums; they visit them. The archaizing is undeniable, but not to be simply recorded without comprehension. Van Groningen does allow that it is possibly connected with the contemporary political situation; I would go farther, and say that it is above all a manifestation of essentially political and civic sentiments of dissatisfaction with the subordinate political role that Greeks find themselves in, once the Roman Empire has established that it is there to stay. The point has been demonstrated in detail, again by E. L. Bowie: he observes that it is only with the advent of Augustus that all political hope is definitively lost in the Greek world.[14] It is only when this fact has penetrated, and when the Greek world is economically in a position to look about it, that the cultural archaizing really gets under way. If the present is unsatisfactory, it *is* tempting to rummage around in the past, to see what you can find to preserve self-respect. Educated Greeks found that in their cultural tradition, their *paideia*; and I have already suggested that there is a positive aspect to that. It is also true that it has a negative side. Literary Greeks very seldom show any interest in Rome. Aristides's encomium *To Rome* is exceptional, and the tone is given rather by a Lucian, who though he certainly knew Rome, and knew Latin, never displays that knowledge; he prefers to talk about Greece. To give Philostratus credit where credit is possible, he noticed that: in his *Life of Apollonius* he makes one of his characters say "You Greeks have ruined yourselves talking about Troy" (3.19). There are some exceptions, among the historians. The example had been set by Polybius in the second century B.C. *He* recognized the power and significance of Rome—he had good cause to do so, since he himself had been taken to Rome as a hostage. In the second and third centuries, Arrian and Dio Cassius, though Greeks, moved in influential Roman circles (they were themselves consuls), and they are altogether more realistic than many of their literary confrères about the political situation. When it came to the pinch, sophists were realistic enough too. Dio Chrysostom and Aelius Aristides speak with one voice when they admonish the turbulent population of this or that Greek city: if you do not live in harmony among yourselves, Rome will impose harmony on you. For all that, Arrian could abandon a highly successful Roman political career at the age of forty, to return to Greece and turn himself into, as he puts it, "a second Xenophon." A generation or two earlier Plutarch had done something similar.

Is this a "romantic" world? And if so, is that a bad thing to be? Perry is near the mark. But, as is often the case with Perry, he puts his finger massively on the right thing for perhaps not quite the right reasons. This romanticism, he tells us, was not, like modern romanticism, forward-looking. I wonder. I wonder who it is who is not forward-looking. Perry himself observes that in the second century intellectual, cultural, and spiritual energies tended to be focused on the individual personality. Individualism, in one form, is of course anything but new in Greek literature; it appears near the dawn of that literature, in Archilochus; it appears in Antigone, in Phaedra. But Archilochus and Antigone were acting in a social context. Now, the basis of individualism is the absolute, independent value of the individual, alone in a vast world. That does not seem to me backward-looking. These are sentiments that *we* recognize. We may of course be reluctant to accept their implications. Some such reluctance, I suspect, colors Perry's assessment of the second century.

Much in that century, indeed, seems positively modern. The elements of old and new are both strong. There certainly is not a break with the past; but equally certainly there is not mere rejection of present or future. And any "rebirth" must look both backward and forward.

CHAPTER 2

The Latin Revival of the Fourth Century

ALAN CAMERON

My brief is to discuss the Latin revival of the fourth century, but first the revival must be set in context. What
was revived, and why, when, where, and by whom? Why and
when did things decline to a point where a revival was possible
or necessary? Scholars tend to assume (1) that cultural decline
was an inevitable consequence of the great economic and military crisis of the Roman Empire in the third century and (2)
that the revival was almost entirely due to the pagan aristocrats of Rome, who were reacting to the combined Christian
and barbarian threat to their traditional way of life. I would
like to present a rather different interpretation.

Early in the second century A.D., the direction of Latin letters began to change sharply, to move away from the rhetoric
and point and polish of the Silver Age toward archaism. The
term "Silver Age" is modern. Many no longer consider it a
helpful label, since it attributes a greater homogeneity to the
literature of the first century A.D. than it actually possessed.
But we are not here concerned to do justice to the variety of
first-century literature, but rather to trace the fortune of a few
of its most conspicuous representatives, mainly poets, who do
share an artificiality, a striving for effect, a taste for exotic
learning, bravura descriptions, and impassioned speeches that
does set them apart.

There had always been a marked strain of archaism in Latin
literature;[1] it is enough to mention Sallust and Virgil. Old and
even obsolete words were thought to convey the appropriate

degree of dignity for a history of Rome's past or an epic poem. But what had formerly been no more than one prominent element in the style of historical writing and epic became the all-pervading goal of writers in every genre in the age of Fronto and Aulus Gellius. Its distinguished historian, R. Marache, thought that the second-century archaizing movement could be explained solely in terms of an internal development within Latin literature, as the gradual victory of this archaizing tendency over all others.[2]

This explanation is surely inadequate. An affectation for linguistic archaisms is one thing; the utter rejection of the literature of the preceding century is quite another. And yet this is just what the Latin writers of the second century A.D. did. It cannot be a coincidence that Greek literature was undergoing precisely the same change of direction at this time: the movement we know as the Second Sophistic.[3] It seems to me that the archaizing movement is best explained as a combination of both these factors. On the one hand, Latin writers of the late first and early second centuries felt dissatisfied with the increasing stridency and artificiality of Silver Latin poetry. On the other, they could not but be impressed by the glittering revival of Greek letters. And the key to the Greek revival had been a rejection of the present and a return to the great old writers of a Golden Age. If Latin writers could just do the same, perhaps Latin literature would be restored to sanity.

This hypothesis is neatly illustrated by a story in Aulus Gellius. A number of Greeks were praising the elegance of the early Greek poet Anacreon and taunting a Latin rhetor called Julianus because Latin had nothing comparable to offer. He then astonished the gathering by quoting the epigrams of three very early Roman poets: Valerius Aedituus, Porcius Licinus, and Q. Lutatius Catulus.[4]

But however disquieting the excesses of Silver Latin rhetoric, it was not possible to renew Latin literature simply by turning back the clock. The Greek classical authors to whom the Second Sophistic looked back—Demosthenes, Plato, Thucydides—were of course among the greatest writers who had ever lived. The same was not true of the revered models of Fronto and Gellius: the elder Cato, Ennius, Accius, Lucilius.

Rightly or wrongly, the Romans had always looked back on the age of Cato as a *moral* Golden Age; but as literature, the writings of the second and early first centuries B.C. were not classics by any definition. For all their merits, these were writers fumbling for a style, a vocabulary, above all for an identity, as they sought to come to terms with the all but overwhelming influence of a recently discovered Greek literature.

Imitation of these early Roman writers could not form the basis of a vital new Latin literature, nor did it. What Latin writing we have from the second century seems predominantly concerned with linguistic archaism, with reproducing quaint and frequently obsolete words and forms attested in second-century B.C. writers rather than current usage—the latter seldom mentioned without a shudder.[5] Words, not ideas, were the business of the Antonine man of letters. The only notable work of the age, significantly enough, is the *Golden Ass* of Apuleius, from the linguistic point of view an unmistakable child of the archaizing movement, but in its subject matter and its treatment a version of a Greek novel. Indeed, we actually possess an abridgment of its Greek original.

The crisis of the late third century doubtless had its effect. Patronage of the arts would inevitably be affected by wars and inflation. But it is not so clear that such things stop writers from writing. War had always been the prime theme and inspiration of ancient historical writing, and the third century saw the production of a large number of histories in Greek. There is the massive chronicle of all Roman history compiled by Dio Cassius; there are Herodian and Dexippus. It may be true that the Greek provinces suffered less during the third-century invasions. Yet unlike Rome, Athens was actually besieged by the Herulian Goths—and none other than the historian Dexippus led the Athenian defense.[6] Even in the West, the second and third centuries produced some remarkable and important Christian writers: Minucius Felix, Tertullian, Cyprian.

It is particularly striking that one of the most influential intellectual movements of Late Antiquity was born precisely in Rome in the darkest days of the third-century crisis: Neoplatonism. I refer to Plotinus and the brilliant and learned pupils who attended his school for so many years, Porphyry and Iamblichus. But of course they were all Greeks.

The truth is that it was only secular Latin literature that suffered this catastrophic decline in the third century. I suggest that the decline owed less to the public misfortunes of the Empire than to the false trail laid by the archaizing movement. This trail led nowhere, and nowhere is just where secular Latin literature went.

We come now to the revival itself. No one familiar with the fourth century would question that during its course some sort of cultural revival took place in the West. But it is not so easy to pin down its essential features or to trace its inception and spread. In fact, there has so far been no proper attempt to write a *history* of this revival at all.

The single most serious obstacle to a true understanding of the movement has been, I think, the prevailing view that it was a reaction of Rome's pagan aristocracy against the growing intolerance and philistinism of Christianity. The standard accounts, the most influential and best known of which are by Herbert Bloch and Philip Levine,[7] in effect treat the revival of letters as just one aspect of the pagan religious revival of the last quarter of the fourth century. I shall try to show that it was a much wider and more complex phenomenon than usually supposed.

The determining element in this prevailing conception has been the notion of the "Circle of Symmachus." In 384 Q. Aurelius Symmachus delivered a justly admired plea for the restoration to the Senate House in Rome of the altar of Victoria, which had been removed two years earlier on the order of the Emperor Gratian as part of his disestablishment of the pagan cults. In 394 Symmachus's lifelong friend Nicomachus Flavianus died at the battle of the river Frigidus in what Christians later represented as the final defeat of paganism by Christianity. He had been fighting for the cause of the usurper Eugenius. Thanks to the survival of Symmachus's extensive correspondence, we can see him at the center of a wide circle of like-minded friends.[8] Modern scholars have added to this circle all sorts of contemporary pagans, indeed any man of letters not demonstrably a Christian—and even a few who actually were Christian, such as Ausonius. Having thus artificially bolstered the "Circle of Symmachus," these scholars then identify it as the source of the revival of pagan letters.

The other document on which this interpretation rests is the *Saturnalia* of Macrobius, a long and learned dialogue in which the interlocutors are, precisely, Symmachus, Nicomachus Flavianus, the Virgil commentator Servius, and a number of other prominent pagans. I have treated the Circle of Symmachus and the *Saturnalia* elsewhere and I do not intend to repeat myself. My own view, now widely accepted, is that Macrobius was not, as used to be thought, a contemporary of Symmachus.[9] He wrote a full generation later, and most if not all of the impressive learning he puts in the mouths of his interlocutors he took directly (often without acknowledgment) from much earlier sources. Quite apart from his obvious nostalgic idealization of Symmachus and his friends, Macrobius does not even purport to give a true picture of their culture. His use of their names is merely a literary device. The real Symmachus, to judge from his letters, was a man of very limited culture who read only the most traditional authors and had no philosophy and little Greek.

It is striking that Macrobius did not include among his dinner guests the two really major Latin writers of later fourth-century Rome: Ammianus Marcellinus and Claudian. His omission was appropriate in the sense that neither is mentioned in Symmachus's letters. Yet both were pagans who wrote in the traditional pagan genres and style. Clearly then there was no united pagan front even in the last quarter of the fourth century, when paganism was truly threatened by Christianity. Especially significant in this respect is the fact that Ammianus himself, who lived and wrote in Rome in the 380's, the period in which the *Saturnalia* is set, complains at length and with some passion of the hostility of the aristocracy to all culture.

It is worth dwelling a moment longer on Ammianus and Claudian, for they nicely illustrate the problems of tracing the Latin revival. Both were Greek by birth and upbringing, with

Greek as their first language, and both can only be understood in terms of a *Greek*, not a Latin, literary tradition.[10]

Ammianus wrote the first full-scale history of Rome in Latin since Tacitus. In the intervening two and a half centuries almost nothing was produced in Latin but superficial and often scandalous imperial biographies and astonishingly bald epitomes, potted histories with one paragraph per reign.[11] In Greek, by contrast, there was an unbroken tradition of large-scale contemporary historical writing, and it is to this tradition that Ammianus belongs.

Claudian was but one in a thriving school of Egyptian poets.[12] In the fourth and fifth centuries, there were literally scores of these Greek poets, wandering from city to city seeking new patrons. They wrote panegyrics, epithalamia, and the like, according to the established Greek pattern. There is not a trace of such a tradition in third- and fourth-century Latin literature before Claudian. Claudian fused these Greek traditions with the style of Silver Latin poetry to produce something totally new to the West. (I would add that the important Latin Neoplatonic movement at the end of the fourth century, of which I cannot speak further here, was likewise entirely derivative of its Greek sources, mainly Porphyry.[13])

The receptions accorded to Claudian and to Ammianus make an interesting contrast. Claudian had many devoted successors in the West. It is uncanny to read the panegyrics of Merobaudes and Sidonius; every thought, every trick of style can be traced back to Claudian. Yet Ammianus had no successor. If the text of his wonderful history (which in any case hangs by a thread) had perished, we should have had no idea that a work of such scale and quality ever existed.

So why did Ammianus and Claudian abandon their native language, go to Rome, and write in Latin? Claudian probably saw better prospects in the West precisely because poet panegyrists were so common in the East. His knowledge of Latin gave him an edge over his Greek competitors and an entrée to the far wealthier patrons of Rome.

Ammianus had just one rival in the Greek world. While he was working on his own history, a Sophist named Eunapius from Sardis published a parallel work, a large-scale history of the fourth century down to about 380.[14] Eunapius had a flashy style and his work was to be very influential. This factor surely contributed to Ammianus's decision to try his fortune in Latin. He undoubtedly had a genuine admiration of Rome, but it was an admiration he had picked up from books. When he finally met the living *senatus populusque romanus,* Ammianus was bitterly disillusioned.

That Claudian and Ammianus chose to write in Latin does not mean that Latin was regarded as the dominant cultural language of Late Antiquity. Quite the reverse. Both chose Latin because they knew they would have no serious competition. If they had written in Greek, their works would almost certainly have perished without trace, like those of most of their Greek competitors. Claudian and Ammianus illustrate perfectly one of the great truths of Latin literature: at all decisive moments it was heavily dependent on what we might almost call blood transfusions from Greek. Without these two intruders, our picture of a Latin revival would look very different.

One area in which pagan aristocrats are supposed to have been especially influential was the patronage of the minor arts. Obviously I cannot fully discuss here the question of the artistic renaissances that art historians discover with such gay abandon throughout the fourth century. But I would like briefly to indicate how uncertain even the apparently most clear-cut example of pagan initiative is.

I refer to the famous and highly classicizing ivory diptych inscribed Nicomachorum/Symmachorum. The names (see Figure 1) are those of two of the families most prominently involved in the "pagan reaction." According to E. Kitzinger, in a notable recent book, the "studied and conscious classicism" of these panels reveals them as "exercises in nostalgia undertaken in the service of a very specific cause."[15] He further maintains that the classicizing revival that the diptych embodies had a profound impact on the whole development of Western art. He sees this influence in the long series of consular diptychs and in two fine Christian ivories of the late fourth century, the Munich Ascension and the Milan Marys at the tomb of Christ. Kitzinger finds "rich irony in the thought that it was the Nicomachi, Symmachi, and other like-minded patrons who thus helped to bring about a massive transfer of pure classical forms into Christian art." This argument sounds persuasive. Yet while there is certainly a *logical* sense in which a style derived from the study of classical models was at this period adapted to both official and Christian art, what Kitzinger has done is to treat a logical sequence as a *chronological* sequence. I have no space for details, but another interpretation and dating of the secular ivories would put Symmachorum/ Nicomachorum *last* in this series, in 402—long after the collapse of the last pagan revival. Certainly the diptych reflects the paganism of the families named, but we can no longer associate it with a militant pagan cause.

We might also consider the *Consecratio* panel now in the British Museum (Figure 2). The only persuasive solution of its monogram yet proposed is "SYMMACHORUM." I myself believe that the panel was commissioned for the same occasion as the other Symmachan diptych, but I will not press the point. It is a Symmachan commission. And if the other diptych is the high-water mark of fourth century classicism, the *Consecratio* panel is its very antithesis, what Kitzinger himself, in an earlier book, called nothing less than "the dawn of the Middle Ages in the late pagan art of Rome."[16] So we cannot interpret the classicism of Symmachorum/Nicomachorum as a straightforward testimony to the paganism of the patron. The same man, incidentally a pagan, could at the same time patronize the old and the new in art. As for the Christian panels, it is quite arbitrary to date them later than the pagan panels. They may be later, but how can we tell? More relevant is the realization that a Christian patron wanted the visit of the Marys to Jesus' tomb (Figure 3) to be portrayed in as classicizing a manner as possible. Just so Claudian's greatest successes were won before the Christian court in Milan.[17] Evidently the superficial paganism of his polished verses caused his patrons few pangs of conscience.

As for the source of the classicizing ivory carving, one can only speculate. The two aristocratic families must have had veritable treasures of ancient art works in their centuries-old palaces. The appeal of a statue or relief is much more direct

1. *Left:* Nicomachorum panel, Cluny Museum, Paris (museum photo). *Right:* Symmachorum panel, Victoria and Albert Museum, London (museum photo).

2. *Consecratio* panel, British Museum, London (museum photo)

3. Women at the Tomb of Christ, Castello Sforzesco, Milan (museum photo)

than that of a musty papyrus roll. It can catch the eye at any time. I am dubious of attempts to link the so-called classicizing style in art with a classical revival in literature. I am far from certain that, for example, Symmachus had any clear concept of "style" in this sense. He would probably have seen certain styles as appropriate to certain subjects: e.g., a classicizing style would be right for a scene of a priestess sacrificing but not for an imperial or ceremonial theme such as a *consecratio*. This, I suspect, is how Symmachus himself would have explained the stylistic difference between the two panels, though of course we cannot even be sure to what extent the initiative here came from the craftsman rather than the patron.

The area in which pagan aristocrats have been thought to have exercised a decisive role in the history of Latin culture is in the preservation and copying of Latin texts.[18] It is true that in the course of the fourth century classical texts were systematically transcribed from fragile papyrus rolls into the far more durable parchment codex. There can be little doubt that, but for the belated adoption of the codex as the form of the book, many texts would simply have perished. Papyrus rolls were too bulky and fragile. Undoubtedly this was a decisive moment in the transmission of classical texts.[19]

It is also true that many of our manuscripts of Latin Classics end with subscriptions stating that a certain person has "read and corrected" the book.[20] These persons are often Roman aristocrats, who obviously spent a lot of time lovingly copying and correcting their classical manuscripts. But do these facts justify the following conclusion of H. Bloch?

And yet, while their fight for the ancient religion ended in failure, they gained on another front a victory which has made their names immortal: they rescued the works of the great Latin authors out of the darkness into which they had fallen during the anarchy of the third century, copied and emended them in the fashion inherited from the great scholars of Alexandria, and so prepared editions which were improved texts, and which were to form the starting point for the mediaeval tradition of these authors. Without the assiduous activity of these men, much of Latin literature that has come down to us would have been irretrievably lost. . . . This is the historical achievement of the pagan revival at the end of the fourth century.[21]

Before we could accept any part of this extravagant claim, we would need to know at least four things that we do not:

1. That the works for which subscriptions are attested *were* in danger of being lost in the fourth century. All of them were, in fact, standard school texts or popular works.

2. That the subscribers were pagans. Remarkably, not *one* has been identified as a pagan. Most were quite certainly Christians. Even in the case of the most famous of all subscriptions in a Latin text, those to the first decade of Livy, it is necessary to warn that the chief subscriber, the younger Nicomachus Flavianus, converted to Christianity after his father's death. Modern scholars like to think that this conversion was merely a facade and that Flavian continued to fight his father's battles underground, by copying Livy.[22] I prefer to suspend judgment.

3. That the subscribers were activated by their religious beliefs rather than simply by their love of literature. Since we cannot prove in the first place that they were pagans, *a fortiori* we cannot infer their intentions.

4. That they were deliberately preserving for posterity texts at risk. Yet the subscriptions are all routine notes—"legi et emendavi," for example—in what are clearly *personal* copies.[23] Nothing at all supports the view, still repeated, that these aristocratic copies were intended as *editions,* as critical texts. They are simply calligraphic copies that the owner proofread— the only way to get a satisfactory text when scribes could not be trusted. This is not to criticize these aristocratic subscribers for only making personal copies of well-known texts. There may have been no pressing need for multiple copies of these texts at that time and place. Yet it is relevant to observe that in 356 the Christian Emperor Constantius II established a scriptorium in Constantinople for the express purpose of copying classical texts.[24] Nor did his successors neglect this foundation. In 372 Valens addressed the following rescript to the prefect of Constantinople: "We command that four Greek and three Latin copyists, skilled in writing, shall be selected for copying the manuscripts of the library and for repairing them on account of their age."[25] The order goes on to provide for the payment of these copyists and for the appointment of custodians to look after the library. The Christian emperor of the Eastern

capital was thus seeing to the preservation and copying of Latin no less than Greek Classics a quarter of a century before the earliest Roman subscription—and at public expense. No pagan prefect of Rome made any such request for the public maintenance of the doubtless fast-decaying papyrus rolls in the public libraries of Rome. The culture of Roman aristocrats was aristocratic: they just wanted books for their own libraries, which (according to Ammianus) they kept locked up as tight as their family tombs. No doubt works were being transcribed from roll to codex quietly and haphazardly all over the Empire. If people want to read books, they have to have copies.

A final, key issue revolves around the timing and locations of the revival. When and where did people start reading again the books that had been gathering dust throughout the second and third centuries? The main objection to modern preoccupation with the alleged cultural initiative of the Roman aristocracy is that the revival itself must have begun long before Symmachus's day. At best, the activity of Symmachus and his pagan (and Christian) friends reflected a movement already under way.

The first signs of the movement can be seen in early fourth-century Gaul. Gaul had suffered badly from the unrest of the third century, and Constantius I, the father of Constantine, is said to have devoted much effort to restoring schools and education there. The state was thus playing a role in the revival in the last decade of the third century. The schools of Gaul prospered throughout the fourth century; Roman aristocrats would send their sons to Gallic rather than Roman professors. Symmachus himself had studied with a Gallic rhetor, and he made his own son do the same.[26]

The best-known representative of the culture of early fourth-century Gaul is Ausonius. Ausonius knew all the usual school authors (Virgil by heart, as illustrated by his erotic Virgilian cento, composed in just one day, without lexica). He also knew all the Silver Age poets: Lucan, Statius, Juvenal he quotes from easily and often.[27]

Nor did Ausonius stand alone. Our knowledge of Constantius's rebuilding of the schools of Gaul derives from the earliest Panegyrici Latini, nine Gallic panegyrists dating from the 290's to the 390's. It is often overlooked that not even the earliest of these panegyrists were archaizers. Their models were Cicero and the younger Pliny. That is to say, they saw themselves in the logical and historical tradition of Roman oratory as it developed from the late Republic into the Silver Age.

Thanks to his brief exchange of letters with Symmachus (confined to the period when he was politically important), Ausonius has usually been classified as at least an honorary member of the Circle of Symmachus. This is doubly misleading. In the first place, Ausonius was a much older man than Symmachus, and he certainly derived his culture from the schools of Gaul, not from contact with Symmachus. In the second place, Ausonius was a Christian. He does not parade his Christianity in his works, to be sure, but that does not justify the sneers and aspersions so many moderns have cast on his beliefs, calling him a lukewarm, nominal, or time-serving Christian. A recently discovered catalogue of Ausonius's works mentions the titles of three hitherto unknown lost works: (1) a poetical history of usurpers from Decius to Diocletian, according to Eusebius; (2) a book on the traditions of the Jews; and (3) a book on the names of the months of the Jews and Athenians.[28] Ausonius's source for the last two works was probably also Eusebius. These discoveries add a new dimension to Ausonius's Christian culture, though it is his pagan culture to which we must return. In addition to the Silver Age poets, like his colleagues the Gallic panegyrists, Ausonius was familiar with the younger Pliny. One of the panegyrists even seems to know Tacitus.[29] The implication is clear: by the middle of the fourth century Gaul had already experienced a full-scale revival of Silver Latin literature.

For the middle of the fourth century, we also have fairly precise evidence for Rome. One of the greatest scholars of the age, St. Jerome, recorded in his *Chronicle* that in the year 353 his own teachers Donatus and Marius Victorinus were flourishing at Rome. Donatus was undoubtedly a major figure in the Latin revival, though his precise role is hard to pin down. He wrote three works: an *Ars grammatica* and massive commentaries on Virgil and on Terence. Most later grammarians wrote commentaries on Donatus's *Ars,* and all later writers on Virgil and Terence pillage his two commentaries. The extant Virgil commentary by Servius is little more than a patchwork compiled from Donatus. But there are two respects in which Servius's commentary differs from Donatus's. Donatus's commentary does not survive intact, but its general outlines can to some extent be reconstructed. And it looks as if Servius himself added virtually all the hundreds of quotations from the Silver Age poets that appear in his commentary. Certainly there are no such quotations in Donatus's *Ars,* nor in the interpolated version we have of his Terence commentary.

The difference can be illustrated by comparing successive treatments of the same point. In his *Ars (Grammatici latini* 4.378), Donatus discusses the two genitive plurals of *domus: domorum* and *domuum.* In his Virgil commentary (on *Aen.* 2.445), Servius quotes Juvenal 3.72 (*"viscera magnarum domuum"*), though he had not done so in his (? earlier) commentary on Donatus's *Ars (GL* 4.434). The latter grammarians Pompeius (*GL* 5.192), Cledonius (*GL* 5.47.7), and Priscian (*GL* 2.309.18) all quote the Juvenal passage, whereas the pre-Servian Diomedes (*GL* 1.307.8), like Donatus, does not.[30] The only Silver Age poet Donatus can be proved to have quoted is Lucan. His most famous pupil, St. Jerome, knew only Lucan and Persius of the Silver Age poets, and he mentions that he studied commentaries on both poets at school.[31]

The other respect in which Servius consistently differs from Donatus is that he omitted the older and more obscure quotations that he found in Donatus. Until recently it was assumed that Servius did so because he was only an elementary teacher who did not want to subject his students to such obscure stuff. But if there is only so much time in a class, there is also only so much room in a commentary.[32] If new poets were added, some of the old ones had to go. At the aesthetic level, moreover, those who were becoming attuned to the polish and rhetoric of the Silver Age were not likely to have much time for Ennius and Cato.

It appears then that the changes in literary taste that characterized the fourth century did not all occur at one time or in one place. In Gaul, it seems, people were reading virtually the whole corpus of Silver Latin poetry by the middle of the century. In Rome they had hardly started on Silver Latin by then, although the teaching of Donatus and of his colleague Victorinus (whose specialty was Cicero) had at any rate shifted the balance toward classical and away from archaic writers. It was left to Servius, at the beginning of the fifth century, to complete the process in both directions by adding the new and eliminating the old.

Servius has in fact been credited with the rediscovery of Juvenal, on the basis of a subscription in a Juvenal manuscript: "legi ego Niceus apud M. Servium Romae et emendavi."[33] But it is improbable that any grammarian, however celebrated, could effect such a change of taste single-handed, and in any case Ausonius knew Juvenal at least half a century earlier. Servius surely reflected rather than initiated this change of taste. We may compare him with Symmachus. Ninety years ago W. Kroll made a thorough study of Symmachus's knowledge of classical writers, only to discover, somewhat to his surprise, that Symmachus knew very little of the archaic writers beyond Plautus and Terence.[34] One hundred years ago, another doctoral candidate demonstrated the same gaps in St. Jerome's reading.[35] St. Augustine reveals similar deficiencies. These scattered observations have yet to be fitted into one picture.

The contrast with the love of archaism displayed by Fronto and Gellius is clear. Though a stylist like Symmachus naturally affected a certain number of archaisms to give a touch of color (mainly after Plautus), the exclusive fascination with the archaic poets in and for themselves has definitely receded. It is against this background that Claudian's instant success is to be understood. He wrote the most polished verses seen since Statius. Every Silver Age trick of style, point, and word order that makes Lucan and Statius what they are is there in Claudian. Indeed whole stretches of Claudian might pass for Lucan or Statius, and his savage invectives have more than a touch of Juvenal's spirit as well as his language and manner. Audiences were ready for it. Many a passage in Claudian depends for its very comprehension on the listener appreciating the neat adaptation or reversal of a phrase in Lucan or Juvenal.[36]

Here was a living poet who could vie with the once-more fashionable masters of the insidious style of the Silver Age. No wonder he found both admirers and imitators. The fact that his immediate audience was the Christian court at Milan rather than some paganizing salon in Rome merely underlines the power and universality of the Silver Age revival.

This change in taste was real and important. If by chance the Empire had not survived the third-century crisis, if something like the Middle Ages we know had descended around 250, then we might well have had many works of Cato, Ennius, and other archaic writers that are now lost, but few or no works of Lucan, Statius, Juvenal, and other Silver Age writers that we now possess. Imagine Renaissance drama without the tragedies of Seneca! Or modern historiography of the Roman Empire without Tacitus! But the Empire did survive its political crisis, and Cato and Ennius were decisively ousted by Lucan and Juvenal and by the younger Pliny and Tacitus.

Not the least interesting aspect of this Silver Age revival is that it ran alongside of and in no way counter to the growth of a specifically Christian literature in the fourth century. After all, Statius was in no sense more anti-Christian than Virgil. Indeed the Silver Age poets were actually less imbued with the traditional Roman religion. As C. S. Lewis pointed out, the deities who people Statius's epics are abstract personifications rather than the old Olympians, and the tendency was carried much further in Claudian.[37] The potent medieval figure of Natura came directly from Statius and Claudian.[38] It is hard to imagine Prudentius's *Psychomachia* without Statius's *Thebaid.*

Ultimately, then, the revival was important because it was the literary tastes of the fourth century that were passed on to the Middle Ages.

CHAPTER 3

The Carolingian Renaissance

JOHN J. CONTRENI

W hat was the Carolingian renaissance and why was it significant? A summary response to that question might
read as follows. The Carolingian renaissance formed part of a
program of religious renewal that Carolingian political and
clerical leaders sponsored and encouraged in the hope that it
would lead to the moral betterment of the Christian people. As
a conscious effort to improve man through knowledge of the
Scriptures, the renaissance emphasized study, books, script,
and schools. Although conceived and initially executed by an
elite group of scholars, the first generation of which was largely
foreign-born, the renaissance was aimed at society as a whole.
It had a spectacular effect on education and culture in Francia,
a debatable effect on artistic endeavors, and an unmeasurable
effect in what mattered most to the Carolingians, the moral regeneration of society. The renaissance deeply influenced the
material, institutional, and intellectual future of Western European civilization. Although this attempt to capture what
seems to be an emerging consensus among students of the Carolingian renaissance is highly distilled and lacks both the authority and the antiquity to be canonical, it can serve here as
the subject of an extended gloss.

There is no denying that within the space of a few years, say
from about 750 to 800, something special began to occur in the
Carolingian realm. For want of a better word, we can call this
development a renaissance.[1] It was not only that important in-

tellectual work was going on. Such work had been going on throughout the early Middle Ages, in phenomena historians have called the Ostrogothic, the Vandal, the Isidorian, and the Northumbrian renaissances. What was unusual in the latter half of the eighth century was that individual efforts were brought together, coordinated, and marshaled in a new direction. Francia, at first glance, was a most unlikely candidate for a program of cultural renewal. The major centers of cultural activity, the loci of the earlier renaissances, lay outside Francia's borders like so many oases around a desert.

It had not always been so. In the early medieval, post-Roman period, Gaul had been divided into two parts: the heavily Romanized south and the heavily barbarized north and east. The union of Gaul under Clovis and his truculent brood produced a curious intellectual amalgam. The southern Roman culture, with its emphasis on writing and Latin literacy, was imported into the north, just as the columns of the south's classical buildings were hauled north to grace new, Christian structures. Classical culture and religious culture, lay literacy and clerical literacy, Christian ethics and barbarian values all coexisted through the seventh century—for a period longer, as Pierre Riché has shown, than many modern scholars used to think.[2]

If the sixth and seventh centuries were not such very dark ages, then what created the conditions that necessitated a Carolingian renaissance? A sustained cultural life requires institutional support and stability. Men and women of talent may flourish under the most adverse conditions, but the history of the later Roman Empire and certainly of the Merovingian dynasty suggests that intellectual and cultural life on a large scale is more fragile. This is not theory: the record of the ruin and subversion of Gaul's educational centers, its monasteries and cathedrals, either by fire and devastation or by mismanagement in the hands of warrior abbots and bishops and their minions is eloquent on this point.[3] The later Merovingian kings were in no position to provide guidance and example, nor did the early Carolingians help matters much. In their political struggles against rival aristocratic families, the Carolingians did not shrink from secularizing cultural centers. In effect they added to the instability of Francia by their continual military activity. Roman Gaul suffered most under the Carolingians.[4]

By the middle of the eighth century, the Carolingian mayors of the palace had consolidated and were soon to legitimize their hold over the Frankish kingdom. Concurrently, two cultural shifts had begun to provide the essential ingredients for the program mentioned in the summary definition above. First, Carolingian expansion brought the Franks into contact with active cultural centers in Spain, the Lombard kingdom, and Rome. Second, while the monarchs reached out to the periphery of their realm, learned foreigners were arriving in Francia. Some, such as Boniface of Crediton and his follow Anglo-Saxons, were animated by missionary fervor. Others—for example, Visigothic and Irish masters—had Moslem and Viking raiders to thank for their decision to leave their homelands in search of refuge and patronage in Francia. Both developments concentrated the material and human resources for cultural revival in the hands of the Carolingians.

All that was needed was the impetus to start the program. That agent or motive force must be credited to the Carolingian leaders themselves, for they were not only warriors and power politicians but men of religion and culture. Charles Martel despoiled church lands, but he also supported Boniface and Chrodegang of Metz. Charles's son copied out the *Life* of his Carolingian ancestor Arnulf of Metz, and Charles's brother wrote out the "deeds" of the Franks, in which he linked the Franks to a far older race, the Trojans. Pepin the Short was the key figure in a political strategy that saw him depose the last of the Merovingians, become anointed king in his own right, and in the process fashion an important liaison with the bishop of Rome. He also was interested in religion and learning. He requested a revised version of the lectionary and began the reform of the Frankish Church. Charles the Great succeeded his father in 768. An admirer of Augustine's *City of God,* Charles was prepared to think not only of the Saxons, Frisians, Lombards, Britons, Spain's Moslems, and his own recalcitrant magnates, but also of the shape of the society he served as rector and minister of God.[5] Dead authors were not his only teachers. He recruited and listened to an international constellation of Italian, Anglo-

Saxon, Irish, and Visigothic men of letters. Together they fash-ioned an ambitious program for the shaping of a fundamentally Christian society; one element of that program constituted what we call today the "Carolingian renaissance." To a degree probably unmatched in the other medieval renaissances, its chief figures—from Alcuin at the end of the eighth century to Heiric of Auxerre at the end of the ninth—were cognizant of the program and unanimous in singing its praises. This renais-sance did not need a Charles Homer Haskins or a Robert Sa-batino Lopez to discover it.[6]

From the time of the Renaissance humanists to the present day, scholars have echoed the Carolingian masters in welcom-ing the Carolingian renaissance, coming as it does after what they view as the barbarity and aimlessness of post-Roman civi-lization in Europe. The recognition that the Carolingian age was a special moment in the cultural history of the West does not mean, however, that scholars have agreed in their assess-ment of the program's significance. The first commentators claimed that the Carolingians sponsored a literary renaissance whose principal effect was to preserve civilization, which they defined essentially in classical terms. Thanks to the Carolingi-ans civilization survived by the skin of its teeth, remarked Kenneth Clark.[7] Other researchers, principally those whose patient labors in the shadowy corners of the pre-Carolingian Dark Ages have gone far to rehabilitate that period, would have us believe that the Carolingians were not at all original but simply imitated programs and texts proposed earlier and else-where. Less pessimistic about the early Middle Ages, they are, in turn, less enthusiastic about the Carolingian achievement.[8] A third and more persuasive school sees the renaissance not so much as a scholarly or literary or classical phenomenon, but as a fundamentally religious movement. The Carolingians did not intend to revive Athens or Rome, their rhetoric sometimes to the contrary, but rather to cleanse and sanctify society. The purpose of the renaissance was to "reform" society and to "cor-rect" abuses. From Charles the Great to Charles the Bald, Car-olingian leaders kept before them the example of King Josias, who, the Book of Kings relates, dedicated himself to cleansing

Israel and to observing the covenant with God. The court scholars were the advance men, so to speak, of an effort to "re-generate" Christian society.[9]

Thus broadened, the concept of the Carolingian renaissance expands beyond the effort to preserve texts and to write better Latin to include almost everything the Carolingians did: their attempts to achieve political stability, their economic legislation, and their papal policy, to mention only a few examples. This view of the renaissance, though dangerously broad, is supported by the words and actions of the Carolingians themselves. Only by placing the renaissance in its broad societal and programmatic context can we clearly perceive its ultimate significance.

Both art and the liturgy, in their different ways, proclaim the aims of the Carolingians. Carolingian art, which has long been celebrated by art historians and which can be viewed in sumptuous books, favored classical forms and motives at the expense of the more Germanic tendencies evident in earlier Frankish and barbarian art.[10] The beautiful pages and ornate bindings of Carolingian gospel books rank among the masterpieces of medieval art. Only two brief comments can be made here about manuscript illustration. First, it must be remembered that the vision of empire that Carolingian patrons sought and that artists tried to achieve was that of the fourth-century Christian Empire. Secondly, it must be admitted that not many Christians outside the palace, cloister, or cathedral were privy to this pictorial extension of the Carolingian ethos.

Other forms of art served a more public function. The faces of Carolingian coins conveyed an unmistakable image of royal power, justice, and Christian religion to those fortunate enough to possess them.[11] On a grander and even more visible scale, people could not help but be astounded by the building program undertaken throughout Carolingian Europe. Some 1,700 buildings have been dated to the Carolingian period. The little more than eight decades from 768 to 855 alone saw the construction of 27 new cathedrals, 417 monasteries, and 100 royal residences.[12] Only about one-seventh of these buildings have been studied systematically; nevertheless, historians of Carolingian architecture have been impressed by their functional nature, especially that of the religious buildings. For Carolingians, churches filled the role of the Roman *munici-pium* and the Greek *polis*.[13] They provided the *locus* where theory and spirituality were acted out through the liturgy.

The liturgy, liturgical texts, and sermons transmitted the Christian ethos to the European population. In each field, Carolingian legislation and patronage had its effect. Pepin the Short and Charles the Great put the full weight of their authority behind the evolution of a Romano-Frankish liturgy.[14] The revision of the biblical text was an endeavor closely related to liturgical reform, as was the improvement of the antiphonary.[15] Sermon collections were compiled.[16] Pastoral material from many sources was gathered together between the covers of manuscripts to support priests in their work with the people.[17]

But we are chiefly concerned here with the implications of the Carolingian program for scholarship and intellectual life. We can begin by discovering what the Carolingians had in mind when they fostered—one might say demanded—more rigorous attention to scholarly activity.

Carolingian leaders from Charles Martel on supported and commissioned the work of scholar-reformers. It was Martel's grandson, Charles the Great, who provided the focus and direction for the program. Two documents, the *Admonitio generalis* of 789 and the circular letter known as the *Epistola de litteris colendis*, were its manifestoes. They set out a program of educational reform, one that would make the king a worthy Josias.[18] The program was an extremely modest one. Students were to be taught reading, writing the Psalms, the Roman *nota*, that is, stenography, chant, *computus*, and grammar, as well as the corrected versions of the Catholic books. Great care was to be taken with the copying of sacred texts, as negligence and the youth of scribes could cause many errors in transmission. These legislative documents, it is important to note, devote not one word to the liberal arts or to the Classics, and certainly not to theological speculation. The goal was to produce not scholars but men whose "bona conversatio" would draw many to the service of God.

To commission the maintenance of schools for the training of youth was not alone sufficient. Consistent example and exhortation would be necessary if these documents were not to become dead letters. The court provided example and leadership. Charles's palace served as both a magnet and as a point of dissemination for the learned men of his time. Alcuin, an Anglo-Saxon from York whom Charles met in Parma, became one of the stars of the court circle before he was given the monastery of St. Martin of Tours. Under Alcuin's direction, this abbey became a vital cultural center. Theodulf, a Visigoth, also participated in the life of the court before he received the bishopric of Orléans.[19] Later Carolingian kings continued to participate actively in intellectual and cultural affairs. Lothair's Capitulary of Olonna in 825 envisioned a network of schools in northern Italy, all under the supervision of the Irishman Dungal.[20] Canons of the Roman councils of 826 and 853 and of the Council of Savonnières of 859 encouraged biblical studies.[21] Charles the Bald maintained an active palace school and was especially keen to sponsor Latin translations of Greek works.[22]

The example took. All through the ninth century, Carolingian abbots and bishops repeated for their own congregations the prescriptions first announced by the kings and their advisers.[23] Scholars emended ancient texts and wrote new works designed to undergird both the study of the liberal arts and sacred studies.[24] Teams of scribes toiled in scriptoria, or writing centers, to produce manuscripts for their own libraries or for loan or donation to less fortunate libraries.[25] The latinity of Carolingian authors improved.[26] Theological controversy and philosophical speculation were part and parcel of the Carolingian scene. Carolingian masters, confident of their own achievements, began to cite each other along with the great patristic authorities.[27] Genealogies of masters were composed, tracing what Carolingians considered the orderly transmission of learning from one generation to another.[28]

Schools proliferated.[29] The Carolingians certainly had not invented cathedral, monastic, and parish schools, the primary institutional agencies of the program for reform and renewal. These had a long history behind them. Indeed, several of the earlier schools had even flourished, for a moment or two: Caesarius of Arles's *domus ecclesiae*, Cassiodorus's Vivarium, or Bede's school at Wearmouth–Jarrow, for example. What was new in the Carolingian period was the *public* school. This was not a school open to the public but rather one under the patronage and jurisdiction of public authority. When Charles the Great and his sons wrote to abbots and bishops, they wrote to men whose establishments they had endowed and could thus influence.

The palace school has always absorbed the lion's share of modern scholarly attention. The importance of the palatine scholars, their patrons, and their works has obscured the scores of less well-known *magistri* and their *discipuli*. It was upon the latter, however, that the program of reform and regeneration depended. Unfortunately, no contemporary historians recorded for us the work and ambience of these schools, as Einhard did for Charles's palace school in his *Vita Karoli magni*, as Richer of Reims did for Gerbert's school in the tenth century, or as John of Salisbury did for Bernard of Chartres's school and the Parisian schools of the twelfth century.[30]

While the narrative record of their activities is rather sparse, these more obscure masters and students did leave behind them their manuscripts and their texts, and with these we can begin to reconstruct their contribution to the Carolingian renaissance. The products of the first fifty or so years of the period are, fortunately for us, covered in E. A. Lowe's *Codices Latini Antiquiores*.[31] Many of the approximately six thousand surviving books from the ninth century have been surveyed by Bernhard Bischoff and other scholars, and new studies and new discoveries continue to add to our knowledge.[32] The manuscripts and the occasional remarks of the masters enable us to enter the Carolingian schoolroom.[33]

The first step in the child's intellectual formation consisted of learning the rudiments: reading and writing. These skills went hand in hand. Students copied letters by rote and at the same time learned to recognize them. Letters led to syllables, syllables to phrases, phrases to texts. The first important text the students read was the Psalter, from which they imbibed both spiritual and educational nourishment. This first and deep study of the Psalms remained with the students the rest of their lives. Those few who went on to become authors found that verses from the Psalms came to mind involuntarily when they wrote. The Psalter is the most frequently cited biblical book in Carolingian writings.

Acquaintance with the Davidic hymns also introduced the beginning students to another important phase of their education, mastery of chant. The appearance of neumic notation in odd places in many manuscripts proves that instruction in chant, reinforced daily in the liturgy and the Divine Office, made a lasting impression. Calculation or the *computus* was another subject beginning students were expected to learn. Computational skills had a wide variety of applications, from measuring the harvests of fields to fixing important dates in the calendar.

All the while the students were being drilled in Latin, a language that was essentially foreign to them. Grammar was the art supreme in Carolingian schools. Not only language, but even theology passed through the prism of grammar. Not unlike the avatars of another renaissance, the Carolingians appreciated the philological approach to problems.[34] The other arts, both liberal and mechanical, received more or less attention depending on the training and interests of the master.[35]

Some students, blessed with natural talent or with high birth, were expected to go beyond the rudiments to prepare themselves as the masters and prelates of the next generation. Whether they became masters in their own schools or active abbots or bishops, they continued to teach and to be interested in learning. Their approach to the world and to the problems they faced was largely fashioned in the schoolroom.[36]

The Carolingian program of intellectual, spiritual, and educational reform was not announced, nor was it implemented in the schools, in as structured and as uniform a manner as the royal letters and decrees and the institutionalization of culture in the schools would lead one to believe. The plan, the program, was often compromised.

Any account of the Carolingian renaissance that omitted its detours, contradictions, and idiosyncrasies would make it seem too schematic. Carolingian rulers and prelates could provide an impetus, but they could not control intellectual activity and debate no matter how much they desired standardiza-

tion and unanimity. The immediate effect of the official involvement in learning and culture was to stimulate activity
on a broad front. Over distances of time and space, however,
the original impetus was transformed by individual talent, local differences, and changing circumstances. The ultimate
product and contribution of the Carolingian renaissance was
precisely this tension between the demands of an official culture and its diverse manifestations. The diversity of expression, of opinion, and of methods we observe on the Carolingian
scene should not surprise us. The Scriptures themselves, at
once the foundation and goal of the program, have always
yielded multiple meanings and justified divergent intellectual
attitudes. It is also no criticism to observe that the most astute
thinkers of ninth-century Francia wrestled with intractable
problems that have been of perennial concern in the history of
Western thought. The renaissance also furnished the occasion
for considerable displays of humor, egotism, camaraderie, ped-
antry, and intense self-satisfaction, traits that strike a discor-
dant note in a program so consumed with grand ideals and
moral concerns.[37]

Nor was all serene among the Carolingian scholars themselves, even in the court circle under the watchful eye of the
great Charles. Almost all the authors and textual scholars who
comprised the first generation of Carolingian intellectuals
came from outside Francia. Theodulf the Visigoth and Alcuin
the Anglo-Saxon enjoyed Carolingian patronage alongside the
Italians Peter and Paul and the Irishmen Clement, Josephus,
and Dungal, to name but a few. To be sure, some Franks, such
as Angilbert and the young Einhard, could be found in this
small but influential circle, but the predominant tone was a
foreign one. This community of disparates produced interesting results—Theodulf's edition of the Bible, for instance, differed markedly from the corrected version prepared by Alcuin.[38] Approaches to fundamental pedagogical issues also
varied. Irish masters were often chastised for being out of step,
as we learn from Theodulf's satirical attacks on their learning,
and particularly on their penchant for dialectic and compilation.[39]

A half-century later, what one might call nationalistic differences were less significant. By the generation of 850–875, the overwhelming number of scholars and masters whom we know by name were Franks. Foreigners such as John Scottus, Sedulius Scottus, and the English Bishop Marcus still found their way to the Carolingian realm. They came, however, not as cultural missionaries but rather, to paraphrase Heiric of Auxerre, as scholars drawn to the Continent by the fame of Charles the Bald's court.[40] Their work supports Heiric's observation, for their interests and methods show no appreciable differences from those of their continental colleagues. The learned John Scottus was a thoroughly Carolingian master.

There was always room for debate, sometimes strident and usually acrimonious, on matters of theology and ideology. Alcuin and Felix of Urgel differed on the question of Adoptionism.[41] Godescalc of Orbais and John Scottus disagreed with each other and with almost everyone else on the question of predestination.[42] The brilliant but unknown author(s) of the Pseudo-Isidorian decretals and those who drew on them in the ninth century challenged the role of the Frankish monarchy in ecclesiastical affairs and the concept of the episcopal church favored by some.[43] The most profound question in the Carolingian world centered precisely on the issues of reform and correction, the motive forces behind the renaissance. How was consensus to be achieved on the twin tasks of establishing norms and recommending correction when men strayed from Christian ideals? There was more to this question than the resolution of monarchical and episcopal views of Christian society. That could be done, at least intellectually. The difficulty came when theological formulations ran up against institutions working in time.[44]

Even the Scriptures did not yield to the desire for uniformity and concord. Alcuin was certainly not commissioned to produce an official Carolingian Bible, but, thanks to the productivity of the scribes at Tours, his corrected version was used in many places throughout the realm. Other versions competed with it. Theodulf of Orleans produced a truly scholarly edition of the Bible that was replete with alternate readings. At least four other versions circulated. Later in the ninth century, unknown masters combined elements from the different Carolingian Bibles to produce yet newer syntheses.[45]

The sermon and the saint's life, potentially two admirable means of communicating the ideals of the renaissance to society as a whole, became in the hands of some authors highly specialized and exclusive genres. Carolingian authors made the saints' lives vehicles for the celebration of monastic virtues, especially of the well-regulated life of the community.[46] And it is doubtful whether the sermons that have come down to us were originally addressed to the lowest levels of society, as Walter Ullmann would have it. Henri Barré, in the first synthetic work on Carolingian sermon literature, came to a different conclusion. Having studied a large body of ninth-century sermons, he described a Carolingian homiletic tradition that anticipated the interests of the Scholastics of the twelfth century rather than the needs of the people of the ninth century. Carolingian sermons were often more like commentaries intended for private study and meditation.[47]

In art, the court style was undermined by what Jean Porcher has called "provincial painting," a kind of art that developed free from court influences.[48] Carolingians wrote literature of all kinds—letters, poems, biblical commentaries, histories, polemic, sermons, and treatises on special subjects—in Latin, making the period an important one in the history of Latin literature.[49] Yet Marc Bloch's comments on the feudal age's disjuncture between Latin, the language of the scholars, and the vernacular language of the people apply even more strongly to Carolingian times.[50] Charles the Great's efforts in the waning years of his life to collect the national songs of the Franks testify to the ambiguity of the program.[51] So does the success of the *Song of Roland,* that great epic of aristocratic courage, valor, and bellicosity that was told over and over again in Carolingian halls.[52] The aristocracy's warrior ethos and the peasantry's rustic culture vitiated the scriptural view of society fostered by the court and promoted by the schools. The aristocrats, the farmers, and even some of the clerics were more attuned to magic, sorcery, and a still vital paganism than to the bookish culture of the educated.[53]

★

It was inevitable, given the instability of the Carolingian world, that the cultural program launched by the court would be distorted by individuals, by time, and by all the attendant forces that work on ideals entrusted to humans and human institutions. Nor is it surprising that increasingly specialized and sophisticated intellectuals, set loose among an amorphous and inconsistent set of doctrines, would fall into contention and dissonance. The Carolingian experiment had shortcomings, unresolved tensions, and failures, but our recognition of these should not blind us to the fact that it nonetheless achieved a broad cultural uniformity in the Carolingian realms.

One victory was the establishment of a basic canon of school authors, consisting of Roman grammarians and poets and commentaries on them, as the foundation for the education of youth.[54] None of these authors had been prescribed by legislation; however, if students were to achieve a proper understanding of Latin and especially of the tropes found in the Scriptures, they had to study the Latin authors. The liberal arts were "Christianized" for much the same reason. Earlier generations of masters, particularly conservative monks, had looked with suspicion on the liberal arts program. But Carolingian masters eagerly embraced it, not for the sake of the arts themselves but as a propaedeutic to the study of Scripture. The arrangement and definition of the liberal arts, and their relationship to the mechanical arts (such as surveying and stonecutting), were never determined in the schools. Nevertheless, the arts in a variety of guises—principally in the form of several Carolingian commentaries on Martianus Capella's treatise on the arts—were another key element of Carolingian education and thought. Alcuin saw them as the supports for the temple of Christian Wisdom. John Scottus wrote that, as rivulets flow together into one stream, so too do the arts unite in the contemplation of Christ.[55]

Higher education led ultimately to the Bible, to the divine pages, in which might be read God's message for people and for society. In addition to improving the text of the Bible, one of the great achievements of Carolingian scholarship was the adaptation of the exegetical works of the patristic age to the new audience of medieval Europe. The authority of the Fathers made them indispensable guides to the wisdom embedded in the Scriptures, yet the eighth- and ninth-century masters did not teach the Fathers by rote. The educational and cultural conditions of the Carolingian period were not those of the patristic age. For most, the Fathers had to be rearranged, combined, simplified, and supplemented. We usually reserve the word "synthesis" for a later medieval century, but it might also be applied to the way in which Carolingian masters approached the Fathers and used them in their teaching. The work of Carolingian masters and scribes may have won the Fathers their first major audience.[56]

Beyond focusing on the school authors, the liberal arts, and the Fathers as the ingredients essential to Christian wisdom, the Carolingians fostered a network of schools throughout Francia to undertake the kind of instruction envisioned by the capitularies. The Carolingian renaissance was both an intellectual and an institutional phenomenon. At least fifty monastic and cathedral centers were sufficiently active or fortunate to leave behind some record of their contributions to the renaissance. Although only a few of these schools have been studied in any detail, enough is known about them to permit a few generalizations. The network of schools was surprisingly interdependent. As a young student, Lupus of Ferrières, for example, traveled from his own foundation to the school at Fulda to train with a superior master. Furthermore, masters at the different centers were in continual contact with each other; they exchanged letters, books, and ideas as well as students. Although Carolingian scholars were not professional intellectuals, in the sense meant by Jacques LeGoff to describe the masters of the twelfth and thirteenth centuries, they formed a fraternity of men linked by their common desire to learn, to teach, and to observe the demands of the religious life.[57]

The burden of transmitting the Carolingian message to the world outside the schoolroom fell on the students, only a few of whom became cathedral or monastic masters in their own right. It was the job of the archdeacons and priests to bring Christian wisdom to their parishioners. We have no progress reports or reflections on this, the most important phase of the Carolingian program. The evidence suggests, however, that

Carolingian clergy, goaded by their bishops' numerous statutes, worked hard to communicate what they thought to be the principles of a Christian life to society at large. Inventories of country churches reveal that they were equipped with the tools necessary to carry on the ceremonies of the Christian cult.[58] Preachers were bidden to speak in the native tongue so that listeners ignorant of Latin might not be excluded from the salvific message.[59] Treatises on baptism, the Mass, the Lord's Prayer, and on marriage abound in the manuscripts. They are just beginning to receive the study they deserve.[60] Already it is apparent that their chief purpose was to help clergy to communicate the ideals of the renaissance to the illiterate and unschooled. We should not underestimate the difficulty of this task. Large portions of the Carolingian realm were only marginally Christian, and others had to face a resurgence of paganism. For the first time, however, the political and religious leaders of society had a plan, a network, and the personnel to combat what they regarded as evil and to lead their charges on to the City of God.

The eighth and ninth centuries were the heyday of the Carolingian dynasty and their renaissance. Although the last Carolingian monarch was deposed late in the tenth century, by the beginning of that century we find it increasingly difficult to speak of a Carolingian Europe. How did the cultural revival fare, once the dynasty and the political unity it had fostered succumbed to invasion and to the resurgence of pre-Carolingian localism? Briefly put, the renaissance was one of the most durable and resilient elements of the Carolingian legacy.

The famous Carolingian minuscule script survived and even appeared outside the land of its development as what paleographers call English Caroline script.[61] As textbook writers are fond of noting, Carolingian minuscule forms the basis of our modern typefaces.

The example the Carolingians provided as patrons of culture was even more significant. The legislation, the palace table talk, the dedication of scholarly works to Carolingian princes, the princes' personal educations, the support they gave to scholars and to schools—all these examples were not lost on subsequent generations of rulers. Already enshrined in Notker of Saint Gall's near-legendary account of the great Emperor Charles was the notion that learning was important, not for itself but for the spiritual health of the individual and of Christian society. The Ottonians, the Capetians, and the descendants of Alfred the Great (an Anglo-Saxon Charles the Great in matters cultural) all valued and patronized Christian learning.[62]

Cathedral and monastic schools continued to function as the primary centers of intellectual life through the tenth, eleventh, and twelfth centuries. From them came the pioneers of a new order: Berengar, Abelard, Anselm of Laon, Lanfranc, Anselm of Canterbury, Peter Lombard. The schools continued to offer a curriculum based on the arts, the Latin authors, and the Fathers. By the twelfth century, that curriculum had been modified by the masters' growing acquaintance with Greek learning and by an increasing emphasis on dialectic instead of the Carolingian favorite, grammar.[63] The new learning, however, never eclipsed the old. The High Middle Ages would never have seen a Bernard, a Peter Damian, a John of Salisbury, a Bonaventure, or a Thomas Aquinas if it had. The great cultural task of the High Middle Ages was to accommodate the new learning to the Christian, European culture created during the Carolingian renaissance.[64]

CHAPTER 4

The Macedonian Renaissance

WARREN TREADGOLD

As with many terms for cultural movements, the term "Macedonian renaissance" is an imperfect one. The "Macedonians" in it were Byzantine emperors of the ninth and tenth centuries who were known as "Macedonians" only because the founder of the dynasty was born in a part of Thrace that the Byzantines, for some reason, called the province of Macedonia. The dynasty's name may have been attached to the cultural revival of the ninth and tenth centuries partly because of the literary accomplishments of two of its members. The second Macedonian, Leo VI the Wise, was the nominal author of several works, and Leo's son, Constantine VII Porphyrogenitus, wrote or commissioned scores of volumes. By and large, however, "Macedonian" refers to the period when the revival took place rather than to the people who brought the revival about. The reigns of the first four Macedonian emperors (867–959) covered nearly a century during which Byzantine scholars wrote, read, and copied an extraordinary amount of literature.

About thirty years ago, when the term "Macedonian renaissance" was already in common use, most scholars considered it a satisfactory name as far as the dates went. In art and architecture, revival did seemingly set in at about the time the Macedonian dynasty took power, if only because figural religious art was reappearing after the long period of Iconoclasm, when such art had been under an official ban.[1] According to recent scholarship, however, learning and literature began to revive as early as eighty years before the first Macedonian clawed his way to the throne. Here I shall consider the revival of learning throughout this whole period of some 180 years, during only the latter part of which Macedonian emperors reigned. In fact, because the revival originated during the movement's non-Macedonian half, I shall devote most of my attention to it.

As for the word "renaissance," it has by now become imprecise enough to avoid the misleading connotations of the alternate name given by Paul Lemerle in the title of his book *The First Byzantine Humanism.* If "humanism" simply means reading and understanding Greek literature of the classical period, humanism had never died out at Byzantium. On the other hand, if "humanism" means a secular spirit that takes classical literature on its own terms, no Byzantine of the period would have admitted to such a thing, and only one or two can reasonably be accused of it.

The Byzantine phrase for "secular learning" was "the outside learning" (τὰ θύραθεν μαθήματα). *Inside* learning, which the Byzantines considered their own, was of course Christian learning. Anything else was foreign to them and of secondary importance. Certainly, every Byzantine who prided himself on his education wanted to know more than the minimum that was basic and essential, and men of real learning, as in every society, particularly wanted to acquire specialized knowledge of exotic and superfluous subjects. But this sort of attitude toward the Classics is not what we usually call "humanistic." This being said, interest in earlier Greek literature did revive strongly around the year 800, in a major change from the comparatively "dark" preceding period. This change does not appear to be primarily the result of any emperor's official policy. It was a gradual process that passed through several phases.

The Second Sophistic began some five hundred years of steady and substantial production of literature in Greek. The extent of this literature is easy to overlook because today much of it is lost, much more of it is hardly ever read, and what *is* occasionally read is read by people in different disciplines. But, put together, the pages written in Greek between A.D. 100 and 600 would easily outnumber those written before them.

The great secular and Christian authors of these five centuries are more or less familiar, at least as names: Lucian and Plutarch, Plotinus and Origen, Libanius and John Chrysostom, Proclus and Dionysius the Pseudo-Areopagite, Procopius and Romanus the Melode. They and other authors of their time account for nearly all the Greek Fathers, Neoplatonists, medical writers, and novelists; they also produced many volumes of history, oratory, poetry, and so on. But, even a little before 600, the pace of literary production slackened; in the seventh century it fell off drastically; and by the eighth century Greek literature seemed almost to have ended. To judge from the manuscripts that survive today, between the years 600 and 800 people even stopped copying most earlier works.[2]

The blame for these "Byzantine Dark Ages" has often gone to the Empire's military problems. These were the years in which Persian, Avar, Arab, and Bulgarian invaders were raiding and conquering all over the Empire. Certainly the Arabs' conquest of Syria and Egypt, with their great cultural centers at Antioch and Alexandria, was a blow to Greek literature. Still, before the invasions Constantinople had already become a cultural center of more importance than any of those that were lost. And the impoverishment and military preoccupations of the remaining Byzantines cannot by themselves really explain the cultural decline. After all, the far worse military problems of Byzantium under the Palaeologan dynasty did not prevent voluminous literary production. For that matter, neither did disastrous defeat in the Peloponnesian War cut off Greek literature at Athens. A society must be poor and preoccupied indeed to be unable to produce some writers.

But in the Byzantine Dark Ages there were other complications, some of which were not related to military events. In the first place, in the sixth century the imperial government, nearly completing the process of extinguishing paganism, forbade pagan scholars to teach. Secular literature naturally suffered with the disappearance of pagan teachers, who had valued the Greek Classics on their own terms and for their own sake. The disasters of the seventh century then compounded the damage by convincing many Christians that the world was coming to an end, and consequently turning their attention to spiritual matters.[3] At the same time, the decline of secular education and secular literature affected even Christian literature adversely.

The most important cause of the decline in literary production, however, was probably the decline of the group of people who produced and read literature. Though around its fringes this group is hard to define, defining its center is easy: it was the Empire's civil and religious officials. The continuing military crisis advanced the influence of generals and the army at the expense of the bureaucracy and the church hierarchy. In addition, the years around 700 were a time of frequent revolutions and changes in official church doctrine, during which the bureaucracy and the Church were repeatedly purged, and the army usually came out on top.

The final stage in the decline of the Empire's civil and religious officialdom came with the introduction of Iconoclasm in 726. The emperors imposed Iconoclasm with military support against the opposition of most of the old civil and religious governing class. Most of the men and women of this class deeply resented what seemed to them to be arbitrary interference in the forms of public worship that they considered unchangeable and in the doctrines of a church that they and their relatives administered. Some protested or rebelled, and were exiled. Monks in particular led the theological opposition, and were exiled, tortured, or even martyred as a result. Other civil servants and clergy who were also disaffected prudently made themselves inconspicuous. Religious literature suffered because few writers cared to write in defense of Iconoclasm, but even fewer cared to suffer the consequences of writing against it. The one prominent Greek writer of the mid-eighth century, John of Damascus, was able to write against Iconoclasm only because he lived in Arab territory, safely outside the reach of the Byzantine government.

The luck of the disgruntled civil servants and clergy finally changed in 780, when the Empress Irene took power after the death of her husband, Leo IV. Irene was herself opposed to Iconoclasm and acted on her opinion almost at once. She recalled the exiled iconophiles and allied herself with the civil service and the monks. The contemporary chronicler Theophanes, himself a monk from a family of civil servants, records under the year 781: "The pious began to express themselves freely, and the word of God began to spread, . . . and the monasteries began to be restored, and every good thing began to show itself."[4] Such was the situation at about the time when, according to recent scholarly opinion, the revival of learning began. Before following the revival's course, however, I would like to survey briefly the state of the Empire's educated class about 780.

Most of the responsibility for maintaining education in the Empire fell upon the members of the civil service, because they, unlike monks and bishops, could marry and have children. Indeed, the most prominent bishops and monks were usually former civil servants or the sons of civil servants. The importance of the civil service was further enhanced by its being heavily concentrated in Constantinople, where, along with the leading clergy, it formed a cohesive elite. This elite was never very large. About six hundred officials manned the central bureaucracy, and perhaps three hundred more were attached to the staff of the Imperial Palace. The staff of the Church, under the Patriarch of Constantinople, might have added another hundred; the important urban abbots and monks might have made two hundred more. By including the chief military officials and private lawyers, notaries, teachers, and stewards, we might bring the total to two thousand or so. This total, small as it seems, could have been nearly a tenth of the adult males in Constantinople.[5] These men had to be well educated in order to hold their positions in government and society. A few others, among the merchants, nuns, and wives and daughters of civil servants, might also have had a fairly advanced education, but in 780 their numbers were probably very low.

The members of this elite group had studied in their youth with private schoolmasters of the better sort. These taught them to read and write *koine* Greek, the language of the New Testament and of many postclassical authors. By the eighth century, spoken Greek differed markedly from what it had been in classical or even New Testament times. It had evolved into something more like modern Greek, but the literary language remained frozen in the first century A.D., with an archaic spelling, vocabulary, and above all grammar. Grammar was therefore the most important subject in a first-class Byzantine school, though some attention was also paid to rhetoric, which in this context meant the art of using and appreciating an archaic style.[6]

Most students probably learned to read on the Septuagint and the New Testament, but ideally they were then supposed to read some of the Classics, works written in an even more archaic language, usually Attic Greek. The Byzantines' list of "Classics" included some authors familiar to us, such as Homer, Euripides, Aristophanes, Demosthenes, Pindar, and Theocritus. The list also included some less expected authors: Theognis, Pseudo-Menander, Aelius Aristides, and St. Gregory of Nazianzus.[7] During the Byzantine Dark Ages, many students probably did not get much beyond the Bible, and read only a little of only a few of the Classics. But their education enabled them at least to understand and to draft state orders, documents, and letters in literary Greek.

A very select few within the elite acquired more than the basic education I have outlined so far. But since ordinary schoolmasters offered no more, the more serious student had either to teach himself or to seek the help of a particularly distinguished scholar, who was probably not a teacher by profession. At least one student of the time was fortunate enough to learn not merely poetry but the principles of classical metrics from St. Tarasius, head of the imperial chancery.[8] But such advanced knowledge was rare before 780, and specialized knowledge of mathematics and the natural sciences seems to have been particularly unusual. The same skills that the educated used to compose government orders, documents, and ordinary letters could of course have been turned to composing formal literature. But apparently this happened very seldom before 780.

Naturally, even around 780, the educated elite of the capital formed only a fraction of the literate people in the Empire. Not only in Constantinople but throughout the provinces tens of thousands of priests, monks, military officers, tax collectors, landowners, traders, and others must have learned to read and write from the Psalms and the New Testament.[9] Homer and Aelius Aristides were probably too hard for them, but they could read simple texts such as saints' lives and keep simple records and accounts. Besides these people, a few members of the elite were scattered over the provinces as provincial officials, bishops, or abbots. But the provinces were not a promising place to look for a revival of learning. Constantinople had the Empire's only important concentrations of educated men, schools, rewards for scholarship, and, above all, books.

Though little specific information is available about books in Constantinople around 780, we know that the Emperor, the Patriarch of Constantinople, and various churches and monasteries all maintained libraries there.[10] Subsequent events were to show that these libraries and others still held not only the ancient Greek literature that has been directly transmitted to us, but about as much again that is lost today.[11] Some literature had already been lost. The Quinisext Council of 692 had sternly condemned those who destroyed or sold for packing material copies of the Bible or the Fathers, unless these had already been damaged by bookworms or moisture.[12] That such a condemnation was necessary for religious books is a disturbing sign, and nothing at all forbade someone from using a manuscript of Aeschylus to light the stove or wrap up fish. In the ninth century we hear complaints that the people of earlier years had discarded many useful books as useless.[13] That some books were discarded and virtually none copied certainly shows that during the Byzantine Dark Ages many books were left unread. Relatively few texts, however, seem to have perished altogether at the time.

When the Empress Irene took power in 780 and recalled the exiles, she was not setting out to begin a classical revival. But she soon did begin to sponsor patristic research. Her aim was to condemn Iconoclasm for good and all, and to that end she gathered scholars to lay the theological groundwork for an Ecumenical Council. In 784 she appointed as the new Patriarch of Constantinople the most learned man she could find: St. Tarasius, head of the imperial chancery, former teacher of classical metrics, and a staunch defender of icons.[14] Tarasius directed his staff to search the works of the Fathers for passages that could be used to defend icons and refute Iconoclasm. Though Tarasius's assistants chiefly used the library of the Patriarchate, they consulted other collections as well. At the Seventh Ecumenical Council of 787 they presented the results of their research, and did so meticulously. Since they argued that the iconoclasts had defended their heresy by citing patristic passages out of context, Tarasius and his librarian and notaries took care to read out their citations at length and to produce the actual volumes for verification.[15]

The research done for this council was the beginning of a trend. At about the same time, monks and monasteries in and around the capital embarked upon a program of manuscript copying. Though the texts they copied were overwhelmingly theological and the effort was undertaken largely to help defend the icons, the manner in which the manuscripts were copied itself represented a scholarly advance. The scribes used the minuscule hand, which unlike the former uncial indicated the divisions between words and included accent marks and punctuation. This hand not only made manuscripts easier to read and understand, but because it was cursive, unlike the uncial, it was also quicker to write.[16] The new wave of copying was evidently a sign that the reading public was expanding, certainly among the monks, and apparently among others who had developed an enthusiasm either for religious literature or for the high offices Irene might award to them if they knew religious literature. And, finally, some new works began to be written and copied. Among the first examples were some sermons and letters of St. Tarasius and saints' lives of iconophiles whom the iconoclasts had persecuted.[17]

At about the same time, two historical works were also written, each of which was significant in its own way. Naturally, both say unpleasant things about the iconoclasts, and to put the deeds of the iconoclasts in a justly unfavorable light was no doubt one of the purposes of their authors. But both histories extend so far back before Iconoclasm that they must also represent something more: a desire to record properly the events that had been recorded inadequately during the Dark Ages.

One of the two texts, begun as the *Chronicle* of the church official George Syncellus, is more a work of reference than of literature. George begins with the creation of the world and narrates biblical and secular history up to the reign of Diocletian. With Diocletian, the chronicle, now bearing the name of George's friend Theophanes, is organized into annual entries, elaborately labeled according to various chronological systems. George's chronicle with Theophanes' continuation fills two good-sized volumes and extends up to the year 813, approximately the time of its completion. Its style is straightforward, not very elegant, and somewhat more popular than that of the New Testament. No one counts it among the world's great histories; it is often looked down upon because of its rigidly annalistic form (which seems to be considered a weakness in middlebrow historians, though not in highbrow ones like Thucydides or Tacitus). Yet today the chronicle of "Theophanes" is much our most important source for the Byzantine Dark Ages. It provides our only chronology for the period. Moreover, every later Byzantine historian who goes back so far either paraphrases Theophanes or begins where Theophanes left off. In view of its cautious attitude toward its disorderly and inadequate sources and its innovation in the absence of a true model, the chronicle of George Syncellus and Theophanes is not entirely unworthy of its position at the foundation of Middle Byzantine historiography.[18]

Probably a bit earlier in date is the historical work of Nicephorus, then an imperial secretary, and later Patriarch of Constantinople. It is brief—about eighty pages—and covers only the Dark Ages, supplying little information that is not also in Theophanes. Its claim to distinction is that it is, as far as we can tell, the first explicitly classicizing work written in the Empire for almost two centuries. In fact, it is formally a continuation of the last known classicizing history, that of Theophylact Simocatta, and was probably intended to be copied in a single manuscript with Theophylact, as at an early date it was.[19] A recent critic has called Nicephorus's history a "rather feeble effort," and admittedly it reflects the spirit of Thucydides less successfully than it imitates his language.[20] But the striking thing about Nicephorus's work is that in it he self-consciously revived history of the classical type at Byzantium after a long lapse. Once again, Attic Greek was not only being read but written. Nicephorus plainly expected his example to be followed, and it soon was.[21]

Such was the very earliest stage of the Byzantine revival of learning, which lasted from about 780 to 815. Its course suggests the revival's cause: the reaction of the Byzantine educated elite against Iconoclasm. This is not to say that the iconoclasts had caused the Dark Ages by persecuting the elite and that when Iconoclasm departed enlightenment automatically dawned—though that is more or less what Theophanes would have us think. According to him, the first iconoclast Emperor, Leo III, "punished many because of their piety, . . . especially those distinguished in family and reputation, so that he also extinguished the schools and the pious learning that had prevailed from [the Emperor] St. Constantine the Great up to that time; of [that learning], among many other good things, this . . . Leo was the destroyer."[22] It was only under Irene, says Theophanes, that "every good thing" (presumably including learning) "began to show itself" once again. In fact, the Dark Ages had been pretty dark well before Iconoclasm. But accurate or not, the idea that the iconoclasts had gone wrong by rejecting and distorting Christian learning served to impress iconophiles with the importance of knowledge in general.

It might seem therefore that when the Emperor Leo V shocked the Empire's elite by reintroducing Iconoclasm in 815, Byzantine learning would have suffered. Yet if anything the opposite occurred. The iconoclasts had evidently been stung by the charge that they had misinterpreted patristic literature, and they were determined to prove the charge false. Leo V found his own scholars—with the resources of an emperor it was not too hard to do—and appointed them to a patristic research commission of his own. The commission naturally arrived at the conclusion that the iconophiles were the ones who had misinterpreted the Fathers, and iconophilism was duly condemned. For their part, the iconophiles did not take this decision lying down and began an extensive underground iconophile literature. At the same time, the scholarship of both iconophiles and iconoclasts was beginning to include secular subjects as well as religious ones. I shall concentrate here on this secular knowledge.

The iconoclasts' leading intellectual light was John the Grammarian, to judge from his epithet a former schoolmaster, who served as head of the iconoclast research commission in 814. When the historian St. Nicephorus was deposed as Patriarch of Constantinople because of his defense of the icons, the emperor wanted to appoint John the Grammarian to the office but was dissuaded because of John's relative youth and low birth. John still went on to have a brilliant career, first as an abbot, then as a high church official and tutor to the future Emperor Theophilus. Finally, after Theophilus became emperor, John was appointed Patriarch in 838. Although the few fragments of John's writings that survive are iconoclast theology, John seems also to have been famous for scientific knowledge, which at the time was uncommon at Byzantium. What precisely he did as a scientist is unclear. The iconophiles charged that John practiced divination and magic in an underground laboratory, where beautiful nuns assisted him in a variety of professional and unprofessional capacities. John also supervised the planning and construction of a palace for Theophilus.[23]

The leading scientific scholar of the day was John's cousin, Leo the Mathematician. Though at the start of his career he was identified as an iconoclast, Leo appears to have been one of the very few Byzantines of his time who did not care much about icons one way or the other. He may even be an example of that greater rarity, a Byzantine who was mainly interested in secular learning for its own sake. Leo certainly began his career as a schoolmaster. The story goes that, despite the prominence of his cousin John, Leo lived in poverty and obscurity until the middle of the reign of Theophilus. But in 838 one of Leo's students was captured by the Arabs and taken to the court of the Caliph. The student displayed a knowledge of Euclidean geometry that none of the Caliph's court geometers could match, and attributed his erudition to Leo the Mathematician. The Caliph then wrote to Leo in Constantinople, inviting him to come to the Arab court to teach. Leo shrewdly reported the Caliph's job offer to the Emperor Theophilus, and Theophilus responded by founding a public school under Leo's direction in the Magnaura Palace.

The disappointed Caliph continued to write letters, asking at least to have Leo sent to him for a short time. But Theophilus refused, saying, "It would be senseless . . . to divulge to the infidels the knowledge of the universe for the sake of which the Roman race is marveled at and honored by all."[24] Shortly thereafter, as a special honor, Theophilus appointed Leo Metropolitan of Thessalonica. The poor mathematician seems to have been somewhat out of place in that role, to judge from a surviving sermon in which he discusses the Pentecost in terms of the properties of the numbers 1, 7, 8, 49, and 50.[25] Leo was not apparently much disappointed when the iconophiles returned to power and deposed him.

The reign of Theophilus, patron of John the Grammarian and Leo the Mathematician, marked a major advance for Byzantine learning. From then on it was taken for granted, as it had been before the Dark Ages, that the emperor would patronize research on secular subjects. Once again, as before the Dark Ages, there was a public school under imperial sponsorship that had a secular curriculum. Certainly, Theophilus did not consider secular learning mainly an end in itself. The emperor was a devout iconoclast, and could think of no better place for John and Leo than at the head of the Empire's two greatest bishoprics, Constantinople and Thessalonica. Theophilus may even have allowed his school at the Magnaura to lapse during the three years that Leo served as Metropolitan of Thessalonica. But Theophilus did set some value on secular knowledge, at least as a means of glorifying his reign. He spent large sums to outfit his throne room with golden machines: mechanical lions that roared, mechanical birds that sang, and a large organ. Perhaps he simply regarded Leo the Mathematician as another sort of court ornament that did marvelous things (though sometimes useful ones—Leo devised an optical telegraph that linked Constantinople and the Arab frontier). Still, by such means technology and knowledge can advance.[26]

I shall pass over the theological works written by the members of the iconophile underground, including the deposed Patriarch Nicephorus. The most interesting member of this group for our purposes was a young man who gained prominence only after the death of Theophilus and the second condemnation of Iconoclasm in 842. This was Photius. Though his family connections have been the subject of some confusion, several facts have now become fairly clear. He was related to St. Tarasius, the Patriarch whom Irene had chosen to direct the first, iconophile research commission. Photius's father was a civil servant and the author of a lost history that apparently continued the classicizing history of St. Nicephorus.[27] Like his father, Photius went into exile under Theophilus. He acquired a superb classical education, in large part through private reading. When the iconophiles came back into power in 842, he was about thirty years old and ready to begin a promising career as a scholar.

The second and final restoration of the icons in 843, the work of a regency headed by Theophilus's widow Theodora, virtually ended the division between iconophile and iconoclast scholars. The Patriarch John the Grammarian, too thoroughly identified with Iconoclasm to accommodate the new order, was sent off into exile. But many other iconoclasts recanted and were forgiven, though those who held church offices had to relinquish them. Leo the Mathematician had no scruples about joining the iconophiles and returning to teach at the School of the Magnaura. Bardas, the Empress's brother, now established the school on a more permanent basis, with a faculty of four. Leo directed the school and taught philosophy, while a former student of Leo's taught geometry and two others taught astronomy and grammar.[28]

As far as we know, this was the first Byzantine school since the early seventh century to have more than one instructor and to offer a formal program of what might be called higher education. Byzantinists have argued hotly over whether this public institution deserves to be called a "university." The level of its curriculum probably does justify the name, but the label "school" seems more appropriate to its small size.

At about the time this school was reorganized, Photius evidently made himself available as a private teacher—a very high-class one, with whom a discriminating student could study while also studying at the Magnaura. Photius, who was independently wealthy, later described his teaching almost as an avocation, which he pursued simultaneously with duties in the civil service. He was plainly interested in earning a reputation as a brilliant scholar, and chose to specialize in fields distinct from the science and philosophy for which Leo the Mathematician was famous. Photius's main interests—history, rhetoric, and theology—are on display in his *Bibliotheca*, a description of his reading that he probably composed in 845. Photius's fame spread, and by 858 the Caesar Bardas, who earlier had enlarged the School of the Magnaura and was now the most influential figure in the government, arranged Photius's appointment as Patriarch of Constantinople. After a patriarchate whose most notable accomplishments were the conversion of the Southern Slavs to Christianity and a bitter dispute with the Papacy, Photius was deposed in 867 by Basil I, the first Macedonian emperor.[29]

We can stop at this point, the beginning of the properly "Macedonian" part of the Macedonian renaissance, to survey the progress that had been made since the movement began around 780. The progress did not lie in any major expansion of the educated class in Constantinople. The size of that elite was held down by the small number of positions available for civil servants, church officials, and abbots in the capital, a number that grew only marginally down to the fall of the Empire. My earlier estimate that the educated class had about two thousand members is based on ninth- and tenth-century guest lists for imperial banquets and on a tenth-century account of the payment of officials; these documents reveal little if any growth.[30] For the tenth century, Paul Lemerle has estimated from evidence in the correspondence of a schoolteacher in Constantinople that at any one time between two and three hundred students under a dozen teachers were receiving a proper literary education in the capital. The estimate suggests that the total number of the educated elite was then about three thousand.[31] Such a number would generally not include the city's monks, who might obtain a fairly good education in monastic schools, or the wives and daughters of the elite, who could be educated at home by private tutors. One possible sign that women's educational opportunities improved is the appearance in Theophilus's reign of a woman writer, the abbess

Cassia. Theophilus is said to have declined to marry her because she once talked back to him in verse, but her epigrams and hymns became popular and survive today.[32]

The best indications of the extent of knowledge in the ninth century appear, naturally, in the surviving literary works of the period. These are in fact more successful as proofs of their authors' erudition than they are as literature. Leaving aside a number of minor authors, whose hagiography, poetry, histories, and letters show an improving literary style without being otherwise very memorable, we can focus on Photius, the archetypical Macedonian renaissance man. And leaving aside Photius's letters, sermons, and theological works, we come to his compilations, the archetypical Macedonian renaissance writings.

Photius produced three compilations, ostensibly more for his own amusement and that of his friends than for any wide circulation. The first is a lexicon, which Photius dedicated to one of his students. It is important as the first of a series of Byzantine lexica that indirectly preserved ancient lexicography and show that people were reading enough ancient literature to create a need for fairly detailed dictionaries. The second compilation is the *Bibliotheca*, a description of some four hundred books read by Photius, which he addressed to his brother. The third work is the *Amphilochia*, which contains answers to some three hundred questions asked by Photius's friend Amphilochius. All three are multivolume works, consisting of excerpts, summaries, interpretations, and criticisms of earlier Greek literature. But which earlier Greek literature?

Only to a very limited extent was it what *we* call classical literature—that is, works written up to the fourth century B.C. Photius explains in the *Bibliotheca* that in it he deals with only fairly rare books and no standard texts, by which he evidently means a list like that I gave earlier: Homer, Aelius Aristides, and so on. On the other hand, Photius describes only a few works of the classical period that were *not* standard—only three historians, including Herodotus, and eight orators, with no poets. Photius does not even seem to have had an especially high regard for classical authors; he refers to Thucydides three times, each time merely to note how much less clear Thucydides is than other writers.[33] Photius's favorite authors wrote during the Second Sophistic and the patristic age, in the five centuries of Greek literature that preceded the Dark Ages. For Photius, the main part of Greek literature was the part that we hardly ever read today.

Photius's favorite historian is Arrian, the author of the *Anabasis* of Alexander of the second century A.D., who today is considered quite mediocre. "Even many of the ancients," says Photius, are inferior to Arrian.[34] Photius criticizes the classical orator Isocrates sharply for his affectation and verbosity, though many classicists today admire Isocrates' style, and he praises the orators of the Second Sophistic, whom most classicists now condemn for their affectation and verbosity.[35] In a revealing passage in one of his letters, Photius tells a friend which authors to imitate in writing letters and which are inferior. The authors whose style he rejects are Aristotle, Plato, and Demosthenes. The best style, says he, can be found in the letters of Pseudo-Phalaris, Pseudo-Brutus, Isidore of Pelusium, and several other late writers—all of whom have little reputation today for good or ill, because they are almost never read.[36] To be sure, Photius levels many criticisms at various obscure authors of the period from the second to the sixth centuries. But for him the authors of that time bulk so large that they naturally get much the greatest share of his literary praise. Of the books described in the *Bibliotheca,* about five-sixths date from the half-millennium that began with the Second Sophistic.[37]

In the importance he assigns to this period of Greek literature, Photius is typical of the Byzantine scholars of Macedonian times. Leo the Mathematician wrote some poems about *his* favorite books, all of which are of this post-classical age. The books include not only scientific treatises, which largely date from that period anyway, but philosophical works and novels.[38] George Syncellus took his ancient history not from classical authors but from the chronicles of two fifth-century monks and perhaps from the third-century Christian chronicle of Julius Africanus.[39] The ordinary well-educated Byzantine plainly modeled his style not on classical Attic authors but on the pagan and patristic authors who had adopted the revived Attic Greek of the Second Sophistic.

It was perfectly natural that the Byzantines of the Macedonian renaissance took up Greek learning and literature from where these had left off before the Dark Ages, and not from the Golden Age of Athens. The Byzantine identified himself as a Christian and a Roman, not as a Greek or "Hellene," a name that meant "pagan." ("Byzantine," of course, is a purely modern term.) The literature of the second through sixth centuries A.D. was the literature of the Roman Empire (minus the Latin literature that the Byzantines could not read because they generally knew no Latin). During those centuries the Empire was increasingly, and in the end completely, a Christian state. The Byzantines liked to think that Christ had chosen to be born at the time of the foundation of the Roman Empire and to have the New Testament written in Greek, the language of the Roman (that is, Byzantine) Empire.

The Byzantines also found the outlook of this period of literature appealing. The primitive and shocking features of Greek paganism, apparent in most classical Greek poetry and drama, were nearly all absent from this later Greek literature. Instead it offered Christianity, Neoplatonism (which had much of the flavor of Christianity), tasteful and amusing fiction, well-told histories of the period, and all sorts of other useful information, most of it couched in an elegant style with clear rules. The interest in knowledge as such and the love of a highly polished literary style were taken over from Late Antiquity to become characteristic of the whole Macedonian renaissance.

Such features are clearly visible in the literature of the remaining portion of the Macedonian period, which I shall only outline here. The reign of Basil I the Macedonian was an extension of the age of Photius, whom Basil soon came to respect and consequently returned to office as Patriarch of Constantinople. Photius had, however, already written his major works. In fact, the reigns of Basil and of his successor Leo VI brought something of a pause in the scholarly revival, though manuscripts continued to be copied and the schools continued to function. One substantial achievement was a new law code compiled under Basil and completed under Leo VI; Leo also commissioned manuals of court ceremonial and military tactics. Though such works were of practical use and showed that the emperors now had competent researchers and writers on legal and military matters in their service, the main progress in scholarship came during the reign of Leo's son, Constantine VII Porphyrogenitus.

Since Leo died when Constantine was seven years old, the government passed into the hands of regents and coemperors. They kept Constantine from taking any significant part in governing until he was nearly forty. With little to do as emperor, Constantine retired to the imperial library and read. Even after he finally managed to assume real power in 944, he remained interested in research and commissioned a number of research projects, to some of which he contributed personally. By Constantine's time the Byzantines' interest in learned compilations, already evident in the works of Photius, had become a reigning fashion. Constantine gave the fashion ample encouragement from the throne, but the compilers of the majority of the tenth century's encyclopedic works worked independently of imperial patronage.

Even more than the works of Photius, these compilations of the tenth century are selections or arrangements of earlier material. Photius at least made lengthy judgments on the books he described in the *Bibliotheca*. Though he includes many excerpts from the books, a substantial part of the *Bibliotheca* is still his own work. By contrast, the scholars of the tenth century produced volume upon volume to which they added little or nothing of their own.

The most extreme case is what must surely have been the longest compilation of the period: a gigantic set of fifty-three encyclopedias compiled for Constantine Porphyrogenitus, containing excerpts from ancient and Byzantine historians on a medley of ill-assorted subjects. Of the whole collection, now called simply the *Excerpta* for lack of a known title, only two encyclopedic sections survive entire: one on embassies and another on virtues and vices. Some better-known and better-organized compilations of the time probably owe nothing to Constantine's patronage. Among them is the *Palatine Anthology*, our largest collection of Greek poetry. It was compiled from earlier collections and updated by the addition of Byzantine poems, including some by the compiler, Constantine Cephalas. Another important compilation was the *Suda*, a massive encyclopedia of Greek history and literature. Its thirty thousand or so alphabetical entries, drawn from various earlier works, cover authors, terms, and topics right down to the tenth century.

Though such compilations consist almost entirely of excerpts, their compilers do reveal a good deal about themselves by their process of excerpting. Like Photius, they have a unified view of Greek literature: from Homer to the middle Byzantine period, it is one literature, including both Christian and pagan authors of both earlier and later times. Apart from the classical authors studied in schools, the later and the Christian authors get most of the attention. The four longest articles in the *Suda* are on Homer, "Jesus, the Christ and our God," Origen, and Dionysius the Pseudo-Areopagite.[40] A great number of the poems in the *Palatine Anthology* are by early and middle Byzantine writers; the classical poems are definitely in the minority. Exactly half of the twenty-six historians excerpted in the surviving sections of the *Excerpta* are later than the fourth century A.D.[41] At the same time, these excerpted histories, like the poems in the *Palatine Anthology* and the articles in the *Suda*, leave no period of Greek literature wholly unrepresented.

To a remarkable extent, even the works written in the tenth century about recent events show the mentality of an antiquarian compiler. These works include the lengthy manuals of court ceremonial, provincial organization, and imperial foreign policy composed by Constantine Porphyrogenitus as well as several histories that cover the preceding century and a half and end with Constantine's reign. In all of these the authors lose most of their interest in their subjects when they come to deal with contemporary events. Even as late as the reign of Constantine's father, Leo VI, they enthusiastically retell their sources. But as soon as they confront events that occurred within their own memories and run out of sources written by other people, their enthusiasm evaporates. The reason cannot have been inhibition about writing on a sovereign who was still living; in their earlier narrative some of the historians are

loud in their denunciation of the Macedonian dynasty and
others fulsome in their praise—and their vehemence evidently
has much more to do with their feelings about Constantine VII
than with any views on his dead forebears and their enemies.
Nor did the historians neglect contemporary events from lack
of inside information: the group included men commissioned
by Constantine, a chief minister of the imperial government,
and Constantine himself.[42]

It seems as if literary research was in fashion and original
composition was not. No one wanted to write mere memoirs,
because real scholarship came out of books and archives. A
similar mentality lay behind the accelerated copying and editing of manuscripts in the tenth century. Then, to a greater extent than even in the ninth century, men considered that the
proper function of the writer and scholar was to copy and com-
pile—to collect all the information that had been so long neglected and to classify and preserve the writings that were finally being appreciated.[43] With so much digesting of works
already written to be done, taking time to write new material
seemed hard to justify. So the Macedonian renaissance was
much more a revival of knowledge than a revival of literature.

This survey of Macedonian literature may seem to vindicate
the long-accepted orthodoxy about Byzantine learning, an orthodoxy that was already well established seventy years ago,
when J. B. Bury summed it up:

It is notorious that the Byzantine world, which produced many men
of wide and varied learning, or of subtle intellect, . . . never gave
birth to an original and creative genius. . . . Age after age, innumera-
ble pens moved, lakes of ink were exhausted, but no literary work remains which can claim a place among the memorable books of the
world. . . . Classical tradition was an incubus rather than a stimu-
lant; classical literature was an idol, not an inspiration. . . . Yet if the
literature of the world is not indebted to the Byzantines for contributions of enduring value, we owe to them and to their tenacity of educational traditions an inestimable debt for preserving the monuments
of Greek literature which we possess today.[44]

Obviously, by "Greek literature" Bury meant classical Greek
literature; he would scarcely have given the Byzantines much

credit for passing on their own productions. Along with the same backhanded compliment, this attitude continues to prevail today. In a recent review of Paul Lemerle's *Le Premier Humanisme byzantin*, Ihor Ševčenko quotes with approval one of Lemerle's conclusions: "We are indebted to Byzantium for no contribution to progress."[45] Even more recently, Cyril Mango has asked: "Why is it . . . that the Byzantines, who lavished so much attention on the pagan classics, never comprehended their spirit?"[46]

Before accepting this judgment as the whole story, however, we might consider precisely what else we would have had Byzantine scholars do in the ninth and tenth centuries. Presumably their mistake was not that they rediscovered, appreciated, and studied the bulk of earlier Greek literature instead of contenting themselves with their small canon of school texts and going on at once to compose charming epics on their wars with the Arabs or incisive biographies of their contemporaries. If the Byzantines were to rediscover and copy earlier Greek literature, they were plainly not going to have much time to do anything else. We should recall that the scholars were part of a small educated elite, most of whom had heavy duties administering the Church and state and correspondingly little leisure for scholarship. Under the circumstances, the Byzantines' high regard for the literature they had rediscovered almost compelled generations of scholars to occupy themselves more with copying, compiling, and classifying it than with writing original literature of their own. The enormous mass of rediscoveries more or less overwhelmed the small band of Byzantine intellectuals.

The implied criticism of many modern scholars seems to be not that the Byzantines should have disregarded earlier Greek literature, but that they should have concentrated only on what we call the Greek Classics and forgotten about all that rubbish written in the Hellenistic period and later. The mistake of the Byzantines might therefore appear to be that they studied all Greek literature indiscriminately instead of choosing the very best and ignoring the remainder. Certainly Photius, for example, read just about every book he could find, but he was by no means an uncritical reader. He praises and blames authors of every period, and is quite capable of praising the style or content of a work by a pagan or heretic and of condemning the style or content of a work by a Christian saint. He gives reasons for his judgments, and almost all of them are at least defensible. Anyone who has read Thucydides in Greek knows that he often *is* obscure; and anyone who has read Isocrates knows that he *is* artificial and verbose. Like modern critics, Photius also knew that many later Greek and Byzantine authors were just as guilty of obscurity, artificiality, and verbosity; unlike many modern critics, Photius realized that many classical and later works with those characteristics nonetheless have merit and even beauty.

What Photius and other Byzantines lacked was a preconception that Greek works written before Alexander the Great were inevitably superior to later ones. In this, the men of the Macedonian renaissance had something in common with those of the Renaissance proper, who counted authors like Lucian and Plutarch among the Classics. From the standpoint of the literary historian, the Byzantines' view that Greek literature was a unified whole is hard to challenge. It gave Byzantine scholars a far more balanced picture of the development of Greek historiography, oratory, and poetry, and of the connections between Greek philosophy and theology, than most modern scholars have. Besides, every people have a natural tendency to study their own traditions, and the Byzantines were quite right to think of all earlier Greek literature as their literary heritage.

Given that what the Byzantines did during the ninth and tenth centuries was worth doing, and that they had little time for anything else while they were doing it, we might still criticize them for not going on to make an original contribution after the task of rediscovery was mostly completed. It is true that in the years around 1000 Byzantine literary activity paused to some extent after its period of revival. After that fairly brief hiatus, however, certain Byzantines did get around to composing a romantic epic on their wars with the Arabs and a set of incisive biographies of their contemporaries. I refer to the epic *Digenes Acrites,* which may even date as early as the tenth century, and to the memoirs of Michael Psellus, called the *Chronographia.* Other outstanding examples of Byzantine literature written during the eleventh and twelfth centuries are the classicizing histories of Anna Comnena and Nicetas Choniates and the poetry attributed to "Theodore Prodromus."[47]

Not even the harshest critics of Byzantine literature in general remain entirely unmoved by this innovative literature of the eleventh and twelfth centuries. Somehow, however, they imply that it does not count, as if by being a part of Byzantine literature a work was guilty of lack of originality merely by association. Bury grudgingly admitted that Psellus's "descriptions of the emperors and empresses whom he knew give an impression of reality and life" and that Psellus's influence on one school of Byzantine historiography was lasting.[48] Cyril Mango, despite his negative judgment on most Byzantine literature, calls Psellus's history a "masterpiece" of striking originality, describes Anna Comnena's history as "vivid and full of psychological insight" and Nicetas's as "remarkable," and finds the *Digenes Acrites* "meritorious" for its presentation of "a truly heroic milieu."[49] One might even say that such qualities give several of these works what Bury said none can claim: "a place among the memorable books of the world." By this stage, the Byzantines' self-appointed task of mastering earlier Greek literature had progressed to the point where their best minds were ready to add their own contributions to that literature. No doubt the very best minds of the time of Psellus were few, perhaps half a dozen—but the very best authors of most civilizations are not much more numerous and are often drawn from a larger educated group.

Mango goes so far as to say that the period that followed the Macedonian revival showed promise of still further intellectual development, though he believes that the Seljuk Turkish invasion and the Fourth Crusade prevented this potential from being realized. In his words: "Byzantine society could have been transformed, and the generation of Psellus gives us some reason for supposing that its intellectual habits, including its relation to the classics, might have evolved in a new direction. Unfortunately, events decided otherwise."[50] But those events do not negate what actually was accomplished in the eleventh and twelfth centuries. Like the Renaissance proper, the Macedonian renaissance should not be judged only by its own accomplishments—the actual rediscoveries—but also by its consequences, a major opening up of culture to activities of a new kind. I do not mean to exaggerate the merits of the Macedonian revival of learning. I would suggest, however, that its merits have been undervalued for a long time because some modern attitudes have tended to obscure the facts both about Byzantium and about Greek literature in general.

CHAPTER 5

The Anglo-Saxon Monastic Revival

GEORGE HARDIN BROWN

L ike any great enterprise, a cultural renaissance requires two ingredients: strong, visionary leadership and considerable resources of wealth and personnel. Moreover, these ingredients must reach a certain critical mass to produce a cultural renewal that will extend beyond the originating personalities and locale. From the eighth to the tenth century, Anglo-Saxon monks and kings collaborated in several attempts to bring about a renaissance, with results that are instructive, and even sometimes poignant, to modern historians. The success or failure of the movements toward cultural revitalization hinged on the intensity or weakness, the cooperation or hostility of the monks and their royal patrons.

Our familiarity with the cultural legacy we owe to the monks tends to mask the historical irony inherent in that indebtedness. The transmission and preservation of culture, the love of learning, anything that might be called formal education, the production of books, the development of art and architecture, indeed the cultural foundation of Western civilization owe their very existence to monasticism. Yet the monastic ideal calls on men and women to retreat from society and the City of Man in order to make an unencumbered pilgrimage to the City of God. Nonetheless, it was these societal dropouts and ascetics who were the principal preservers and purveyors of culture from the fifth to the thirteenth century.[1]

Yet although it preached asceticism, Western monasticism also adhered to the Judeo-Christian premise that God is inher-

ent in the world he created, that he acts in it, and is revealed in
it. Thus through the right use of the material world in life and
art, humans can glorify God and progress to him. Furthermore,
monastic Christianity is a religion of the book, and monks are
a people of the book. The choir monks and officers of the con-
vent had to be literate in order to understand and communicate
the Bible, the Rule, and the liturgy. Because reading promotes
thought and meditation, St. Benedict (c.480–c.550) ordained in
his *Rule* that each monk read for at least four hours on regular
days and for even longer on Sundays and feast days. Oblates,
novices, and young monks were trained in grammar and literature, both sacred and profane. Benedict enjoined literacy for
both private and public reading and allowed for the work of ar-
tisans, but made no special provisions for the arts. Cassiodorus
(c.485–c.580) established all the liberal arts as a basic propaedeutic for the study of Scripture and theology. Over the course
of medieval history the ideals of Benedict's Monte Cassino
merged with those of Cassiodorus's Vivarium.[2]

Early medieval handwriting and book production were directly linked to the vicissitudes of monasticism. When monastic discipline throve in England, learning throve—and almost
exclusively in the monasteries. Diocesan clergy did not usually have the tradition or collegial resources to educate themselves beyond a primitive level. The canons' secular attach-
ments and individualistic functions and attitudes rarely inclined them to pursue learning, much less to promote an educational system. Until the Benedictine reform, cathedral
schools were totally dependent on the quality and resources of
the bishop and had a lamentable record. Thus in early England,
the state of learning depended on the spiritual and cultural direction of the monks.

To become a successful center of learning, an English monastery needed both patronage and such independent resources
as buildings of some importance and beauty, a library that contained at least the basic texts, and a staff adequate to teach the
basic disciplines of grammar, rhetoric and metrics, music, and
computus (by which monks reckoned movable dates in the ecclesiastical year). These resources were not easy to come by.
To provide the economic basis for such extensive enterprises,

the monasteries depended on the generosity and endowments of the nobles, and their donations frequently came with not just strings but ropes attached. Many local worthies founded small houses, *monasteriola*, on their own property. They treated these little convents as their own establishments, controlling them and often receiving from them more than spiritual benefits. Many nobles placed lay members of their own family as superiors over a monastery, in a practice known as *saecularium prioratus*.[3] However, no monastery could succeed spiritually or intellectually on such a small, entailed, and dependent estate. A monastery established by a great earl or lady had a greater endowment, but it also had greater problems with dependency and control. As a result, an ambitious, prudent monk who wanted to found an Anglo-Saxon monastery preferred to appeal to the king for an unencumbered endowment large enough and protected enough to insure a relatively independent and safe development. Some of these clerics were astute enough also to secure a papal document confirming the liberties of the house.

Thus the noble, industrious, intelligent, and enormously acquisitive Benedict Biscop (628–690), after a monastic sojourn at Lérins, visits to Rome, and tenure as abbot of St. Peter's, Canterbury, received seventy hides of land from King Ecgfrith's own demesne to found St. Peter's monastery at Wearmouth in 674. He invited the talented and strict Ceolfrith to leave Ripon, Wilfrith's establishment, to become prior of this St. Peter's. Leaving Ceolfrith in charge, Benedict traveled to Gaul to contract masons, sculptors, and glaziers to help build his monastery and then to Rome for more books, vessels, vestments, images, and pictures to adorn it. From Rome he brought John, archchanter of St. Peter's, to instruct his monks in music. Benedict looked to the welfare of his establishment in another important area: he secured from Pope Agatho a letter of privilege, granted with the full consent of King Ecgfrith, that exempted his monastery from all external control.[4] When Ecgfrith granted him another ten hides of land to erect a sister foundation, Benedict founded St. Paul's of Jarrow in 682 with seventeen monks under Ceolfrith as abbot. The plague hit both houses hard—only Ceolfrith and a young lad (who the evidence indicates was Bede himself) were able to continue singing the office at Jarrow—but they were soon flourishing again.[5]

Still, the monasteries were not entirely free from the tyranny of political caprice. When Ecgfrith was killed, Aldfrith became king of Northumbria. Like the niggardly Heremod in the epic *Beowulf*, Aldfrith liked to collect treasures but not to distribute them. Benedict now had to buy what he had previously been given; he presented the king with his two silk pallia from Rome in exchange for three needed acres, and Ceolfrith sold the king a splendid cosmography that Benedict had acquired in Rome. Benedict died on 12 January 690, exhorting the brethren to hold fast to the pure Benedictine Rule and commanding them to preserve carefully "the glorious library of a very great store of books which he had brought with him from Rome."[6] Ceolfrith carried on as abbot of both Wearmouth and Jarrow. Having learned the lesson well from his master Benedict, he obtained from Pope Sergius a letter of privileges, which he had confirmed by King Aldfrith and his English bishops. In 716, with the twin monasteries and their six hundred monks doing well, Ceolfrith determined to make a final saintly pilgrimage to Rome, taking with him the deluxe copy of the Scriptures his monks had prepared for the Pope.[7] He died en route.

Benedict's and Ceolfrith's energy and Ecgfrith's generous and Aldfrith's grudging patronage ensured a good education for the Venerable Bede (c.673–735), their greatest alumnus. As a teacher and writer he was to excel his mentors. In his monastic library, Bede had access to about a hundred authors and about two hundred books.[8] Under the patronage of relatively minor kings, two monasteries thus created monastic history and left a legacy of beautiful books. As successful as they were, however, the institutions were too few and the patronage was too limited for the Northumbrian cultural renewal to merit the sometimes conferred title "renaissance." Nonetheless, the two monasteries, whose story Bede recorded for posterity in *The Ecclesiastical History of the English People* and the *History of the Abbots of Wearmouth and Jarrow*, provided a positive English example for the greater tenth-century revival to come. Some historians trace the source of Carolingian culture as well to Wearmouth–Jarrow and the great Bede, whose learning was carried to the Continent by Anglo-Saxon missionaries and teachers, most notably by Alcuin of York (c.732–804), protégé of Egbert, Bede's disciple.

The career of Benedict Biscop's fellow aristocrat and childhood friend, Wilfrith (634–709), exemplifies what could happen when inspiring drive did not attract supporting patronage. An abbot of Ripon, originally trained at Lindisfarne but converted to Roman practice, Wilfrith attained his greatest success at the Synod of Whitby (663–664). There he championed the Roman traditions against the Irish and was rewarded with the see of York. However, his feuds with King Ecgfrith (the patron of Benedict Biscop) led to the division of Wilfrith's diocese in 678 by Archbishop Theodore of Canterbury and to Wilfrith's loss of both lay and ecclesiastical support at home. Although he successfully appealed the archbishop's actions to Pope Agatho, he was rendered powerless and indeed imprisoned by Ecgfrith. When Ecgfrith died in 686, Wilfrith was reconciled to Archbishop Theodore and received the see of Ripon and the abbacy of Hexham—only to be banished after a dispute with King Aldfrith. Further struggles and another appeal to Rome brought him a victory in theory and a loss in practice. Secure in his belief that he had divine support and papal patronage, at the end of his career Wilfrith nonetheless had little to show for his great expenditures of talent and industry. He had contributed to education and building in York, Ripon, and Hexham, and through his monastic foundations in both the north and south of England he may have been responsible for the spread of the Benedictine Rule. Yet Wilfrith's religious and cultural enterprises were tied to him alone, and with his passing they went into partial eclipse or disintegrated. He helped win England for Rome, but his attempts at cultural renewal were scattered and therefore soon dissipated.

If Wilfrith provides an example of great intelligence and ambition neglecting to pay due attention to diplomacy, King Alfred (871–899) offers a poignant example of a great king struggling with few resources and fewer leaders to renew learning. The Viking conquest of northwestern England had sapped the

Anglo-Saxons' spiritual strength and resources until the monasteries and the educated clergy had practically disappeared. Alfred himself recalled in his Anglo-Saxon preface to Pope Gregory's *Pastoral Care* how England had formerly been a source of knowledge and instruction for the Continent, but "so completely had learning decayed in England that there were very few men . . . who could apprehend their services in English or even translate a letter from Latin into English." He explains his intention to have translated a few essential books (what he viewed as "required reading"): "I began in the midst of other various manifold cares of this kingdom to turn into English *The Pastoral Care,* sometimes word by word, sometimes by paraphrase, as I had learned it from my Archbishop Plegmund, my Bishop Asser, and my priest Grimbald and my priest John."⁹ No doubt Alfred, in his efforts to bring about uniform law and to restore learning, was looking back to the example of Charlemagne. Alas, great as were his accomplishments as king and Christian, Alfred's efforts were supported neither by resources as great as Charlemagne's nor by ecclesiastical leaders quite the caliber of Alcuin, Paul the Deacon, and the other luminaries of the Carolingian court school.

However, Alfred did lay the foundations for a unified political entity, and each of his immediate successors consolidated and enlarged that intrepid king's realm in southwest England. The martial Edward the Elder concentrated on warfare and on secular administration, adding Essex, Mercia, East Anglia, and the Five Boroughs to his kingdom of Wessex. His strength was statesmanship, not learning. During his fifteen-year reign Edward's son Athelstan added Bamborough and York to the Wessex domain, partly through negotiation but also through warfare: after a series of lesser victories, in 937 Athelstan and his young stepbrother Edmund soundly thrashed the Vikings, Irish, and Welsh at Brunanburh.¹⁰ Athelstan, whose contemporaries acclaimed him more than they did his grandfather Alfred, was not only a great leader but also a patron of religion and the arts, a donor of manuscripts, and a collector of relics. Nonetheless, during Athelstan's reign organized monastic life simply did not exist in England. The houses built in earlier days either lay in ruins or were occupied by clerks who performed the liturgy and trained children to succeed them.[11]

Yet it was in Athelstan's court that Dunstan and Aethelwold, two of the three leaders of the coming tenth-century monastic and cultural revival, were introduced to Anglo-Saxon aristocratic life. Dunstan (909–988) was called to that court in 924, the year Athelstan became king, and made a remarkable impression. Dunstan had been educated at Glastonbury. Though no longer a monastery, this ancient abbey was then a house of secular clerics, with itinerant Irish scholars who had set up a school, in a part of England where the memory of the former monastic life was strong. There Dunstan studied his letters, Scripture, poetry, mathematics, and music; he became adept at the organ, and the harp was a constant companion. He earned fame as a scribe, illuminator, organ- and bell-maker, and ecclesiastical artist. King Athelstan, a collector of beauty, liked this bright young man given to introspection and visions. But the other young men of Dunstan's rank, and even his own family, deemed such gifts dangerous. Charged with "studying the vain poems and trifling histories of ancient paganism to become a worker of magic,"[12] he was literally thrown out of court into the mud. Then a serious illness convinced Dunstan to take the monastic vows that his uncle, Aelfheah the Bald, Bishop of Winchester, had previously urged on him.

When Edmund succeeded his brother Athelstan, he recalled Dunstan to court, only to exile him again when some of his thanes leveled new jealous accusations at the young man. This second exile was short-lived, however. Miraculously saved from a fall over a cliff, Edmund repented, sent for Dunstan, and in 945 installed the twenty-one-year-old monk as abbot of Glastonbury. Finally Dunstan's position was secure enough for his greatness to manifest itself. Abbot Dunstan at once began a reform of the house, and over the next fifteen years firmly established the first organized community of monks to exist in England for at least two generations. When Edmund's brother Eadred became king in 946, he supported Dunstan royally, entrusting title deeds and many other treasures to his custody.

Backed by royal patronage and with the wealth he had inherited from his own family and from the lady Aethelflaed, Dunstan made Glastonbury into a flourishing community with extensive buildings and furnishings. He attracted to the life other men of talent, often with temperaments quite different from his own. The monastic life at Glastonbury became the core from which monachism was to spread throughout England. So many of the monks whom Dunstan had trained were eventually promoted to new or reformed monasteries that he well deserves the title of founder of the monastic movement. In his later role as Archbishop of Canterbury, Dunstan let Aethelwold become the more active monastic leader; nonetheless, it was his initiative and support that made the movement a success.[13]

Although Dunstan and his associates were aware of the early tenth-century monastic reforms in Burgundy and in upper and lower Lorraine, the Glastonbury reform was originally very much an English affair. We have no evidence to indicate that the communal life there was based on the codes of Benedict of Aniane or even on the Benedictine Rule. It was Dunstan's followers who reestablished that Rule in other monasteries. Dunstan's greatest friend, disciple, and fellow artist was the formidable Aethelwold, who was ordained with Dunstan by Bishop Aelfheah and subsequently became dean of Dunstan's monastery. Aethelwold wished to seek wider learning and more perfect monastic discipline abroad but was thwarted when in 954 King Eadred commissioned him instead to restore the decayed monastery of Abingdon. Dunstan himself soon became involved in the Continental Benedictine reform through the backwards expedient of being again sent into exile, this time because his public rebuke offended King Eadwig's future queen.[14]

Dunstan found refuge with the monks of St. Peter's at Ghent, under the patronage of Arnulf, count of Flanders. Founded as part of the tenth-century reform movement that originated at Brogne, St. Peter's proved the ideal location for Dunstan's maturation as a monastic prelate. He stayed there two years until recalled in 957 by the fourteen-year-old Eadgar, newly elevated to power by the nobles of Mercia. Two years later, Eadgar became monarch over the united realm of the West Saxons, Mercians, and Northumbrians. He set about establishing orderly government and peace. Known to history as "the Peaceable," he gained much and lost nothing, while shedding no blood. He appointed Dunstan as his chief minister and adviser. In rapid succession Dunstan became bishop of Worcester, bishop of London, and finally Archbishop of Canterbury. (The combination of young king and experienced prelate was to be repeated in a more ambitious enterprise half a century later on the Continent when Otto III made the learned Gerbert of Aurillac Pope Sylvester II, in a failed effort to resurrect the Caesaro-Papal Roman Empire of Late Antiquity.) Unlike Henry II, Eadgar never interfered with the ecclesiastic or monastic polity. He received the unqualified support of the monastic clergy and bishops in his efforts at consolidation and national education. Meanwhile, Aethelwold and his monastery of Abingdon, under a cloud during Dunstan's exile, prospered once more. Aethelwold sent his monk Osgar to study the customs of Fleury. The great monastery, later called St-Benoît-sur-Loire, was renowned for its scriptorium and library and had been reformed by Odo of Cluny. Aethelwold also imported skilled chanters from another great northern French monastery, Corbie, also famous for its scriptorium, to regularize and maintain the liturgy and chant at Abingdon. In 963, three years after Dunstan became Archbishop of Canterbury, Aethelwold was raised to the see of Winchester, the capital of the realm.

From the tenth century to the present, English historians have considered Aethelwold the most energetic and harsh of the reformers. He forced rather than urged monastic rule on the clergy of the decayed abbeys of Wessex. He peremptorily expelled the secular clerks with their wives from the monasteries and set others willing to follow monastic discipline in their places. He drove out the priests from the old and new minsters at Winchester and from Chertsey and Milton Abbas, and replaced them with monks. He reestablished monastic life at Ely, Medeshamstede (later Peterborough), and Thorney. The extant records of these three monasteries also reveal how assiduously and capably Aethelwold negotiated adequate endowments and resources for his foundations. He defended their claims in local courts and ardently supported their rights.[15]

The third member of this monastic triumvirate was Oswald. Of Scandinavian descent, he was related to Archbishop Oskytel of York and to Archbishop Odo, Dunstan's predecessor at Canterbury. At Winchester, he had lived in worldly ease as head of the monastery that before Aethelwold's reforms was a community of married clergy or canons. But then he begged his uncle Odo to send him to Fleury to learn the perfect observance of the Benedictine Rule. After a second sojourn at Fleury and a stint as assistant to Oskytel, he succeeded Dunstan at Worcester and in 972 became Archbishop of York. More diplomatic and circumspect than Aethelwold, Oswald managed to convert the dean and canons of Worcester to Benedictine monasticism, established monks at Winchcombe under his friend Germanus, and inaugurated the monastery of Ramsey. He brought the most learned man on the Continent, Abbo of Fleury, to teach at Ramsey for two years. One of Abbo's students at Ramsey, Byrhtferth, composed the most important encyclopedic scientific treatise of that age, *Byrhtferth's Manual.*

Their experience with the vicissitudes of patronage both in their native England and on the Continent enabled Dunstan, Aethelwold, and Oswald to survey the options and, from their own rare positions of power and political leverage, to choose those that posed the least threat of impoverishment and unwanted control. Of course, in seeking endowments and gifts, the prelates called not only upon the king and powerful lords. They also solicited aid from wealthy ladies. Dunstan's relative, the rich lady Aethelflaed, left him all her riches; the dowager queen Eadgifa constantly aided both Dunstan and Aethelwold; and several other noble ladies are also remembered as great benefactresses. Queen Aethelthryth, Eadgar's second wife, was disliked by the monks for her extracanonical marriage to the king. Yet by political astuteness she secured her position and that of her son Ethelred Unready (978–1016), and was named special patroness of the nuns and nunneries in England.

From the beginning of the reform movement at Glastonbury, when no organized monastic life was to be found in England, until their deaths, Dunstan, Aethelwold, and Oswald created or reestablished some fifty monasteries and convents. Located mostly in the south, where the king's property and power were both extensive, these institutions were thriving generally. But their practices diverged at a number of important points, due to the movement's lack of uniform customs and rules. The reformers therefore called a synod at Winchester, with the backing of the king. Under Aethelwold's leadership, they produced the *Regularis concordia,* whose roots lie in the Benedictine *Rule* and Benedict of Aniane's *Concordia.* A set of customs and regulations that draws on the practices and experiences of Fleury, St. Peter's in Ghent, and other houses, the synod's *Concordia* was to provide a common customary for all the English houses.

Its proem begins, significantly, "Gloriosus etenim Eadgar . . . rex egregius," indicating that the document had royal as well as ecclesiastical support. The proem goes on to delineate the history of the reform and to record the synod's support for the free election of superiors and its rejection of "saecularium vero prioratum." "On the other hand," the document continues, "the assembly commanded that the sovereign power of the King and Queen—and that only—should ever be besought with confident petition, both for the safeguarding of holy places and for the increase of the goods of the Church."[16] The *Concordia* is unique among Benedictine customaries in that it adds to the liturgy a constant round of prayers for the king. By commanding all monks to pray for the one king and queen, it helped transform the royal family of Wessex into the royal family of England and thus merits a place in the annals of both monastic and constitutional history.[17]

The tenth-century reform movement resulted in many solid achievements. It led to the restoration or foundation of many great monasteries, including Glastonbury, Abingdon, and Ramsey. Through its excellent educational program, the movement provided England with most of its bishops from the reign of Eadgar to that of Cnut. It was under these monastic bishops that there evolved the peculiarly English institution of monastic cathedrals, of which Canterbury, Winchester, Worcester, and Sherbourne are examples. Furthermore, the reform's influence spread outside England, through the English missionaries to Scandinavia and through the outstanding quality of its best artistic products, many of which were exported or emulated abroad.[18]

The cultural impact of the monastic reform was dramatic. Aelfric (c.955–1020), abbot of Eynsham and great English stylist, wrote, "No English priest could either write a letter in Latin or understand one until Dunstan and Aethelwold revived learning in the monastic life."[19] Even though Aelfric was probably imitating King Alfred's lament about the state of learning in his day, what he said contains much truth. The restoration and foundation of the monastic schools in fifty houses changed all that, at least south of the Humber. Education in letters, writing, art, architecture, and the early medieval sciences flourished. Of the approximately 950 extant manuscripts written in Anglo-Saxon England, most were produced during the period of the reform, a testimony of the burst of book production. We know that the surviving manuscripts represent but a small fraction of those actually produced in the scriptoria. Though the majority of the manuscripts are of a religious nature, we also have a large number of school texts (grammars, rhetorics, *computus*) and classical literary works from the period. Latin letters thrived as never before. Not all the tenth-century Latin written in England is pristine or even correct—scholars have pointed out numerous solecisms even in the liturgical texts of the period.[20] However, given the very little they had to start with, these monks wrote a remarkably good Latin. Two styles flourished: (1) the aureate Latin of Late Antiquity, curiously augmented by Aldhelm and others of the eighth century and now imitated particularly at Aethelwold's school at Winchester; and (2) the serviceable, direct Latin practiced by Bede and imitated in the tenth century by Aelfric and Wulfstan. Latin of both the high and medium styles and a literary vernacular were written by many monastic authors. They even showed a smattering of Greek.

Tenth-century England excelled in book production. Drawing both on continental sources and earlier Insular (Irish and

English) models, the monastic scribes produced both service-able and elegant books, of which the lovely *Benedictional of St. Aethelwold* is a good example. For Latin texts, the monks used the continental Caroline minuscule, writing the display lettering in a hierarchy of Roman Square and Rustic Capitals and Uncial; they kept that most attractive hand, the pointed Insular, for the Old English texts. The coexistence of foreign and native traditions was unique to England and Ireland and is manifested in their poetry, manuscript illumination, bell-mak-ing, metalwork, and many other art forms.

The tenth-century Anglo-Saxon reform was special among medieval revivals of learning in two other ways. First, follow-ing precedent set by King Alfred, it emphasized translation, good translation, of Latin texts into the vernacular. Aethel-wold led the way by translating the Rule at the request of King Eadgar and Queen Aelfthryth. Many other texts, mostly reli-gious, were translated into Old English at Winchester. We now have positive evidence that Aethelwold and members of his scriptorium consciously tried to establish a "standard Old English." He and his circle at Winchester thus have some claim to be "the first English philologists."[21]

The tenth-century revival was also significant in that it fos-tered and preserved vernacular literature. All medieval renais-sances rediscovered the Classics, though they did not study them with the passionate energy of the Renaissance itself. Comparatively few of the extant manuscripts written in En-gland during the tenth century contain classical authors, al-though standard works by authors such as Cicero and Virgil are represented. However, the English reform also welcomed Old English literature into the scriptorium and the meeting hall. Nearly all the Old English poetry now extant comes from four manuscripts written between 970 and 1020. Although some of the poems may have been composed at an earlier date, their final and only redactions are these late tenth- and early eleventh-century versions.

British Library Cotton MS. Vitellius A.xv contains the great Germanic epic of *Beowulf* and the religious narrative, *Judith*. The bold paraphrase of Genesis, with illustrations by masters of the Winchester School, as well as portions of Exodus, the Book of Daniel, and the poem *Christ and Satan* are contained in Oxford Bodleian MS. Junius 11, "the Caedmon manuscript." The third manuscript, now at Vercelli on the ancient pilgrimage route across North Italy to Rome, includes the poems of the one Anglo-Saxon author whose works are extensive and signed, Cynewulf. This anthology is most notable for the poignant religious poem on the cross, *The Dream of the Rood.* The fourth manuscript was described in the list of gifts from Bishop Leofric (d. 1072) to his cathedral at Exeter as "a large English book composed in verse about all kinds of things." It is an extraordinary miscellany of religious and secular poems (e.g., *Christ, Guthlac, The Wanderer, The Seafarer, Riddles*). The legacy of Old English poetry, while small in bulk (some thirty thousand lines in all), is enormous in its quality and solemn richness. Although literary historians do not praise Anglo-Saxon prose as highly as they do the poetry, no one denies the real literary merit of Aelfric and Wulfstan (d. 1023). Both men were products of the Benedictine reform. The learned theologian Aelfric wrote in a direct, clear, yet rhythmic prose. He created an instructional sermon that impresses us with its deep devotional simplicity. Like Aelfric, Wulfstan earned his reputation not only as a great homilist but also as a prelate whose official publications provided guidance for the clergy and nobility. His *Institutes of Polity* are not as exciting as his fiery *Sermo Lupi ad Anglos*, but were just as important historically.[22]

Anglo-Saxon prose and verse both survived because of the Benedictine reform that occurred in the tenth century under the patronage of Eadgar. That great reform in England owed only its implementation to the monastic reforms on the Continent. Dunstan and his colleagues were inspired to begin a native reform movement by the obvious need for a religious and cultural revival. They were fortunately able to meet, at St. Peter's of Ghent and at Fleury, the experienced reformers who had brought reformation from Cluny, Brogne, or Gorze. From them the English prelates learned how to implement the English reforms. In this effort they had the support of Eadgar, the young and capable monarch who brought glory and peace to the Anglo-Saxon peoples. Eadgar had also learned well from his continental peers, to whom he was connected by marriage through his father's sisters.[23] He knew the value to the state of gifted and devoted monastic clerics, and they in turn found him a bulwark for their reforms. The results were spectacular and unique. Even though the tenth-century English reform depended heavily on continental precedents, it also developed into a truly English cultural phenomenon, quite distinctive and in many aspects quite superior. English education, books, and works of art experienced a new life and brilliance. The tenth-century reform fostered both classical and vernacular letters. England would not experience such a cultural revival again until the more secular one three hundred years later under the patronage of Richard II and the literary leadership of Chaucer.

CHAPTER 6

The Twelfth-Century Renaissance

STEPHEN C. FERRUOLO

That Western Europe experienced a renaissance in the
twelfth century comparable to *the* Renaissance that began in Italy in the trecento is an old and well-established idea
among medievalists. It can be traced back as early as 1840,
twenty years before Jacob Burckhardt published his classic
study, *The Civilization of the Renaissance in Italy.* In 1840
the French scholar Jean-Jacques Ampère proposed that there
had been not one but three significant renaissances of Western
culture: the first at the time of Charlemagne in the ninth century, the second beginning at the end of the eleventh century,
and the third and last "the great renaissance of the fifteenth
and sixteenth centuries." According to Ampère, the self-conscious intellectual movement in the twelfth century had "all
the characteristics of a true renaissance."[1] As this idea gradually gained acceptance, scholars began to view the considerable
achievements of the twelfth century from a comparative perspective. The period was seen either as one of three distinct
cultural revivals or else as the middle segment of the three-
stage rebirth of classical culture. The twelfth century was said
to share certain common ideas and inspirations with the Italian Renaissance, but its achievements were thought to be neither as brilliant nor as enduring. Dissatisfied with this comparison of the achievements of the twelfth century to those of
the later period, some medievalists reacted against the idea
of a twelfth-century renaissance. In the revised edition of
his *Guide to the Study of Medieval History,* Louis Paetow re-

gretted that the cultural movement that began in the eleventh century had generally come to be called the "twelfth-century renaissance." In his view, the term disparaged the cultural achievements of what he saw as a "new era" and as "the most important turning point in the intellectual history of the middle ages."[2] Paetow's wise warning was not heeded, however. Within a few years of his *Guide*, two major new books used the term "the renaissance of the twelfth century" in their titles. Despite the voices raised in opposition, the use of the term "renaissance" to describe the cultural and intellectual achievements of the period seemed established.

The first of the two new books was the immediately successful and still widely read masterpiece by the great American medievalist Charles Homer Haskins, *The Renaissance of the Twelfth Century* (published in 1927). No book before or since has contributed more to the appreciation of the twelfth century's important achievements in classical studies, poetry, historical writing, law, science, and philosophy (if the book has a fault, it is that Haskins limited his attention exclusively to Latin literature and learning). According to Haskins, the advances in these areas amounted to a considerable literary and intellectual revival but not to a new birth. The achievements of the twelfth century were the result of a "general quickening of spirit," inspired by social and economic changes. They were not sudden advances into new directions of thought or expression but the continued if accelerated development of ideas and methods rooted in the past, above all in "the soil of the Carolingian tradition." Thus Haskins saw little that was truly unique or novel in the actual achievements. Rather, drawing on Henry Osborne Taylor's comment that each medieval century advanced culturally by reaching back into the remoter past, Haskins concludes that the greatness of the twelfth century was that "it reached out more widely and recovered more." The resulting widespread cultural revival made the century an "age of fresh and vigorous life" comparable, in his estimation, to the Italian Renaissance of the fifteenth century.[3]

The second of the two books is less well known, even though it remains the standard textbook for students of the intellectual life in the schools of the period. *La Renaissance du douzième siècle: Les Écoles et l'enseignement* was published in 1933 by a group of scholars: Gérard M. Paré, A. Brunet, and P. Tremblay. As their subtitle makes clear, they wrote primarily to explain the developments in thought and in teaching methods within the expanding urban schools of the twelfth century. The authors conclude that Scholasticism (often considered inimical to the kind of learning that defines a renaissance) was the ultimate achievement and the crowning glory of the great social, cultural, and intellectual transformation that Western Europe experienced after 1100.[4] The decisive role assigned to Scholasticism could have seriously challenged the established conception of a renaissance. But, perhaps because this book appealed to a more specialized audience than did Haskins's, its interpretation of the renaissance had much less impact on scholarly opinion about the twelfth century.

Although Haskins's idea was not novel, the publication of *The Renaissance of the Twelfth Century* set off a lively debate about the validity of applying the term "renaissance" to the achievements of the twelfth century, a debate that continued intermittently in scholarly journals for twenty-five years. The most influential contributor was the art historian Erwin Panofsky, who in 1944 first published his article "Renaissances and Renascences" in the *Kenyon Review*.[5] Using the presence of classicizing tendencies as his criterion for a "renaissance," Panofsky argued against the idea of a "twelfth-century renaissance." According to Panofsky, although there are certain elements that justify the use of the terms "proto-renaissance" for the art and "proto-humanism" for the literature of the twelfth century, these together amount not to a true and complete renaissance of Antiquity, like that which later occurred in Italy, but only to a limited and a transitory "renascence" of some classical influences. Both the artists and the writers of the twelfth century, according to Panofsky, had a much too narrow and distorted understanding of Antiquity. They divorced classical form from classical content; they lacked critical distance from the world of Antiquity and failed to see classical civilization as a coherent cultural system essentially different from their own. These men only selectively borrowed from and imitated classical sources; they did not find novel and enduring inspiration in them as did the humanists of the Italian Renaissance. For Panofsky, the renaissance of the fourteenth and fifteenth centuries was a unique phenomenon, the one comprehensive and permanent revival of classical Antiquity, and for it alone should the term "renaissance" be reserved.

While Panofsky, as far as many art historians were concerned, had settled the issue conclusively, the validity of the idea of the twelfth-century renaissance remained an open question among some American medievalists. Scholarly debate in the United States reached a peak in a series of three articles that appeared in the journal *Speculum* in 1948 and 1951. William Nitze initiated the discussion with his provocatively titled article, "The So-Called Twelfth-Century Renaissance." Nitze, like Panofsky, argues that the term "renaissance" should be applied only to a cultural revival that involved what he redundantly describes as "the new birth or recreation of the ancient world discovered anew." The twelfth century did not qualify because its cultural revival neither rediscovered Antiquity nor was truly inspired by the classical tradition. "The fact remains," Nitze concludes, "that the classical element in it was chiefly background or coloring given themes that were indigenous to the practical life of the age and not freshly imported from the ancients." Such a cultural revival, which subordinated classical sources and ideas to other inspirations and interests, was, in his view, simply unworthy of comparison to the Italian Renaissance, when men truly did strive to return to the classical world.[6]

Three years later, Eva M. Sanford took issue with both Nitze and Panofsky in an article arguing that they had exaggerated the difference in attitude toward classical Antiquity of the writers and artists of the twelfth century and of the Italian Renaissance. Though she thought it was defensible, on these grounds, to apply the term "renaissance" to the twelfth century, she concluded that it might nonetheless be unwise, since such usage has the implicit effect of making the Italian Renaissance the standard for measuring the twelfth century. Quite rightly, Sanford questioned whether the criteria used to evaluate the achievements of the fourteenth and fifteenth centuries ought to be applied to those of the twelfth. "Should we not rather be satisfied," she concludes, "to let the twelfth century stand on its own merits as a dynamic period of medieval culture, which made fruitful contributions to the development of modern man without forfeiting its own essential medieval character?"[7]

In the same issue of *Speculum,* Urban T. Holmes showed that adopting such an attitude did not necessarily require one to reject the idea of a twelfth-century renaissance. His solution was to broaden the definition of "renaissance." Instead of meaning only a rebirth of classical Antiquity, the term would embody the more general idea of a cultural revival as a "sudden increase of enthusiasm for [any] given stream of culture." According to Holmes, the twelfth century's important achievements sprang from increased enthusiasm for three different streams of culture. The rediscovery of classical sources was one stream. But two others were of equal if not greater importance: the enduring inspiration of the Latin Christian tradition, embodied in the Bible and in the writings of the church Fathers; and the introduction of novel ideas and influences from Arabic, Jewish, and Byzantine sources. The renaissance resulted from the confluence of all three streams; it was "a vigorous reawakening of cultural enthusiasm in which dialectic, theology, legal studies, vernacular literature of a worldly type, decorative art, and Latin poetry rose to new heights. This enthusiasm embraced some humanism (in the sense of enthusiasm for classical culture) . . . but humanism was not at the heart of the movement."[8] The obvious purpose of this broadened definition was to expand the established idea of a renaissance to include full consideration of influence and achievements other than those involving classical studies. Holmes maintained that the twelfth century could, as he states it, "stand on its own merits," and thus his article served to bring the debate to a fitting close.

From the perspective of thirty years later, we can see that this debate focused more on the idea of the renaissance than on what of social and cultural significance actually happened in twelfth-century Western Europe. The primary purpose here is to discuss and to evaluate what did happen, but first I must treat the issue of what constitutes a renaissance. This is not, as we have seen, a matter of simple definition. The uses of the term raise substantive historical problems. Too often its use alone, for any period before the fourteenth century, is somehow considered sufficient to establish the greatness and the significance of any apparent increase in cultural activity. By calling an era a "renaissance," many scholars seem to assume that the particular importance of its achievements, whatever they might be, has been assured. Sometimes, however, scholars have used the term with the more explicit purpose of challenging the uniqueness and novelty of the great achievements of the Italian Renaissance. These writers set out to prove that another period, or other periods, exhibited some of the same specific cultural inspirations and ideas for which the fourteenth and fifteenth centuries have long been praised.

Both uses of "renaissance" have been detrimental to historical understanding. The essential question in any discussion of a renaissance should be that of what makes the activities or the achievements of a given period of history more significant and more enduring, socially or culturally, than those of another. The criteria of judgment should be explicitly stated, and the cultural values and assumptions that underlie these criteria should be articulated.

As the debate about the twelfth-century renaissance shows, scholars have held at least two quite distinct ideas of what constitutes a renaissance. One idea embraces all the developments of any given period of time and defines "renaissance" as a general but somehow integrated increase of cultural activity, which draws upon a variety of older or external influences but advances significantly beyond them. The other idea includes only those achievements that can be shown to stem from a revival of classical culture. These two different definitions of "renaissance" entail two different approaches to any period so defined. If one subscribes (as did Holmes) to the broader definition of "renaissance," then one would try to evaluate the full extent and novelty of cultural activity by asking questions like the following: How many people were involved? Who were they? Where and for how long were they active? What were the nature and purposes of their activities, and how original were their achievements? And perhaps above all, how widespread and enduring was or has been the influence of these achievements? On the other hand, if one holds to the narrower definition (as did Panofsky), one looks for the evidence of more specific types of cultural activity and asks a quite different set of questions: Which aspects of classical culture were revived? Were they merely imitated, or did they truly inspire thought and action? Were the classical sources understood and appreciated on their own terms or were they reinterpreted to fit into the preexisting cultural system and despoiled and deprived of their true meaning and content? Were classical models preeminent or were they subordinated to other nonclassical—and therefore less valuable—cultural influences?

The narrow definition measures the achievements of any earlier period against one specific standard of increased cultural activity, the Italian Renaissance, when, as all who have read their Burckhardt know, the rediscovery of classical Antiquity brought the "discovery of the world and of man" and lifted the veil on one thousand years of darkness and God. There is something ironic—and fundamentally misconceived—about evaluating the events of a millennium in terms of such limited and biased criteria. The practice is especially unacceptable in the case of the twelfth century, whose achievements were so great and novel and often of such enduring importance. Only the broader definition of "renaissance" as a general increase of cultural activity can encompass the historical significance of this vital and creative period.

What then was the significance of the twelfth century? Considerable scholarship over the last thirty years has confirmed the enduring importance of the social and cultural advances made in Western Europe during the period roughly between 1100 and 1200. Those scholars who have attempted to assess the importance of these developments have used at least three different approaches. I will discuss each of these approaches in turn, as a preliminary means of suggesting why it is indeed appropriate to speak of a twelfth-century renaissance.

One approach has been simply to accept the established idea of the twelfth-century renaissance and to use it to aggregate all the various developments and cultural advances that occurred in Western Europe more or less within that century. An example is Christopher Brooke's widely known and beautifully illustrated book, *The Twelfth-Century Renaissance* (1969). Brooke discusses the period's major developments in education, religion, thought, and art in terms of a general increase of cultural variety and sophistication, but he does not explain how or why these developments took place concurrently or what inspirations or impacts they might have had in common. He goes no further than to show that the twelfth century produced creative and interesting thinkers, writers, and artists, and he makes little or no effort to define what it means to call the period a "renaissance."[9]

A second and much more fruitful approach has been to describe the achievements of the twelfth century in the cultural terms previously reserved primarily for the Italian Renaissance: "humanism" and "the discovery of the individual." Humanism and individuality are highly valued characteristics of the Western cultural tradition; some have argued that they are the very essence of that tradition. It is hardly surprising, then, that some medievalists try to claim these features for the Middle Ages, arguing that they originated before the fourteenth century. These scholars are not usually interested in comparing the twelfth century and the Italian Renaissance (some have even carefully avoided applying the term "renaissance" to the period). Yet this approach does raise some of the same problems as the earlier debate. What is human (or humane)? What is individuality? These are the fundamental questions one faces when describing or evaluating the cultural achievements of a period in terms of these characteristics. Perhaps it would be better simply to do away with such terms, as Elizabeth Brown has recently argued we should do with the idea of feudalism.[10] But such terms can be useful, if they are explicitly defined and their meaning is clearly understood. The mistake is to assume, as Sir Richard Southern argues in an important article on medieval humanism, that the terms are neutral and that their appropriateness has been incontrovertibly established. Citing feudalism and romanticism as well as humanism as examples, Southern writes:

> As a general rule medieval historians do well to avoid words which
> end in "ism." They are words which belong to a recent period of his-
> tory and their use injects into the past the ideas of a later age. . . . They
> distort but they also summarize; and we are obliged sometimes to ask
> what they mean and whether they correctly describe the main traits
> of the ages to which they have been applied.[11]

If we accept this obligation as a necessary step in evaluating
the second approach to the twelfth-century renaissance, we
must first ask what scholars have meant by "humanism" and
"individuality" and then determine whether the ideas help explain the main achievements of the period.

What has "humanism" meant when applied to the twelfth
century? Southern shows that the term "humanism" has had
two quite distinct meanings, which, although often confused,
are, in some ways, connected.[12] The first and narrower definition points to the study of a specific set of intellectual disciplines based on Latin and Greek literature (as in "studia humanitatis," "literae humaniores," or the "humanities"). These
subjects have traditionally included grammar, rhetoric, poetry,
history, and moral philosophy and have explicitly excluded the
more specialized disciplines of logic, theology, law, and medi-
cine. To refer back to the *Speculum* debate, Holmes was using
this sense of the term when he argued that humanism was
"not at the heart of the movement" that he still believed could
be called the twelfth-century renaissance.[13]

Most recent scholars would probably agree that humanism
in this sense—Southern calls it "literary humanism"—does
not adequately describe the main traits or summarize the major achievements of the entire period. Literary humanism
tends to focus too narrowly on the last decades of the eleventh
century and the first half of the twelfth, when the known
sources of classical Latin literature were being read and imitated enthusiastically—that is, on the period before these
sources were mastered and their study systematized. John of
Salisbury is commonly regarded as the greatest figure of this
humanism and Chartres as its greatest center.[14] One proponent
of this idea of humanism, however, gives the place of honor to
the remote English Cistercian monastery of Rievaulx, which,
in his view, represented "the quintessence of the humanism of

the twelfth century."[15] For such scholars, the middle of the twelfth century marked the beginning of a general decline, decay, or disintegration into a culture that one of them describes as "less universal, less appealing, and in a word less humane than what had gone before."[16]

This is a most questionable evaluation of an age that can count among its great achievements the foundation of the university, the life of that universally popular saint, Francis of Assisi, and the creation of poetry as moving as the hymn "Jesu, Dulcis Memoria"—to say nothing of the concurrent advances in artistic expression, and especially the new Gothic forms in sculpture and architecture that have come, perhaps more than anything else, to symbolize the period. Literary humanism distorts our understanding and appreciation of the twelfth century in several ways. It ignores the contribution to the cultural revival of other, nonclassical influences such as what has been called the "rediscovery of the Gospels"; it deprecates the important role of dialectic and of the scholastic method, which it regards as the lethal adversary of humanist thought, in advancing learning essential to the human experience; and it completely ignores the importance of legal and institutional developments in improving the general quality of human life. I will return to each of these subjects later. How—the proponents of this definition of humanism must first be asked—is reading Cicero or Virgil and writing stylish Latin more "humane" than developing a moral theology applicable to a variety of human situations or than improving legal procedures by substituting trial by a jury of peers for trial by ordeal or battle? This narrow definition of humanism cannot be accepted, because it completely excludes recognition of many of the most significant and enduring achievements of the twelfth century.

The second definition of twelfth-century humanism is both broader and more inclusive: humanism as a preeminent interest in, and commitment to, humanity. Southern himself is probably the best-known proponent of this idea of humanism. To distinguish it from literary humanism, Southern uses the term "scientific" humanism, in the medieval sense of *scientia* as general knowledge. He identifies the three essential elements of this humanism as: (1) a strong sense of the dignity and nobility of human nature; (2) a recognition of the inherent dignity of nature itself and of the meaningfulness and rationality of the natural order; and (3) the belief that this order is intelligible to the human mind and can be understood through the exercise of reason. Each of these elements of humanism, Southern claims, emerged no earlier than the late eleventh century. From that time through the twelfth and thirteenth centuries, these combined concepts of human dignity, natural order, and intelligibility and reason dominated Western European culture and society. They inspired advances in every area of thought and action. For Southern, moreover, the "twelfth-century renaissance" was only one part of a longer period of humanism. "I believe," he writes, "the period from about 1100 to about 1320 to have been one of the great ages of humanism: perhaps the greatest of all."[17]

In my opinion, this broader idea of scientific humanism does go a long way to summarize without distortion the main traits as well as the major achievements of the period it encompasses. But it takes a scholar of Southern's remarkably penetrating insight to see the stigmata of St. Francis of Assisi and the *summae* of St. Thomas Aquinas as manifestations of the same cultural movement and values. Southern is even able to explain quite convincingly some of the period's less humane developments—for example, anti-Semitism and the Inquisition—as "penalties of humanism." "Society," Southern writes of these developments, "does not become more attractive in becoming more human in inspiration. Oppression keeps pace with the growth of freedom."[18]

Nevertheless, this broader definition of humanism still does not satisfactorily explain all the achievements of the period. One is left wondering, for example, where and how a work like Lothario dei Segni's treatise *On the Misery of the Human Condition* fits in. This gloomy tract was written right in the middle of Southern's great age of humanism. Its author was not out of touch with major cultural developments (as one might surmise from the work's tone and content), but one of the most learned and successful men of the time. Lothario dei Segni was a Roman noble educated in Bologna and Paris, who, within three years of completing his treatise, was elected pope and who then, as the great Innocent III (1198–1216), proclaimed and sought to make real the ambitious doctrine of the papal "plenitude of power."[19]

For those unfamiliar with this treatise, I will cite a passage that illustrates its perspective on human life:

> Man was formed of dust, slime, and ashes; what is even more vile, of the filthiest seed. He was conceived from the itch of the flesh, in the heat of passion and the stench of lust, and worse yet, with the stain of sin. He was born to toil, dread, and trouble; and more wretched still, was born only to die. He commits depraved acts by which he offends God, his neighbor, and himself; shameful acts by which he defiles his name, his person, and his conscience; and vain acts by which he ignores all things important, useful, and necessary. He will become fuel for those fires which are forever hot and burn forever bright; food for the worm which forever nibbles and digests; a mass of rottenness which will forever stink and reek.[20]

How different this is from an expression of the dignity of human nature! Although Innocent III intended to follow this treatise with another on that more exalted subject of human dignity, this fact does not diminish the significance of the great success and influence of the treatise he actually wrote.

Colin Morris, a scholar greatly influenced by Southern, has traced the evolution of the term "humanitas." Whereas throughout the early middle ages the term was usually used pejoratively to mean human frailty, in the twelfth century its meaning shifted to encompass the essential dignity of human nature.[21] Semantic change can be an accurate barometer of the transformation of cultural attitudes and values. But in this case, the treatise *On the Misery of the Human Condition* is surer evidence that a deep sense of the frailty and sinfulness of man remained a vital force in the twelfth century. Thus while I am prepared to accept that humanism in its broader sense encompasses much of what happened in the period, I would argue that it was an ambiguous humanism. Underlying the undeniable confidence in human nature and human potential was a strong current of uncertainty and fear.

The mention of Colin Morris brings us conveniently to the "discovery of the individual." Other scholars had written of the discovery or appearance of individuality in the twelfth century, but it was this historian's *The Discovery of the Individ-ual, 1050–1200*, published in England in 1972, that brought the idea to the forefront of scholarly debate. The book's thesis can be quickly summarized. According to Morris, the discovery of the individual was "one of the most important cultural devel-opments in the years between 1050 and 1200." A general and widespread cultural phenomenon, it found expression in a full range of human activities and especially in education, litera-ture, art, and religious life. The central features of the move-ment were a concern with self-discovery and individual expres-sion, interest in human relations and in the relationship be-tween the individual and society, and a system of ethics judged by the standards of inner intention rather than external action.

Other scholars have generally spoken of a brief flourishing of individuality in the twelfth century, which passed with the de-cline of literary humanism, not to reappear until the four-teenth century. Morris, by contrast, believes that there was no sharp discontinuity between the individuality of the twelfth century, that of the Italian Renaissance, and that of modern Western culture. According to Morris, the individual once dis-covered was never lost. Although he is willing—too willing, in my view—to concede that the opportunities for self-expression and self-exploration became more restricted after 1150, with the advance of logic, law, and theology in the schools, Morris insists that individuality remained an important and vital ele-ment of medieval culture.[22]

The key issue that needs to be addressed is how important and vital was this element. The twelfth century may have dis-covered the individual (or, as one of the critics of Morris's book prefers, the "self"),[23] but it also discovered and created new communities, new social groups and orders, and new institu-tions to which these individuals belonged. It is a mistake to focus on the discovery of the individual in describing the achievements of the period. Two vital questions must be asked. First, is individuality, as defined by Morris, a more significant or creative feature of the cultural revival of the twelfth century than the period's new social groups, religious orders, and politi-cal institutions? Second, what was the relationship between these two developments? Did the discovery of the individual diminish the sense of community, lessen the importance attached to belonging to a recognized group, or reduce the need of men and women to conform to established social roles, ethical norms, and religious ideals? Carolyn Bynum argues strongly for what she describes as "a quite self-conscious interest in the process of belonging to groups and filling roles" in the twelfth century. She chides Morris for not recognizing that the "discovery of the group" was no less important a phenomenon of the period than the "discovery of the individual."[24] Without actually conceding the point, Morris has cleverly responded that even so individual initiative and choice must have increased significantly, as there were now more groups for individuals to choose among.[25] This response suggests how these questions can and should be answered.

Whatever the limitations of its thesis, Morris's book stands as a major contribution to our understanding of the twelfth century. The "discovery of the individual" does not encompass all the achievements of the period, but Morris treats the idea in a way that opens up two vital areas of inquiry. First, his book requires us to ask what social changes made this increase in individual initiative and choice possible. Second, it demonstrates the need to explain both what inspirations and influences shaped these initiatives and why the cultural activities proceeded in certain directions and not in others. Morris himself looks at these issues from an especially suggestive perspective. The principal inspiration for the achievements of the twelfth century, he believes, was the combination of increased opportunity and diminished certainty. "If there is one force," he writes in his conclusion, "which may be particularized as creating the new individualism, I have tried to show that it was the uncertainty created in the minds of men by the opportunities and challenges of a more complex world."[26] This is a most perceptive description of the vitality of the period. The compelling need to reorder society, to make sense of the expanding world, and to make choices in a rapidly changing environment shaped the essential dynamic behind the considerable achievements of the twelfth-century renaissance.

Another example of recent scholarship on individuality in the twelfth century shows just how useful it can be to venture into the areas of inquiry opened by Colin Morris. In an article published in 1978, Martin Stevens examines the increased prominence of what he calls "the performing self"—that is, writers' and artists' self-representations in literature and art. Such figures appeared first in autobiographies and prefaces and later in romances, chronicles, lyrics, and manuscript illuminations. Stevens rightly describes this development as a "revolutionary event" in cultural history. "The mode of the artist speaking *qua* artist," he writes, "is a signal departure in the literature and art of Western civilization." Stevens especially breaks new ground by advancing a convincing explanation of why this cultural change happened when and where it did. Only part of the answer, he says, lies in such new or revived cultural inspirations as the style of sources like the *De consolatione philosophiae* of Boethius, the renewed vision in the schools of God the Creator as artist or architect of the universe, and humanism. More important, or at least equally important, were the changing social conditions of literary and artistic production. Artistic works were being performed before courtly audiences or used by the artists to advertise their skills in the search for patronage, employment, or advancement in a society that increasingly valued and was sometimes even willing to reward learning and creativity. The artists began to identify themselves in their works because this was a useful means of gaining support and recognition. The emergence of "the performing self," a key aspect of individuality, was thus directly related to the changing social environment of the artist.[27] Stevens's article is a model of how changing social conditions can help explain the origins of new and important cultural phenomena. One hopes that future researchers on individuality will follow his lead.

There is no need to dwell any further on "the discovery of the individual" or on this second approach to the twelfth-century renaissance. But before moving on to the third approach, I think it is necessary to say something about the institutional achievements of the twelfth century. Scholars writing about the twelfth-century renaissance, whatever their approach, often place too much emphasis on individuals and too little on institutions. The twelfth-century renaissance's most enduring legacy was not the promotion of new forms of individual expression but the creation of new institutions—institutions that were not reborn or revived but newborn and invented. This aspect of the twelfth-century renaissance has long been recognized by historians of political institutions and ideas. In a paper first delivered at Princeton in 1941, the constitutional historian Charles McIlwain declared:

In the field of political institutions and ideas I venture to think that what Professor Haskins has termed the "Renaissance of the twelfth century" marks a more fundamental change than the later developments to which we usually attach the word "Renaissance," that the constitutionalism of the modern world owes as much, if not more, to the twelfth and thirteenth centuries than any period of comparable length before the seventeenth.[28]

Any discussion of the twelfth-century renaissance must at least note the period's important institutional achievements and ask what made them so enduring. Most of these institutions are familiar enough because they have survived, if in some cases modified almost beyond recognition. However, the particular circumstances of their origins and early development are too often neglected. The changing social conditions and values that created these institutions are an important aspect of the twelfth-century renaissance and require further examination.

Unfortunately, I can do no more here than take somewhat of a general approach to the important institutional achievements of the period. In the especially vital area of constitutional development, the evolution of political and legal institutions can best be explained in the context of the struggle of secular rulers to keep pace with the advances of the Church. The "papal revolution" begun by Gregory VII (1073–1085) transformed the Church into an increasingly autonomous, centralized, and powerful institution with ambitions to lead (if not to dominate) and certainly to reform European society. The ensuing struggle between Church and state lasted for more than two centuries, with intermittent pauses for cooperation such as the Crusades. Out of the long and often bitter confrontations emerged administrative institutions as important as the College of Cardinals and the *curia regis;* agents of government as effective as legates and itinerant justices; and legal documents as far-reaching as the canons of the Fourth Lateran Council and Magna Carta. Not all of these achievements may have been truly unprecedented or novel; but there can be no doubt that together they fundamentally restructured and strengthened the religious and political order of Western Europe. Concerning the concurrent development of law, one can argue that Roman law was merely revived but canon law was definitely invented.[29]

No less remarkable and enduring were the institutional achievements of those who chose the religious life. Religion, so often a conservative force in society, in the twelfth century led men and not a few women in new directions. The period produced a full spectrum of new forms of spiritual life and religious institutions, including new monastic orders (such as the Carthusians and Cistercians), communities of canons living according to a prescribed rule (the Augustinians and Premonstratensians), the military orders (the Templars and Teutonic Knights), and the mendicants (Franciscans and Dominicans). Each group claimed—and repeatedly emphasized—its dependence upon biblical or patristic inspiration. But the collective impact of these new orders went beyond broadening or even reviving religious life. Together they fundamentally reoriented the accepted ideas of worship and Christian living. These orders represent the varied expressions of a new spiritual dynamism, of an evangelical awakening in European society, of a religion and culture more active, more open, and more ambitious.

Institutions inevitably depend upon people with particular skills and specialized knowledge. The new political, legal, administrative, and religious institutions of the twelfth century, as well as the commercial and banking institutions that developed with the expansion of long-distance trade, all created a demand for men with new kinds of learning. This need was one of the major factors that encouraged the development of the university, another great institutional achievement of the twelfth century. It has not been generally recognized that this new institution was as much a product of widely shared cultural ideals as it was of utilitarian social needs. This aspect of the university's origins is important and needs to be reexamined.[30]

I can only emphasize here two important points about the role of the university in the twelfth-century renaissance. First, it is simply wrong to assert or to imply that the university brought the renaissance to an abrupt and premature end, because, as some scholars suggest, after 1200 (or even 1150) its teaching became too specialized and utilitarian.[31] Quite the contrary, the university provided a secure place where the period's intellectual advances—in the liberal arts no less than in theology and law—could endure and be expanded upon. Far from destroying the cultural revival, the university actually saved it. Second, not only did the university preserve these achievements of the renaissance, but the activities of its masters and students broadened the impact of the achievements and made their influence felt throughout European society. As Jacques LeGoff shows in his important essay *Les Intellectuels au moyen âge*, the "intellectuals" who first appeared in the early twelfth century and who eventually (by about 1208 in Paris) formed the guild or corporation that came to be known as the university were a wholly new social group: teacher-scholars whose profession was to share and to spread knowledge.[32] This new profession fundamentally changed the nature and purpose of education. In the twelfth century knowledge came to be regarded not as a treasure to be guarded by the small clerical elite or to be opened only for the enlightenment of aristocratic friends, but as a gift of grace to be liberally shared and freely offered to others.[33] Moreover, education came to be valued as a means of improving life and of reforming society. This is why both popes and kings willingly supported the development of the university. When, in 1155, Emperor Frederick Barbarossa granted the scholars of Bologna imperial protection, it was, as his decree states, "because the world will be ruled and illuminated by learning."[34] This was the ideal of learning essential to the foundation of the university.

It was the specific genius of the twelfth-century renaissance to create institutions, like the university, that embodied and exemplified cultural ideals. Although these institutions had a defined purpose, structure, and system, they were flexible enough to adapt to subsequent changes in social needs and conditions and thereby to endure for centuries.

Finally, we turn to the third approach that scholars have taken in trying to explain the significance of the achievements of the twelfth century. This approach involves the effort to investigate the changes in mentality, that is, in the shared habits of mind, that determined the shape and direction of the period's renewed cultural vitality. Following the great Marc Bloch, historians of the *Annales* school have concentrated on the transformation of Western Europe's secular elite from the warriors and robber barons of what has been called "the first feudal age" to the more civilized knights and nobles of "the second feudal age."[35] For example, a recent representative of this tradition, Georges Duby, claims that the habits of the nobility shifted decisively with the rise and growing influence of towns and of urban values.[36] Historians like Bloch and Duby have demonstrated that the rapid change—and the general improvement—in social and economic conditions transformed the behavior, thoughts, and feelings of those who lived in the twelfth century. The establishment of social order and the availability of surplus wealth are indeed essential preconditions of any cultural revival. However, though social and economic changes make a revival possible, they cannot alone effect the significant transformation of thought and action that produces the enduring intellectual advances and cultural achievements of a renaissance. Social and economic changes have the advantage of being measurable. Changes in mentality are more subtle as well as far more difficult for the historian to detect and to explain.

The scholar who has best described the changing mentality of the twelfth century is probably Père Marie-Dominique Chenu. In a volume of collected articles published in 1957 with the misleadingly narrow title *La Théologie au douzième siècle*, Chenu attempts to identify the implicit mental habits (*les mentalités implicites*) that unified the diverse cultural, religious, and intellectual developments of the period.[37] According to Chenu, this involves the threefold task of searching for the common root causes (*les sous sols*) that underlie, the internal laws (*les lois internes*) that inform, and the collective insights (*les lucidités collectives*) that transcend all of the individual achievements.[38] Chenu's explicit purpose is to show that the great achievements of the twelfth century were not primarily influenced or inspired by classical sources and models. "The bringing to light of ancient materials is by no means sufficient cause or the characterizing mark of such an advance in culture," he writes; "it is an effect incidental to a hunger of spirit [*l'âme en appétit*]."[39] Rather, according to Chenu, most of the achievements of the renaissance revealed fundamentally new initiatives and inspirations, which were nourished by but not dependent upon the rediscovery of classical sources. The underlying cause was not the rediscovery of the past but the age's own "hunger of spirit."

What does Chenu mean by this "hunger of spirit"? It is not easy to summarize his richly complex description of the twelfth-century renaissance, but I will try. Chenu believes that the new initiatives behind the renaissance originated in the major changes in the material conditions of life that had begun in the eleventh century. Improvements in agriculture, commerce, technology, and political stability increased people's awareness of the possibility of progress and also made them more mobile, both geographically and socially. As a result, people began to see themselves as having some measure of control over their environment. As they began to apply their energy and their reason to master this environment, they discovered and "desacralized" nature. "Man, confronting the universe," Chenu writes of this new attitude, "did not merely accept the eternal world; he changed it and, with his tools, sought to make it a humanized world."[40] The first significant effect of these material changes, then, was that people began to take a more active and positive role in shaping their physical environment and in improving human life. Human work and effort came to be increasingly valued.

The improved material conditions and increased mobility had a second and no less far-reaching effect on cultural values. People were confronted with the need to make more choices about how to conduct their lives at the same time that the established practices, norms, and ideals were no longer adequate as guides. The new challenges posed by the changing environment, Chenu believes, opened minds as never before in the Middle Ages to a wide range of novel ideas, attitudes, and values, many of which were incompatible with traditional religious teachings and practices. This development, in turn, brought about what he considers the most important and fundamental change: the renewal of Christianity. The search for a way to adapt to the changed material, moral, and intellectual environment led back to the Gospels. The consequent evangelical awakening (*reveil évangélique*) inspired the Christian religion to take a more active role in the world, to increase its level of involvement and thus to keep pace with the new, more dynamic spirit of the age. This renewal manifested itself in an increased commitment to preaching and ministering to the spiritual needs of the laity as well as in a more ardent desire to convert heretics and nonbelievers. But this evangelism, Chenu emphasizes, affected thought no less than action. The schools displayed the same new dynamism as they applied the sharpened tools of dialectic to biblical studies and developed a new pastoral (Scholastic) theology that required masters to embrace a threefold program of teaching (*lectio*), disputing (*disputatio*), and preaching (*praedicatio*).[41] For Chenu, this combination of "the new youthfulness of the Gospel and the discovery of ancient reason" explains virtually every major cultural advance within the twelfth-century renaissance.[42]

Much in this approach is compelling. Far better than "humanism" or "the discovery of the individual," Chenu's idea of "a hunger of spirit," originating in improved material conditions and inspired by an evangelical awakening, gives unity and integrity to the diverse achievements of the twelfth-century renaissance. Advances in religion, thought, literature, art, and politics, all were part of the common effort to humanize—or, to use the word preferred by Chenu, to Christianize—the world.

The scholarship about the twelfth-century renaissance is vast, certainly exceeding that about any of the other renaissances discussed in this collection of essays. I have not tried to summarize that scholarship, since this is neither possible in a short essay nor particularly helpful to understanding the achievements of the twelfth century. Rather, in discussing the three primary approaches to the renaissance, I have tried to show that, although there is now general agreement that what happened in the twelfth century merits being called a "renaissance," there are vastly differing opinions about the meaning, significance, and greatness of the achievements of this renaissance. These differing views are likely to remain part of the scholarship on the twelfth century, because the term "renaissance" will continue to be laden with cultural presumptions, and the divergent cultural values of those who use it will continue to influence their interpretation. Some of my own scholarly opinions and cultural values have been suggested in my discussion of the approaches of others. To conclude this essay, I can do no more than to make my view of the renaissance more explicit, and I do so with no pretense of advancing much beyond what has already been written on the subject. I offer what follows as an *accessus*—a summary why, how, where, who, what, and when of the twelfth-century renaissance.

I will begin with the *why* and *how,* and discuss the essential causes and preconditions of the twelfth century's cultural advances. Certainly important were the social and economic improvements that had begun in the eleventh century with the end of the invasions and the securing of the boundaries of Europe: the pacifying effects of the Peace of God and the Truce of God movement, and the rebuilding of the political order. But probably most important was the fact that as a direct result of these developments, of a few technological advances, and of a somewhat better climate, the agrarian economy of Western Europe began to produce surpluses of food, wealth, and people. These surpluses fueled the revival of trade and commerce as well as the growth of towns. The expansion of commercial activity had, in turn, considerable social and cultural repercussions. Alexander Murray, for example, has recently suggested that as money circulated more rapidly, those men skilled in mathematical and logical reasoning became increasingly valued, and it was their growing influence that made the culture of the twelfth century both more systematic and more rational.[43] With increased trade and expanding towns also came improved means of communication and larger aggregations of people. Both factors helped to overcome localism and particularism and thus to pave the way for the development of a more dynamic and unified culture.

But commerce was not the only force at work here. No less important were the foundation and expansion of the new religious orders. This process began with Cluny, the first of the international orders and the organizational model for subsequent foundations, and above all with Cîteaux, whose rapid growth in size and wealth contributed so much to twelfth-century culture. The increased popularity of pilgrimages and then the Crusades, those bold new ventures of overseas conquest, also improved communication and increased cultural contact and interchange among the varied peoples of Western Europe. Nor must we discount the importance of a common language. Latin, the established language of worship and of learning, was the only means by which people from both the Germanic and Romance speaking parts of Europe could communicate with each other and exchange ideas. I would suggest that this linguistic fact, far more than the inspiration derived from the rediscovery of classical literature, explains the considerable efforts made by twelfth-century scholars to improve spoken and written Latin.

Social order, increased wealth, improved communication, and a common language all helped, but the greatest stimulus to cultural advance must have been the challenges from the outside, as Western Europeans expanded their horizons and discovered the very different peoples who lived beyond their frontiers. Europeans encountered new ideas and new problems as they learned of and from the two great neighboring civilizations of Byzantium and Islam. Thus a widening geographical perspective contributed to a broadened intellectual perspective. It is difficult to explain why Western Europeans, unlike their Greek and Arabic neighbors, remained so open to external ideas and influences. When they first began to travel beyond their own frontiers, at the end of the eleventh century, they moved in a remarkable burst of confidence and boldness. But by the early thirteenth century, the Western Europeans were more aware of and more anxious about how vast the world was and how vastly they were outnumbered by other peoples.

The Crusades were of central importance to this development—not because they facilitated cultural interchange (as virtually all historians now agree they did not), but because they helped to shape European attitudes, feelings, and values. The achievements of the twelfth-century renaissance owe a great deal to the Crusades, to the impact of the few great victories of the Crusaders (the conquest of Jerusalem in 1099 and of Constantinople in 1204), and to the more frequent defeats (such as Hattin in 1187 and Damietta in 1221). For more than two centuries, Western Europeans were preoccupied with the Greeks and the Saracens. The cultural advances they made during this time were undoubtedly influenced by the rediscovery of the classical past, but the greater stimulus probably came from the discovery of Byzantium and Islam, two very different and hostile cultures that shared that same past. Far more than the recovered knowledge of the past, it was the new knowledge of their own expanding present that challenged the minds of Western Europeans in the twelfth century. Their great aggressiveness, both military and intellectual, stemmed not from a confident sense of religious or cultural superiority but from serious anxieties about their place in the world and in history. As Western Europe emerged from several centuries of relative cultural quiescence, its peoples found that they could not just assume their superiority; they had to prove and to defend it.

Where did the renaissance happen? Its principal centers were certainly the expanding towns. Paris, which had the combined advantages of being near the intersection of important commercial crossroads, in the center of some of the lushest farmland in Western Europe, and the chosen capital of what was rapidly becoming the wealthiest, most powerful, and most prestigious monarchy in Europe, has rightly been called "the Florence of the twelfth-century renaissance."[44] Paris may in fact have played a greater role in this renaissance than Florence did in the later one. The presence of several prominent schools and then the first great university was a magnet that drew to

Paris from throughout Europe the increasing numbers of young men who saw learning as a means of advancing in the world. What happened in Paris (*Parisius*), this "paradise [*paradisus*] of letters," was not a local or a regional but an international phenomenon. The young men who came to the city to study and sometimes to teach carried with them what they had learned in Paris when they left. Paris became the primary center of intellectual and cultural diffusion. But Paris was not the only center. It drew most of its men, its inspirations, and its ideas from other cities, then sent them back stamped unmistakably with its influence. Chartres, Canterbury, Toledo, Bologna, and Rome come to mind at once as important origins and destinations, but they were not alone. No major town, court, or monastery remained untouched or unchanged by the cultural, intellectual, and religious currents of the twelfth century. The impact of the new ideas and institutions wherever they arose was rapid and ubiquitous. The cultural revival affected all of Europe. Paris was the vital center, not merely of a local renaissance of limited influence and duration, but of the birth ("naissance") of the unified, distinct, and enduring culture of Western Europe.

Who were the creators and the leading figures of the twelfth-century renaissance? Surprisingly, Haskins, who did so much to advance the idea of the renaissance, concluded that the twelfth century produced "few outstanding individuals."[45] Though it is certainly true that no one individual matches the reputation for brilliance of Dante or Petrarch, of Erasmus or Thomas More, the twelfth-century renaissance produced many men who significantly influenced their own age and whose achievements measure up to those in any other. The problem with mentioning specific names is that one is likely to exclude others equally prominent and important. But few who have studied the twelfth century would deny that Anselm of Bec (later of Canterbury), Peter Abelard, Bernard of Clairvaux, Suger of St. Denis, Peter the Venerable, John of Salisbury, Alan of Lille, Stephen Langton, Pope Innocent III, and Francis of Assisi were outstanding individuals, if not all equally so.

Nevertheless, it is true that many of the most important and enduring achievements of the time were produced by the efforts of the lesser men, who sometimes worked alone but more often in association with a school, a court, or a religious community or order. These include, to cite a few notable examples, the learned scholars in the abbey of St. Victor, Gratian and his colleagues at the law schools of Bologna, the first generation of Paris theologians after Abelard (including Peter Lombard), the practical theologians who later in the century formed the circle of Peter the Chanter, and the learned clerics and capable administrators who gathered in sophisticated courts like those of King Henry II of England, Count Henry the Liberal of Champagne, and King Roger II of Sicily.

Sociologically, the renaissance can be said to have been primarily the work of young men of high birth, the surplus sons of the feudal nobility. Motivated primarily by the practical need to support themselves, these *juvenes* aspired to a level of education higher than that of their fathers or older brothers so that they could select among an increasing diversity of careers and professions.[46] But the renaissance was not the achievement of this noble elite alone. The expanding society of the twelfth century also allowed capable young men of humble birth to rise socially and to make their own cultural contribution. An especially notable example is Maurice of Sully. The son of simple peasants, he attended and taught in the schools of Paris and then served as bishop of the city for more than thirty-five important years (1160–96). It was Bishop Maurice who initiated construction of the beautiful new Gothic cathedral, Notre Dame, which became the great landmark of Paris.

These young men brought a previously unknown vitality to Western European society and culture, an exuberance that constitutes the essence of the twelfth-century renaissance. Their creative response to the changing environment and expanding opportunities—a cultural boldness born of ambition combined with anxiety—was the impetus for a whole range of social and intellectual advances. Nowhere was this more evident than in the schools. The first generations of students to flock to the expanding urban schools found their inspiration in the learning and the achievements of the past. The known past, both classical and patristic, initially provided the new ideas and models for action, and these were for a time studied assiduously and imitated enthusiastically. Then, by about the middle of the twelfth century, the rediscovery of the past appeared to be complete. The "moderns," as the scholars of the time began to describe themselves, had assimilated the available learning of Antiquity and were now confident of their mastery of it.[47] More importantly, they were aware that they could and should learn more and advance beyond what had been known before. Here lies the significance of that familiar image of dwarves standing on the shoulders of giants, which was used repeatedly by the scholars of the time to describe their relationship to the authorities of the past, and which is so often still cited in essays on the twelfth-century renaissance. The image embodies the important idea of the advance of knowledge and of cultural progress.[48] "Our age often knows more," writes John of Salisbury—not, he explains, because we have greater ability but because we have inherited and benefit from the achievements of earlier men.[49] The scholars of the twelfth century may have perceived themselves as dwarves, but they and their contemporaries stood boldly and ambitiously on the shoulders of their giants and maneuvered these beasts of tradition where they would.

To advance beyond what had been known before, those in the schools first undertook to organize and systematize the inherited knowledge of the past. The effort produced an impressive series of textbooks, including the *Glossa ordinaria*, the *Decretum* of Gratian, the *Summa Prisciani* of Peter Helias, the *Sentences* of Peter Lombard, and the *Historia scholasticia* of Peter Comestor. All proved so useful that they continued to be used in universities until the sixteenth century. These textbooks or *summae* did not bring the renaissance to an abrupt halt, as some scholars have implied, but initiated a new phase of learned activity. Such valuable compilations, in establishing and disseminating a common body of knowledge, provided the sound intellectual foundations for advances into as yet untraveled avenues of thought and action.

In the latter part of the twelfth century, the schools emphasized action rather than speculation. There was perhaps less intellectual excitement and creativity as scholars settled down to the difficult task of applying what they had learned to social action and reform. Many of the most capable and ambitious men left the schools as soon as the opportunity came to advance their careers—and their ideals—by serving in the administrative ranks of the Church or in the courts of secular rulers. Those who remained to teach in the schools, like Master Peter the Chanter and his disciples in Paris,[50] focused their attention on practical issues of moral theology, not because they were less intelligent than their predecessors or more fearful of papal censure, but because they believed that this learning was preparation for the essential tasks of reforming society and improving human life. This was the cause to which education became committed.

The changes in the schools can best be understood as a reflection of the more general changes in twelfth-century culture. Two fundamental objectives motivated those who participated in the cultural activity of the period. First, they believed that by organizing and systematizing knowledge they could begin to rationalize the universe and order human experience. Second, they intended to apply this knowledge to the varied interests, needs, problems, and questions of human life in a rapidly changing, expanding, and sometimes frightening world. The considerable and enduring cultural advances that make up the twelfth-century renaissance testify that these men found the inspiration and took the initiative necessary to succeed remarkably well in realizing both objectives.

Finally, *when* did the twelfth-century renaissance happen? This question is more difficult to answer than one might expect. Obviously cultural revivals do not coincide neatly with the convenient but arbitrary division of history into centuries. Scholars who speak of the twelfth-century renaissance never mean to suggest that the movement was specifically or exclusively confined to the years between 1100 and 1200. However, they generally agree that the main period of activity and creativity did fall sometime within the century. The substantial disagreement is over when the renaissance began and when it ended. This dispute fundamentally involves different conceptions of the twelfth-century renaissance. What one considers the period's most significant cultural achievements will determine what limits one chooses for the beginning and end of its renaissance.

The *terminus a quo* of the renaissance has been assigned an especially wide range of dates. Scholars place it as early as the mid-tenth century, when the external invasions ended, and as late as the final years of the eleventh century, when the Crusades began.[51] A strong case, I believe, can be made that the renaissance did not actually begin until the latter part of this chronological range. Certainly, the economic and social changes that were its essential preconditions were well under way before the middle of the eleventh century, and important cultural initiatives had already been taken, especially in intellectual life and in religious reform. But the truly formative period of the renaissance was the fifty years between the Council of Sutri in 1046, when the reform of the papacy began with the deposition of three rival popes, and the Council of Clermont in 1095, when Urban II launched the First Crusade. The major papal initiatives of this half century had an especially great impact upon both the scope and the direction of the cultural revival. Previous cultural initiatives had been local, decentralized, and limited in their influence. It was the reform-minded popes, especially Gregory VII, who provided a common focus and the central leadership necessary to give full impetus to these new aspirations. Moreover, although significant social and cultural changes were already under way, their pace was accelerated greatly when the so-called Investiture Controversy challenged the established order. Papal leadership was the key factor in broadening the nascent cultural revival into a Europe-wide movement.[52] In the last half of the eleventh century Rome played midwife to Paris, which then nurtured the twelfth-century renaissance.

When did the twelfth-century renaissance end? Those who regard the renaissance as a limited revival of classical culture claim it died soon after 1150, a victim either of the increased predominance of theology in the schools or of the reaction of a more rigid Church fearful lest, as one historian writes, "the framework of Christian civilization should be undermined by the popularity of pagan ideas."[53] In the second half of the twelfth century, church officials were clearly worried about the spread of heretical beliefs and practices among the laity, but definitely not about the number of people reading Cicero or even Ovid.[54] The twelfth-century renaissance changed after 1150; however, it did not end. From then on, the culture depended less on classical sources and was more open to other inspirations and to newer ideas. If one understands the renaissance as a diverse yet integrated cultural revival, one cannot fail to realize that the second half of the twelfth century was as active and as creative as the first half. There were movements in new directions, but the motivations and the objectives remained essentially the same.[55]

As for the designation of a specific *terminus ad quem*, probably the year 1215 is the best choice.[56] The major events of that year—the Fourth Lateran Council, the sealing of the Magna Carta, the decreeing of the first statutes for the University of Paris, and the final confirmation of the mendicant orders—summarize many of the greatest achievements of the twelfth-century renaissance. But do these events mark an end or a new beginning? The answer must be both. By 1215 a unified and self-conscious culture had been born in West Europe. That vibrant new civilization, nourished by the continuing vitality of the ideas and the institutions created by the twelfth-century renaissance, proved capable not only of surviving the new challenges posed by Aristotle, the Arabs, and the Mongols in the thirteenth century, but of being further enriched and tempered by them to form a cultural legacy that still endures.

CHAPTER 7

The Palaeologan Renaissance

IHOR ŠEVČENKO

Borrowing a device from the Byzantine rhetoricians, I shall begin my article by defining the two words of its title. In terms of time "Palaeologan" shall mean the period between 1261 and 1453, the reign of the last Byzantine dynasty, the Palaeologi, in Constantinople; in terms of space it shall mean the territory directly ruled by members of that dynasty. By about 1320 that territory did not amount to much. It encompassed a few cities in western Asia Minor (most of them close to the other side of the Straits or to the coast); a fairly narrow strip of land, extending from Constantinople to what is today southern Albania and for a while bulging southward to include Thessaly; the southeastern corner of the Peloponnesus; and a half dozen or so islands in the Aegean. As time went on, the Palaeologan state shrank even further. Some fifty years before Constantinople fell in 1453, the Empire consisted of that city, a few towns along the Black Sea and the northern coast of the Marmara Sea, a coastal strip in Macedonia and Thessaly, a few islands, and the same southeastern part of the Peloponnesus with its capital at Mistra (near today's Sparta).[1] Scholars may wonder how such a small and weak political entity produced such an impressive efflorescence of culture, but they have no difficulty telling us what this entity was and by whom and for how long it was ruled.

I have generally adopted the Greek spelling of proper names, except where the names are more familiar in their Latin or English forms.

The word "renaissance" is less easy to define; coupled with "Palaeologan," it becomes ambiguous. We should remember this ambiguity but we need not dwell upon it: ever since Erwin Panofsky most people have been made aware of the distinction between the Renaissance and renascences.[2] Since I subscribe to that distinction, I prefer to call the event discussed here the "Palaeologan revival" and to reserve the name Renaissance for that unique event in European—predominantly but not exclusively Western European—history. In a Byzantine perspective, the Palaeologan revival of the fourteenth century was only one of several such renascences, the others being the Theodosian revival of the fourth and fifth centuries, the Justinianic revival of the sixth, the so-called Macedonian renaissance of the tenth, and the Comnenian revival of the twelfth.

"Renaissance," "renascence," "revival"; these labels matter little, so long as we explain what we mean by them clearly. But by what criteria should we evaluate Byzantine renascences or revivals? Here too often we Byzantinists begin to mumble, and in practice use as our yardstick the degree to which the creative individuals involved in a revival successfully imitated the high forms of ancient Greek language and literature and of Greek, or rather Hellenistic, art, that is, the degree to which they succeeded in intensifying their contacts with Antiquity. This can be a legitimate yardstick, so long as it is clear that as good historicists we are simply expounding the point of view of the principal creators of the revivals themselves. However much they may have misunderstood the term, these men did set out to imitate Antiquity. But we run into trouble when we unconsciously adopt their point of view as our own. The scale of values we thus unreflectingly employ is the scale inherited from the unique event called the Renaissance, and retained, with some modifications, until the nineteenth century.

But we can avoid the pitfall of measuring a revival solely by its success in imitating the past if we use the term in a neutral way to mean a general intensification of cultural activity. This device also allows us to sidestep the fascinating but difficult question: Was the Antiquity the revivalists thought they were imitating the same as the Antiquity they were in fact imitating or Antiquity as we understand it today?

The evidence that a revival did occur under the Palaeologi was gathered over almost a century of scholarship. Scholars adduce first of all the level and elegance of the language used by Palaeologan writers. So long as the empire existed, the tyranny of high style held sway over Byzantine literati in the form of the worship of Atticism that they inherited from the Second Sophistic.[3] At all times Byzantine intellectuals put a premium on complicated, classicizing prose. In poetry, they followed a hierarchy in verse meters; the hexameter, for example, ranked above the iambic (or to use a term more appropriate to the Byzantine period, the Byzantine dodecasyllable). The remarkable thing is that some Palaeologan writers turned out to be particularly adept at this favorite Byzantine literary game.

Take the dialogue, a genre the Byzantines practiced in the fourth, sixth, seventh, tenth, and twelfth centuries, as well as in the Palaeologan period. In this form, they imitated the ideologically dangerous Plato or the morally reprehensible Lucian. Only in modern times have scholars realized that the dialogue *Philopatris,* long attributed to Lucian (even if occurring only in a few late manuscripts) could not have been written by him but was a skillful Christian imitation of his style. Placed first in the fourth or seventh century, *Philopatris* is by now anchored in the second part of the tenth, that is, in the so-called Macedonian renaissance, or even in the mid-eleventh century.[4] It is instructive to compare this work to the dialogue *Florentios* by Nicephorus Gregoras, one of the prominent representatives of the early Palaeologan revival. Written in order to pulverize Gregoras's enemy, the Calabrian monk Barlaam (who was to become Petrarch's professor of Greek), *Florentios* is a much more graceful imitation of Plato than *Philopatris* is of Lucian. Gregoras assimilated Plato's vocabulary and idioms in an organic fashion. To realize this, we have only to read a single page of *Florentios* in the latest edition by Professor Leone, whose apparatus reveals the large number of allusions to Plato and the mosaic of unobtrusive if literal borrowings from that author.[5]

Aelius Aristides, that shining light of the Second Sophistic, was a model of the high style for all later Byzantine writers. But it was not until the early fourteenth century that two speeches were written which were good enough to pass as his in the eyes of modern scholars for almost two centuries. Not until roughly the mid-nineteenth century did critics become suspicious and redate these speeches to Late Antiquity. Conclusive proof that they were in fact the work of a fourteenth-century philologist-monk from Thessalonica, by the name of Thomas Magister, was offered only about forty years ago.[6]

The linguistic changes that occurred in Greek at the end of Late Antiquity made it difficult to write hexameters. The hexameters that Gregory of Nazianzus composed in the fourth century already seem deficient. Nonnos's *Dionysiaka,* written in the fifth century, was an exceptional tour de force both for the correctness of its hexameters and for its enormous size; Musaeus's *Hero and Leander,* which belongs roughly to the same period, is but a small epyllion. In the seventh century George of Pisidia was able to turn out "correct" iambics, that is, ones that could be read both in the antique and in the Byzantine way; but he used hexameter only sparingly. If we except the fifteen hundred or so didactic hexameters by the self-centered twelfth-century scholar John Tzetzes, the situation prevailed until our period. Yet around 1300, the philologist-monk Maximos Planudes was capable of penning hundreds of passable hexameters.[7] The largest corpus of hexameters that Greek letters had seen since the time of Nonnos emerged a few decades later: the nine thousand hexameters contained in twenty poems by Theodore Metochites, the most prominent representative of the early Palaeologan revival. Metochites's poetry is not very good; he did not follow the standard rules of prosody and his writing was cerebral, devoid of feeling. But that he set out to write in the grand old way is beyond doubt.[8]

Such a high level of technical achievement and, as we shall see shortly, such broad knowledge of antique literature imply a correspondingly high level of technical preparation and competence. The early Palaeologan revival was an age of philology, of antiquarianism, and of love for books, which were expressed both in the quest for texts and in intensive copying activity. Present-day classicists are vastly indebted to the efforts of their Palaeologan predecessors, such as Demetrios Triklinios, Manuel Moschopoulos, Thomas Magister, and Maximos Planudes. These men wrote dictionaries of Attic words. They made new editions of poets such as Hesiod and Pindar, and of the two tragedians Sophocles and Euripides. They wrote scholia to Pindar, the tragedians, and Aristophanes; and a number of their readings—of Sophocles, for example—are still accepted as felicitous conjectures.[9] They rediscovered authors about whom tradition had been silent for hundreds of years, as Maximos Planudes rediscovered Ptolemy's *Geography* and the epic of Nonnos of Panopolis, for example. Their complete editions of various authors remain the basis of our own knowledge—Planudes, again, edited (and partly rediscovered) Plutarch and the *Greek Anthology*, the latter in a version that we call "Planudean" today and that contains almost four hundred epigrams peculiar to it alone. Male antiquarians and aristocratic bluestockings searched for ancient texts, borrowed them from each other, described the process of making a book, and when they could afford to, created vast libraries of both secular and religious works. The collection that Theodore Metochites assembled in his monastery of Chora by the first quarter of the fourteenth century remained the largest library in Constantinople—and therefore in the Empire—until the fall of the City in 1453.[10] Some of Chora's volumes survive today in the libraries of Vienna and Paris.

Ability to write in a *recherché* language, philological acumen, and a vast and often genuine erudition are no guarantee of originality. Much of what was written on secular and sacred topics during the Palaeologan revival was respectable routine. The revival produced three large historical works that treated contemporary events but drew on such models as Thucydides; a body of epistolography, usually very complicated in style despite some epistolographers' professions to the contrary and the antique rules of the genre that recommended brevity and clarity; a great deal of iambic poetry; a relatively large body of hagiography in high style; and a vast amount of theological polemics against the Latins, the Orthodox of the adverse camp, and Islam—the usual subjects for the time.

Still, at least two writers of the period can lay claim to an originality that transcends their own time. The first was Theodore Metochites, who lived at the beginning of the revival and wrote the nine thousand clumsy hexameters mentioned above. The second, who lived at the revival's end, was George Gemistos Plethon.

Metochites was preoccupied with the notion that he and his generation had been left with nothing new to say. Yet his (still unpublished) eulogy of Gregory of Nazianzus is to my mind the very first scholarly appreciation of this Father and the first biographical sketch based on an intelligent reading of his work. Anxious and sensitive, Metochites constantly wrote about himself, unabashedly or in disguise—a trait rare in the Middle Ages. He inherited the belief that the Byzantine Empire was coeternal with the world and consequently would disappear only at the end of days. Yet he was the first Byzantine intellectual on record to regard the Empire as just another political entity and to envision its impending collapse as just another manifestation of the universal law of creation and decay. Unlike his predecessors, Metochites saw Byzantine civilization as neither unique nor superior to all others. A historical relativist, he even considered the infidel Tatars noble, more so in some respects than his Byzantine fellow-Christians. Metochites claimed immortality on earth for himself—another of his unmedieval beliefs. Like most intellectuals, he may have been self-centered, but he saw through many shibboleths of his culture and anticipated its end. It was not his fault that he was unable, either as an intellectual or as a statesman, to avert that end.[11]

George Gemistos Plethon, who died in the Peloponnesus one year before the fall of Constantinople, is the only Palaeologan thinker who has his counterparts among the paganizing writers of the Italian Renaissance. In his philosophical system, Plethon broke with Christianity. He or at least his circle read and appreciated the writings of the anti-Christian Julian the Apostate. He advocated a polytheistic pantheon that, based as it was on antique religion but tempered by Neoplatonic speculations, helped him to create a philosophical counterpart to the Trinity. Zeus stood at the head of the gods and was assisted by Poseidon and by the four types of gods of descending power. Plethon professed a belief both in the message of Zoroaster and in that of the Seven Wise Men, and posited the immortality of the soul *before* its descent into the body. Scholarios, one of his adversaries, accused him of believing in metempsychosis, and he certainly professed a doctrine of fatalism, probably under the influence of Islam. He proposed to Theodore, the ruler of the Peloponnesus, a reform reminiscent of the *Laws* and of the *Republic* of Plato: the division of the population into three classes. No wonder that when some time after his death the master copy of his major work in three books, the *Laws*, was handed over to the Patriarch of Constantinople, Gennadios Scholarios, Scholarios ordered it to be burnt. As a result, we know of Plethon's un-Christian religious system mainly from refutations by the same Patriarch, from numerous fragments copied by Plethon's adherents, and from the page or so of the *Laws* that have survived in Plethon's own handwriting.[12] Some modern scholars view Plethon's system as forward-looking, rather than as the last *summa* of the "Greek Middle Ages"; they do it on the strength of Plethon's influence on Renaissance Neoplatonists.

The most obvious evidence of the Palaeologan revival, even to an outsider, is its art. In fact, to my knowledge art historians were the first to speak of a Palaeologan renaissance at the beginning of this century. Struck by the synchronism between the paintings of Giotto and the mosaics of the church of Chora in Constantinople, they wondered who had influenced whom, if at all.[13] The representative examples of Palaeologan mosaics and frescoes included here begin with the great Deesis mosaic in the gallery of St. Sophia in Constantinople, a work that scholars now think was created shortly after the reconquest of the City in 1261 (Figure 1). The mosaics of the Church of the Holy Apostles in Thessalonica, the second city of the Empire, date from about 1312 (Figure 2). Among the jewels of the Palaeologan art of the capital are the early fourteenth-century mosaics: the Christ in the Pammakaristos Church (Figure 3) and both the conventional and the classicizing examples (Figures 4 and 5) at the monastery of Chora (restored by Metochites). For examples of frescoes, we may turn to the Peribleptos Church of Mistra (Figure 6) in the Peloponnesus, the home city (Figure 7) of the last Byzantine emperor, Constantine XII. As despot of Mistra, Constantine lived in the palace whose ruins still impress us today (Figure 8).

1. Istanbul, S. Sophia, South Gallery:
Deesis Mosaic

2. Thessalonica, Church of the Holy
Apostles: Descent into Limbo

3. Istanbul, Fethiye Camii (Pammakaristos), Parekklesion: Christ in apse

4. Istanbul, Kahriye Camii (Chora), Church of Christ, inner narthex, bay 3 east, lunette: Donor panel

5. Istanbul, Kahriye Camii (Chora), Church of Christ, outer narthex, bay 3 north, NW pendentive: The Wedding at Cana, detail

6. Mistra, Church of the Virgin Peribleptos: The Baptism of Christ

7. Mistra, general view

8. Mistra, Palace of the Despots

9. *Vaticanus Palatinus Gr.* 181, fol. 169^v: Moses Receiving the Law

10. *Parisinus Gr.* 139, fol. 422^v: Moses Receiving the Law

11. Staro Nagoričane, Church of St. George, west wall: Dormition

12. Ohrid, Church of St. Clement, NW pier, west face: St. Mercurius, signed by Michael Astrapas

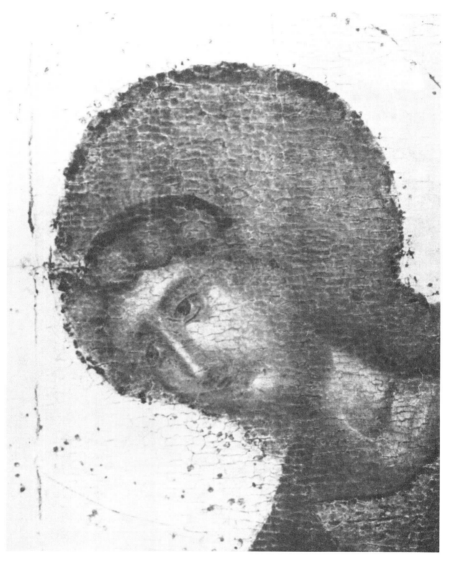

13. Moscow, Kremlin, Annunciation Cathedral, Iconostasis:
Archangel Gabriel, by Theophanes the Greek

14. Calendžixa, Georgian SSR, Church of the Savior, apse: Head of
the Archangel Gabriel, by Manuel Eugenikos

15. Rimini, Tempio di Malatesta, NW corner: foundation inscription, ca. 1450

16. Istanbul, land walls, inscription of 1441 about repairs made by Emperor John VIII

All these mosaics date from before 1320, whereas the frescoes are from the second half of the fourteenth century. The years in between did not favor the production of monumental art—which after all requires a considerably larger outlay of funds than does writing a history or a philological commentary. In these intervening years two civil wars, the first of which started in 1321, ruined both the aristocracy and the imperial court and facilitated rapid Turkish conquests. The Ottomans established their first permanent settlement in Europe in 1354. Soon after 1371 Byzantium became for about thirty years a vassal state of the Ottomans and, after a short respite, relapsed into vassalage again for the last thirty years of its existence. The economic effects of the civil wars explain why there is no known instance of mosaic decoration in Byzantium after 1320. Fresco is an impoverished patron's mosaic; thus it was the only medium used after 1320 even in the Peloponnesus, which enjoyed some prosperity in the late fourteenth and the fifteenth centuries.

Late Byzantium was not only decaying, it was very small. The number of those responsible for the Palaeologan revival was also small, perhaps 150 to 200 people over the two centuries involved.[14] The voluminous correspondence of the time reveals so much crisscrossing of names that it seems everybody knew and wrote to everybody else. In this small milieu subgroups gravitated around the various centers of power that before the civil wars of the 1320's were able to extend substantial patronage. In descending order of importance, that patronage came from the imperial court itself; from peripheral courts like those of Trebizond or Arta; from a few individual patrons, top imperial bureaucrats who had won their own posts by their literary refinement and achievements (this method of recruitment was somewhat reminiscent of the Mandarin system in China); from the Great Church of St. Sophia, with its Patriarch and patriarchal bureaucracy; and from a metropolitan's palace. Imperial or aristocratic ladies, patriarchs, and high officials were not only patrons but prominent writers in their own right: examples are Irene Choumnos and Theodora Raoulaina Palaeologina; patriarchs Gregory of Cyprus and John Glykys;

dignitaries such as Metochites and Nicephorus Choumnos; and John Kantakouzenos, first a high official, then emperor. Since these aristocrats and officials stood high on the rungs of imperial bureaucracy, they were able to retain or amass considerable wealth, some of which they used to further the learning that had helped them climb so high on the ladder of privilege.

It is hardly thinkable that Nicephorus Gregoras could have achieved what he did without the support he received in his early years from his uncle, the metropolitan of Heracleia Pontica (today's Karadeniz Ereğlisi); without the encouragement that the Patriarch John Glykys gave him when he arrived in the capital; without his contacts with Emperor Andronikos II; and without the continuous patronage of Metochites, who declared Gregoras his spiritual heir and gave him a sinecure in his restored monastery. Assuming an uninterrupted tradition of education, quite small groups can produce impressive revivals. All they need are structures that will provide them with a minimum of support—that is, a chance to gravitate around a powerful elite that shares with their protégés the conviction that culture and learning increase the social prestige of both producer and patron.

The Palaeologan revival was no less apparent to the intellectuals of the time than it is to modern scholars. The former derided—not quite fairly—the low state that learning had reached in the years just preceding. Still, awareness of the revival does not necessarily explain why this revival was as Hellenizing as it was, especially in its early phase. The explanation might simply be that the Byzantines, who always imitated Antiquity, just did it particularly well in the early fourteenth century. But another historical factor that began to operate shortly before that time may also have contributed to the Palaeologan intellectuals' intensified consciousness of their Hellenic past. Until the last quarter of the eleventh century, Byzantium had been a multinational entity. Greek culture had provided a veneer—the appearance of uniformity—while Christianity had provided the deeper, unifying bond. Byzantium's elite, and even more, some of its less refined writers, had always seen their Empire as a continuation of the Roman Empire rather than of classical Greece.[15] Now, however, aside from some

Slavs and Albanians and an insignificant number of Latins and
Jews, the Palaeologan state was ethnically Greek. Greek intellectuals were living among Greeks and harkening back increasingly to a different past: Greek antiquity.

A telltale sign of this reorientation is the reappearance of the
words "Hellene" and "Hellenic" in their original meaning.
That original meaning showed up a few times before 1261, but
it was firmly established only with the writings of certain refined Palaeologan intellectuals. Before the thirteenth century
"Hellene" usually meant "pagan," a pejorative term whose origins go back to the apocryphal books of the Old and to the New
Testament. There "Hellene" simply denotes a non-Jew, that is,
a gentile. The usage was reinforced by the strong cultural and
ethnic contrasts present in the world of early monasticism—in
Egypt, the unlearned Christian Copts like Saint Anthony were
poles apart from Greek-speaking pagan champions of Hellenic
culture. Other pagan intellectuals of Late Antiquity also conceived of themselves as the guardians of the old Hellenic values. The negative connotation of "Hellene," whether in its
Greek or in its Church Slavonic form, persisted throughout the
Byzantine period and outlived Byzantium in the Eastern Orthodox world. But in Palaeologan times this connotation survived mainly in the writings of middlebrow Byzantines. The
refined intellectuals actually boasted that they were members
of the "Hellenic nation" or—in moments of despondency—
that they were the "remnants of the Hellenes." Under the new
conditions of relative ethnic homogeneity, and even some
xenophobia, their search for roots led them back to the glorious
Hellenic past.[16]

The Byzantine literati of all periods were fond of imitating
Antiquity, but the average practitioner of letters had a two-di-
mensional conception of that Antiquity. Plato not only stood
next to Aristotle but also to Iamblichus; and Demosthenes's
neighbor was Synesios of Cyrene. The Byzantines imitated the
literary devices of Antiquity at second remove. Their operative
models were the writers of the Second Sophistic—not just the
pagans Lucian and Aelius Aristides, or Philostratos and Libanios, but also the three Cappadocian fathers, Gregory of Nazianzus, Gregory of Nyssa, and Basil of Caesarea, who by their

own literary practice had bestowed a seal of limited approval on pagan literature. We moderns may have singled out the various Byzantine revivals for praise precisely because each in its turn crossed the barrier of the Second Sophistic and made some direct contact with the genuinely classical period.

The Palaeologan revival is an especially good case in point: not only did it make direct contact with classical works, but some of its prominent representatives certainly saw Antiquity in three dimensions. Metochites regretted that Socrates, with his powerful mind, had been unable to avail himself of all the insights that antique philosophy attained after his time. In his critical essay on Demosthenes and Aelius Aristides, Metochites attributed the difference between their two kinds of oratory to the different periods in which they had lived. Demosthenes orated in the heyday of democracy, when one had to speak to the point and answer questions on the spot; Aelius Aristides lived under a monarchy, a condition that favored panegyric and encouraged verbosity—one could disregard objections from the floor, so to speak. But even Metochites, like professional philologists of his time, sometimes quenched his thirst for Antiquity at less limpid springs. One such spring was not surprisingly the Second Sophistic, whose Christian and pagan authors both served as models. Metochites's hexameters imitate those of Gregory of Nazianzus, and his passage on the Hermae of Athens is borrowed from one of Gregory's sermons. Metochites's contemporary, George Lakapenos, published an annotated anthology of 264 letters by Libanios, and made generous use of Libanios in the commentary he provided to his own letters. Metochites even sometimes derives his information on Antiquity from Byzantine sources. He quotes one Attic orator not from the original text but from a passage in the ninth-century *Bibliotheca* of Photius; in his commentaries on Aristotle, a work of his youth, Metochites depends on an eleventh-century Byzantine commentator named Michael of Ephesus. What is true of literature is true of art: the classicizing Psalter miniatures of the thirteenth-century *Vaticanus Pal. Gr.* 381 (Figure 9) are close, if perhaps indirect, copies of the classicizing Paris Psalter (*Parisinus Gr.* 139), a tenth-century work (Figure 10).[17]

Thus, compared to the fifteenth-century Italian humanists, the Palaeologan literati were humanists in only a qualified sense—"Christian" or "surface humanists" might be better terms. Except for the professional philologists and a maverick like Plethon, these literati used antique devices and subjects to gain an advantage in the game of literary one-upmanship, while they simultaneously continued to compose in a conventional vein. Nicephorus Gregoras wrote works of hagiography that update and stylistically upgrade the saints' lives written in the ninth and early tenth centuries. The really passionate writing of the fourteenth century was still reserved for the religious controversies, especially that between the Palamites and the anti-Palamites. (The former claimed that God could be contemplated directly through his uncreated energies, such as the light on Mt. Thabor; their adversaries claimed that the energies of God were created by him and that the only uncreated thing about God was his essence, which could never be directly contemplated.) Controversies over the Union of the Churches and over the use of works by Catholic theologians also kindled considerable passion. But only in the fifteenth century, mostly after the fall of Byzantium and on foreign soil, did controversies about the respective merits of Plato and Aristotle—that is, about philosophy of the classical epoch—acquire a truly passionate character. Plethon's *On the Differences between Plato and Aristotle*, written in Florence at the time of the Council of 1439, and Bessarion's *Adversus calumniatorem Platonis*, first printed in Rome in 1469, are the outstanding examples of such an *engagé* attitude.[18]

The truth is that its competent and admiring utilization of antique sources is the most striking but not the prevalent aspect of the Palaeologan age. As far as form went, even the Palamites admitted that the goal of a writer was to imitate the ancients "correctly" by means of technical rhetoric. But form aside, old attitudes and conservative ways of thinking found expression not only at the Patriarchate, from where Athanasius I (1289–1293; 1303–1309) dictated his turgid letters (most of whose quotations were Scriptural and liturgical, or at best due to Gregory of Nazianzus and John Chrysostom), but even in the highest circles at the court of Andronikos II, the foremost patron of the revival. Constantine Akropolites, that emperor's great logothete, wrote his letters in a language that would earn high marks in Greek composition for any Oxford undergraduate today. But he used that language to write lives of the saints; and Akropolites confessed in a letter that when he came across *Timarion*, a twelfth-century Lucianic satire about Timarion's descent into Hades and some eleventh- and twelfth-century Byzantines he met there, he had wanted to burn the manuscript on the spot. The dialogue deserved condemnation, Akropolites wrote, because its author used Hellenic mythology, because he was anti-Christian, and because by seating Minos and Rhadamanthys in the netherworld he negated Christ's descent into Hades. Needless to say, Akropolites used the words "Hellene" and "Hellenic" in a pejorative sense. But even this staunch defender of traditional religious values reveals himself as a child of his own philological age: we learn from a recently published passage that Akropolites once asked a friend to send him a good copy of the poem on the creation of the world by the seventh-century George of Pisidia. Akropolites needed the friend's text of the poem (he promised to keep it only for a few days), for his own copy was teeming with errors.[19]

By the second half of the fourteenth century, the overbearing stance of the proponents of classicizing erudition was arousing the resentment of the lower tier of Byzantine intellectuals, who characteristically clung to Palamitic beliefs. An unpublished dialogue by Philotheos, Metropolitan of Selymbria (today's Silivri), pitted the anti-Palamites (including Barlaam and Nicephorus Gregoras) against Palamas and his many supporters. Given the values of the upper layer of Byzantine society to which Palamas himself belonged, Philotheos could not directly attack the refined learning of the anti-Palamites in his dialogue. However, he made the point that the Palamites were also perfectly learned in poetry, oratory, and dialectic. They could have employed sophisticated philosophical devices and literary tricks if they had wanted to, but in their quest for the simplicity of religious truth advocated by St. Paul and by Gregory of Nazianzus had chosen not to make a contentious show of these skills.[20] Sour grapes, if you like, but a case worth noting in view of the subsequent victory of the Palamite doctrine in the Orthodox Church.

The further truth is that some of the new achievements of the Palaeologan period, some of the new cultural trends, and some of the new literary forms attested in the last two centuries of the Empire's existence had little or nothing to do with intensified contacts with classical Antiquity. Some of these innovations were established by intellectuals who stood lower on the social scale—if someone's position on that scale is measured by his ability to turn out a Demosthenic phrase. Others can be attributed to literati who wrote both in the classicizing and in the more popular mode.

The scientific revival of the early Palaeologan period, especially the restoration of astronomy to its former glory by Metochites and his pupil Gregoras, meets with nearly universal acclaim today. Gregoras is praised for proposing a revision of the calendar that anticipated the Gregorian reform but was unfortunately suppressed for political reasons.[21] Metochites is justly admired for reading, understanding, and paraphrasing the *Almagest* of Ptolemy.[22] He took three years over the task, no more than would a modern student of that complex, highly technical work. But all that Metochites did was to revive the old system, reintroduce the old parameters of the second century A.D., and adjust these parameters to the new starting point of 1282. Yet by his time, thanks to the efforts of Arabic and Persian astronomers, new and better parameters were current both in the East and in the European West. It was left to the lowlier astronomers—George Chioniades, George Chrysokokkes, and John Abramios—to use the Persian and Islamic tables or to translate them into Greek. These men, who wrote in the early, mid, and late fourteenth century respectively, were the true bearers of objective scientific progress in Byzantium.[23]

We moderns also point approvingly to the elegant, nonliteral, and therefore nonmedieval translations from the Latin of such scholars as Manuel Holobolos (who, as latest research suggests, did in fact translate) and Maximos Planudes and single out such classical Latin authors as Ovid who were thus made available to Byzantine readers in this period. But most of these authors, Ovid included, belonged to the medieval repertoire. This is certainly true of the works translated around 1300: Cicero's *Dream of Scipio* with Macrobius's commentary, the *Disticha Catonis*, Boethius's *Consolation of Philosophy*, and St. Augustine.[24] The most ambitious translation project of the period was to render parts of the *Summa* and other works of Thomas Aquinas into Greek. The task was undertaken in the second half of the fourteenth century by Demetrios Kydones and his brother Prochoros, who were inspired by religious and political concerns of the time and not by a desire to rediscover Latin Antiquity.[25]

In spite of occasional titles such as the *Achilleis* or the *War of Troy*, the popular romances and animal stories, many of which date from the fourteenth and fifteenth centuries, have next to nothing to do with Antiquity and a great deal to do with the medieval West. Some, like the *War of Troy*, were surely translated from the French. Others deal with heroes out of the glorious early Byzantine past such as Belisarius, Justinian's unhappy general, but these may also reflect events of the late thirteenth century. They are written in fifteen-syllable verse and in a language that falls below even the most lenient standards of educated Greek. The authors who composed or at least transcribed these products were not quite unlearned; still, a world separates them from the refined minds of the time of Andronikos II.[26]

A number of works that consciously depart from Atticizing aspirations or literary Greek also seem to date from the fourteenth century. These are the paraphrases or "metaphrases," as they are called today, of works written in the twelfth and thirteenth centuries: e.g., the histories of Anna Comnena, Nicetas Choniates, and George Pachymeres, and the *Mirror of Princes*, by Nicephorus Blemmydes. All these authors wrote in a highly convoluted or at least classicizing language. The "metaphrasts" transposed them into simpler, but still grammatically standard Greek.[27] With one exception, we do not know who the authors of these metaphrases were, but the exception gives food for thought. George Oinaiotes, who was one of the two authors of the metaphrase of Blemmydes's *Mirror*, also left us a collection of letters written in high style; several of them were addressed to the formidable Theodore Metochites.[28] Thus he must have been making his metaphrase not for his sophisticated peers but for a different clientele. Though I do not know for sure who made up that clientele, I suspect that new readers were emerging—yearning for culture and information, but not skilled enough and unable to find their way in the labyrinth of Atticism or simply tired of the mandarin intricacies of high-style literature. It is perhaps for such people that toward the beginning of the fourteenth century at the court of Arta (Epirus), whose despot bore the Italian name of Orsini, Constantine Hermoniakos wrote his paraphrase of the *Iliad* in hopeless anacreontic verse. Hermoniakos read at least some books of Homer in the original and cribbed some lines from Euripides for his description of the sack of Troy, but he derived most of his paraphrases from an allegorical interpretation of the *Iliad* by the twelfth-century Byzantine John Tzetzes.[29]

The outstanding Byzantine intellectuals of the Palaeologan revival were a small elite who wrote for one another and for the powerful. They either stood quite high on the social scale in their own right or they served the mighty. Clinging to a thousand-year-old tradition, they proclaimed their superiority over their unlearned compatriots and over the presumably unsophisticated West. But they came to realize that they could maintain their position only as long as the system of patronage on which they depended kept functioning; and some of them also became aware of and fascinated by the intellectual achievements of the contemporary West. From the 1360's on, they considered emigrating to Italy; there, as one of them said, one could improve one's mind in contact with the Italians, whose Muse was more stately than that of Plato and Aristotle.[30] Some stayed abroad for considerable periods: Demetrios Kydones lived in Venice for about six years. Some embraced the Union with the Catholic Church; others joined that Church outright, or even its Dominican order. But as a rule they eventually returned east, if sometimes only halfway, stopping in the Venetian possessions of Crete.[31]

The first professor to leave Byzantium for Italy and to die in the West embarked at the very end of the fourteenth century. The story of these professors is a well-known part of the story of Renaissance humanism, but two of the most important emigrés deserve to be at least mentioned here. Between them, Manuel Chrysoloras, who died in Constance in 1415, and John Argyropoulos, who died in Rome in 1487, taught in Padua, Rome, Milan, Pavia, and above all Florence. They introduced Byzantine didactic practices, possibly the curricula, and surely the techniques of philology and Platonic and Neoplatonic philosophy to Italy, translated Aristotle's works and Plato's *Republic* word by word into Latin, and taught or influenced such prominent humanists as Leonardo Bruni, Guarino of Verona, Massilio Ficino, Poggio Fiorentino, Filelfo, and John Reuchlin. For the greater part of their careers, they did well in their new homes, though they had to pay a price for this acceptance: Argyropoulos joined the Union and Chrysoloras the Catholic Church.[32]

Painters also sought their luck abroad, though not in the West. In the early fourteenth century, Michael Astrapas and Eutychios[33] traveled from Thessalonica to the Macedonian part of the Kingdom of Serbia, where they painted and—a rare trait for their time—signed frescoes (Figures 11 and 12). At the very end of the fourteenth century, Theophanes the Greek, a daring artist, went to Novgorod and Moscow, where he covered church walls with frescoes (Figure 13), painted icons, and probably illuminated manuscripts.[34] In the 1380's the Constantinopolitan Manuel Eugenikos, working in a more conventional mode, painted the church of Calendžixa[35] in faraway Caucasian Georgia (Figure 14). The scholars who stayed behind—such as Gennadios Scholarios, who was to become the first Patriarch under the Turks—could only bewail the low state of learning in the capital on the eve of the City's fall.[36]

If we claim that the Palaeologan revival failed to turn into a renaissance solely because of the straitened circumstances of the Empire and the Turks, we do not tell the whole story. Even when and where material conditions remained tolerable, the Byzantines did not assimilate some antique forms or develop a feeling for Antiquity as thoroughly as did their contemporaries in the Italian West. Nothing drives this point home better than an inscription that commemorates the building of the famous temple of Sigismondo Malatesta in Rimini. Incidentally, whereas the Patriarch Gennadios Scholarios had the works of

Gemistos Plethon burned, Sigismondo Malatesta had Pleth-on's bones unearthed and placed in a sarcophagus on the out-side of this Christian temple (inside whose shrine there was—and still is—a nude Venus). The Greek inscription, repeated twice on the temple's exterior, expertly handles antique for-mulae and is patterned on a known prototype: a pagan inscrip-tion in Naples. Its lettering imitates most successfully the characters of the fifth to the third century B.C. (Figure 15). The model or models for these characters were probably brought to Rimini by that tireless antiquarian and traveler to Greece and Asia Minor, Ciriaco of Ancona, and Ciriaco must have found these models on Byzantine soil.[37] No Byzantine inscription of any time, including the Palaeologan period, borrows antique formulae to the same extent or uses antique script even re-motely similar to that of the Malatesta inscription. One has only to compare the latter with a carefully executed and roughly contemporary Byzantine inscription from the walls of Constantinople[38] to see the difference (Figure 16). Yet the Byz-antines did not have to travel far to find Greek antique inscrip-tions; the inscriptions were lying around under their very noses. When we look at the two inscriptions side by side, we may not know why but we certainly do know that there was a Palaeologan revival but no Palaeologan Renaissance.

Conclusion

WARREN TREADGOLD

When we consider together the seven pre-Renaissance renaissances discussed in this book, what general conclusions can we draw about their causes and effects?

In the most obvious sense, people started renaissances because they felt that the education and literature of their times were inferior to those of the past, and believed that increased study of past culture would improve culture in the present. But this explanation does not take us very far. Most people, and especially educated people, took the superiority of the ancient Classics for granted throughout Late Antiquity and the Middle Ages. During the dark ages, scholars often deplored the sorry state of education and letters and advised reading good old authors as a remedy. But such lamentations and advice by themselves brought no renaissance. For that, a group of scholars had to take action. During the dark ages no groups did, whether out of despair, incapacity, inertia, or simply failing to have a sufficiently concrete conception of what to do. Some stimulus was needed, even if it was only an idea.

In the various renaissances the stimuli were of different kinds, and the groups they stimulated varied in size. In the barbarian West, imperial or royal patronage was a crucial catalyst for the Carolingian renaissance and the Anglo-Saxon monastic revival, but it was of secondary importance for the movements that began in less backward milieus. In these, ideas played a larger part: changes in literary taste in the Second Sophistic and the fourth-century Latin revival, defense of old opinions in the Macedonian renaissance, adaptation to social change in the twelfth-century renaissance, and nostalgia for the Greek past in the Palaeologan renaissance.

Given the initial impulse, these cultural revivals do not seem to have been very difficult to start. They did not require much money, many scholars, or particularly peaceful conditions. A modest number of teachers or copyists, not necessarily professionals or men of exceptional talent, could begin a process of educating students and copying books that would snowball into an important movement within a generation or two. If no strong force was needed to start a revival, still less was needed to keep it going after it had developed its own momentum. Even when the general level of education had declined, the prestige of learning and literature persisted to such an extent, or was so easily reawakened, that students and patrons were seldom hard to attract. Whenever a few men of some education, for whatever reasons, wanted to learn more about literature than was customary, they met with little opposition and usually with encouragement.

When we turn from causes to effects, we first find two achievements that are fundamental to a renaissance: the copying of manuscripts and the improvement of education. Without extensive copying of manuscripts neither old nor new literature could reach a wide contemporary audience—or perhaps even survive into the future. This essential but unexciting task required a great deal of time and effort that was consequently not available for more creative literary activity. After all, the number of pens at work was limited. The groups responsible for the revivals ranged from a moderately large educated class during the Second Sophistic and the fourth-century Latin revival—and again during the twelfth-century renaissance—to a handful of educated men during the Carolingian renaissance and the Anglo-Saxon monastic revival; the fairly small Byzantine educated class of the Macedonian and Palaeologan renaissances fell somewhere in between these extremes.

In the course of the revivals the educated classes of Late Antiquity and in Byzantium became better educated, but they do not seem to have grown very much. By contrast, in the medieval West the Carolingian renaissance and Anglo-Saxon revival

were intended to spread education and had some success in doing so, and the twelfth-century renaissance brought a major extension of education to a wider group. These expansions of the
educated class in the West surely contributed to the more creative and dynamic character of its culture in comparison with
Late Antiquity and Byzantium, a difference that was becoming
apparent by the twelfth century.

Apart from teaching students and copying earlier texts, the
scholars of all the revivals produced some compositions of
their own. But, with the partial exception of some twelfth-century scholars in the West, none produced particularly original
thought or very great literature. This fact is often emphasized
by those who minimize the importance of the movements, but
it is only what we might have expected. The process of redis-
covering and absorbing earlier knowledge was not only time-
consuming but at least at first humbling, reinforcing the always lingering suspicion that the ancients had known so much
and written so well that it would be foolhardy to try to rival
them. Writers who attempted to adopt the ancients' style and
methods produced works that were usually unoriginal and often merely imitative. For this reason, and also because the classicizing style is not to our taste, we tend not to admire even the
authors from these revivals who were most admired by their
contemporaries. Few today read Aelius Aristides, Claudian, Alcuin, Photius, Aethelwold, or Theodore Metochites, and readers of Abelard are usually more interested in his life than in his
thought. Our implied verdict is not wholly unjust. Since the
scholars of these revivals were more interested in rediscovery
than in creation, few of their best efforts were creative ones.
Even in their own times, they were usually admired more for
their knowledge of earlier literature than for any original contributions of their own.

But even though these cultural revivals produced little original literature of importance, their work still had important effects on later times. What they rediscovered and their way of
looking at what they rediscovered continued to influence
thought and letters for centuries afterward. The revived Attic
Greek of the Second Sophistic and the revived Golden and Silver Age Latin of the fourth-century revival remained the ap-

proved forms of each language throughout the Middle Ages, at the expense of the Hellenistic Greek and archaic Latin that the two revivals ignored. Consequently works in the approved form of the language were read and admired, but those in the disapproved form were mostly lost for good. Each subsequent revival tended to reassert the ascendency of the approved works, together with their classicizing accretions from later times, despite the natural pressure in all periods on written Latin and Greek to become less classical and more like the spoken languages.

In the short term these reintroductions of the Classics took a toll on literary creativity, but as men became more familiar with classical literature they gradually found it less intimidating. As I have explained in the Introduction, the word "renaissance" has been used in this book to refer only to periods of actual rediscovery of earlier literature; but several of these renaissances were followed by periods in which scholars continued to exploit the rediscoveries. These later scholars, able to draw on their predecessors' work, had an advantage in both knowledge and perspective when they did their own writing. We should therefore not be surprised to find that the greatest literature and the most original thought of Late Antiquity and the Middle Ages date from soon after one or another of the cultural revivals. Thus the Second Sophistic formed the literary community that produced Neoplatonism, the Cappadocian Fathers, and the histories of Procopius; and the fourth-century Latin revival provided the cultural background of Augustine and Boethius. The Macedonian renaissance was the precondition for the histories of Psellus and Anna Comnena; the twelfth-century renaissance led to Aquinas and Dante.

And, in the largest sense, each renaissance in East and West provided the materials for the next, until the rediscoveries of the twelfth-century and Palaeologan renaissances became the basis of the Renaissance proper.

Reference Matter

Notes

Introduction: Renaissances and Dark Ages

1. For a selection of books on the general subject of renaissances and dark ages, see the bibliography for this chapter. These works are not cited in my notes, which only point out recent or particularly significant examples from a vast body of secondary literature. I would like to thank Professors Michael Wigodsky and George Brown of Stanford for reading this chapter in draft and making some helpful suggestions.

2. A good discussion of the use and misuse of the words "humanist" and "humanism" appears in "New Learning and New Ignorance," C. S. Lewis's introduction to his *English Literature in the Sixteenth Century* (Oxford, 1954).

3. On the decline of classical literature, see Gordon Williams, *Change and Decline: Roman Literature in the Early Empire* (Berkeley, 1978), and his references.

4. On the ancients' lack of technical innovation, see M. I. Finley, "Technical Innovation and Economic Progress in the Ancient World," *Economic History Review*, 2d series, 18 (1965), 29–45. On the superiority of the Middle Ages in this respect, see Lynn White, Jr., *Medieval Technology and Social Change* (Oxford, 1962), and Jean Gimpel, *The Medieval Machine* (New York, 1976).

5. See H.-I. Marrou, *A History of Education in Antiquity*, trans. G. Lamb (London, 1956), for the best available survey.

6. For a recent and reasonable judgment on the disputed fate of the Alexandrian Library, see P. M. Fraser, *Ptolemaic Alexandria* (Oxford, 1972), I, 320–35, esp. pp. 334–35.

7. For a recent and convincing judgment on the disputed fate of the .

schools at Athens, see John Glucker, *Antiochus and the Late Academy* (Göttingen, 1978), pp. 330–79.

8. For a recent treatment of this continuation of the Second Sophistic, see Ihor Ševčenko, "A Shadow Outline of Virtue: The Classical Heritage of Greek Christian Literature (Second to Seventh Century)," in Kurt Weitzmann, ed., *Age of Spirituality: A Symposium* (New York, 1980), pp. 53–73, with references and bibliography.

9. On the continuation of the fourth-century Latin revival, see P. Courcelle, *Histoire littéraire des grandes invasions germaniques* (Paris, 1964), and *Late Latin Writers and Their Greek Sources*, trans. H. E. Wadeck (Cambridge, Mass., 1969).

10. On the great dark age in the West, see Pierre Riché, *Education and Culture in the Barbarian West, Sixth Through Eighth Centuries*, trans. John J. Contreni (Columbia, S.C., 1976).

11. The current fashion for comparative studies has exaggerated the cultural significance of such East-West contacts as occurred. A refreshingly frank admission of the unimportance of these contacts for culture is in Anthony Bryer, "Cultural Relations Between East and West in the Twelfth Century," in Derek Baker, ed., *Relations Between East and West in the Middle Ages* (Edinburgh, 1973), pp. 77–94. On the estrangement between the churches, see esp. Steven Runciman, *The Eastern Schism* (Oxford, 1955).

12. On the tenth century, see Lynn White et al., "Symposium on the Tenth Century," *Medievalia et Humanistica*, 9 (1955), 3–29. These short but lucid papers note that there is little secondary literature on the period and generally reject the idea of an "Ottonian renaissance" (see esp. p. 20). For a more recent study of culture during the Ottonian period, see Uta Lindgren, *Gerbert von Aurillac und das Quadrivium* (Wiesbaden, 1976), which includes a full bibliography.

Chapter 1. The Second Sophistic

1. The most reliable brief account is in A. Lesky, *A History of Greek Literature* (London, 1966; translation by J. Willis and C. de Heer of the German 2d ed., Bern, 1963). A fuller account appears in B. P. Reardon, *Courants littéraires grecs des IIe et IIIe siècles après J.-C.* (Paris, 1971), to which general reference may be made here (hereafter cited as *CLG*). For many of the Greek writers mentioned in this article there exist convenient Loeb editions, to which the reader is here referred. Only some particular cases and more recent work will be indicated in the following notes. See also G. W. Bowersock, ed., *Ap-*

proaches to the Second Sophistic (University Park, Pa., American Philological Association, 1974), pp. 30–40, for bibliography and references.

2. Croiset, for instance, remarks that in the early Roman Empire "se prépare une renaissance, qui ne sera sans doute ni très complète, ni très durable, mais qui aura néanmoins son éclat" (M. Croiset, *Histoire de la littérature grecque*, V [Paris, 1928], p. 320). A historian can write "Hellenism, in the period of the 'Second Sophistic,' experienced yet another renaissance" (J. Keil, in *Cambridge Ancient History*, XI [Cambridge, 1954], chap. 14, "The Greek Provinces," p. 556).

3. See Philostratus, *Lives of the Sophists*, trans. W. C. Wright (London, 1921; Loeb Classical Library). Quotations in this chapter will be taken from this translation. The term "historian" is used at this point for simplicity, but it is not wholly accurate and will be qualified in due course.

4. That is, if we regard the rhetorical movement of the fourth century—Libanius, Themistius—as a different thing. It operated in a different, Christianized world, and many decades of chaos and social upheaval had intervened. But it rested on the same tradition.

5. Only vol. 1 of the Loeb edition of Aristides has appeared (C. A. Behr, 1973; it contains *Panathenaic* and *In Defence of Oratory*). Greek text: B. Keil's partial edition (1928) has now been completed by C. A. Behr, 4 vols. (Leyden, 1976–80). *Sacred Tales:* C. A. Behr, *Aelius Aristides and the Sacred Tales* (Amsterdam, 1968). *To Rome:* J. H. Oliver, "The Ruling Power: A Study of the Roman Empire in the Second Century after Christ Through the Roman Oration of Aelius Aristides," *Transactions of the American Philosophical Society*, 43 (1953), 871–1003.

6. An excellent study has now appeared: T. Hägg, *The Novel in Antiquity* (Oxford, 1983). There is a brief account in B. P. Reardon, "The Greek Novel," *Phoenix*, 23 (1969), 291–309; cf. *CLG*, pp. 309–403. See also G. N. Sandy, "Recent Scholarship on the Prose Fiction of Antiquity," *Classical World*, 67 (1974), 321–59.

7. The only reasonably up-to-date account in a standard history of literature is in Lesky. All others are more or less seriously misleading.

8. E. Rohde, *Der griechische Roman* (Leipzig, 1876; 3d ed., 1914, reprinted Hildesheim, 1960); the "standard" book by reason of its massive scholarship.

9. B. A. Van Groningen, "Literary Tendencies in the Second Century A.D.," *Mnemosyne*, 18 (1965), 41–56; quotations from p. 52 et seq.

10. Ben Edwin Perry, "Literature in the Second Century," *Classi-*

cal Journal, 50 (1955), 295–98, and *The Ancient Romances* (Berkeley, 1967).

11. See B. P. Reardon, "The Second Sophistic and the Novel," in G. W. Bowersock, ed., *Approaches to the Second Sophistic,* pp. 23–29, for the following remarks.

12. G. W. Bowersock, *Greek Sophists in the Roman Empire* (Oxford, 1969); the quotation is from p. 58.

13. E. L. Bowie, "The Importance of Sophists," *Yale Classical Studies,* 27 (1982), 29–59.

14. E. L. Bowie, "Greeks and Their Past in the Second Sophistic," *Past and Present,* 46 (1970), 3–41. (This is an important essay for the present topic.)

Chapter 2. The Latin Revival of the Fourth Century

1. R. Marache, *La Critique littéraire de langue latine et le développement du goût archaisant au IIe siècle de notre ère* (Rennes, 1952); cf. W. L. Lebek, *Verba Prisca* (1970).

2. Marache, *La Critique littéraire,* p. 111.

3. For the Second Sophistic, see Chapter 1 of this volume.

4. *Noct. Att.* 19.9, with Cameron, "Poetae novelli," *Harvard Studies in Classical Philology,* 84 (1980), 161 et seq.

5. Marache, *La Critique littéraire;* and Marache, *Mots nouveaux et mots archaiques chez Fronton et Aulu-Gelle* (1957).

6. F. Millar, "P. Herennius Dexippus: The Greek World and the Third Century Invasions," *Journal of Roman Studies,* 59 (1969), 12–29.

7. Herbert Bloch, "Pagan Revival in the West at the End of the Fourth Century," in A. Momigliano, ed., *The Conflict between Paganism and Christianity in the Fourth Century* (Oxford, 1963), pp. 193–218; Philip Levine, "The Continuity and Preservation of the Latin Tradition," in Lynn White, Jr., ed., *The Transformation of the Roman World: Gibbon's Problem after Two Centuries* (Berkeley, 1966), pp. 206–31.

8. Inevitably so, since O. Seeck made his classic edition of Symmachus (*Q. Aur. Symmachi quae supersunt,* Mon. Germ. Hist., Auct. Aut. vi.i; Berlin 1883) a prosopographical study of the late Roman aristocracy.

9. Alan Cameron, "The Date and Identity of Macrobius," *Journal of Roman Studies,* 56 (1966), 25–38.

10. See Alan Cameron, *Claudian: Poetry and Propaganda in the Court of Honorius* (Oxford, 1970), pp. vi–vii.

11. The best introduction to this subject is A. Momigliano's chap-

ter, "Pagan and Christian Historiography in the Fourth Century," in idem, *Conflict*, pp. 79–99.

12. See Alan Cameron, "Wandering Poets," *Historia*, 14 (1965), 470–509.

13. The basic work remains P. Courcelle, *Late Latin Writers and Their Greek Sources* (Cambridge, Mass., 1969).

14. T. D. Barnes, *The Sources of the 'Historia Augusta'* (Brussels, 1978), pp. 114–23.

15. E. Kitzinger, *Byzantine Art in the Making* (Cambridge, Mass., 1977), pp. 34 et seq.

16. E. Kitzinger, *Early Medieval Art* (London, 1940), pp. 13–14.

17. See Cameron, *Claudian*, p. 190.

18. Both Bloch and Levine lay heavy emphasis on this point.

19. L. D. Reynolds and N. G. Wilson, *Scribes and Scholars*, 2d ed. (Oxford, 1974), pp. 30–32.

20. For an up-to-date list of these subscriptions, see J. E. G. Zetzel, *Latin Textual Criticism in Antiquity* (New York, 1981), pp. 211–31.

21. Herbert Bloch, "A New Document of the Last Pagan Revival in the West, 393–394 A.D.," *Harvard Theological Review*, 38 (1945), 199–244; the quotation is from pp. 240–41.

22. E.g., W. Hartke, *Geschichte und Politik im spätantiken Rom* (Wiesbaden, 1940), pp. 164 et seq.; cf. A. Chastagnol, *Fastes de la Préfecture de Rome au Bas-Empire* (Paris, 1962), p. 242.

23. Alan Cameron, "Paganism and Literature in Late Fourth Century Rome," *Entretiens* (de la Fondation Hardt), 23 (1977), 5–6, 26–28; cf. Zetzel.

24. C. Wendel, "Die erste kaiserliche Bibliothek in Konstantinopel," *Zentralblatt für Bibliothekswesen*, 59 (1942), 193–209.

25. *Codex Theodosianus* 14.9.2 (ed. T. Mommsen, Berlin 1904, p. 787).

26. Symmachus, *Epp.* 9.88.3, 6.34. In general, see T. J. Haarhoff, *Schools of Gaul*, 2d ed. (Oxford, 1958); and R. Etienne, *Bordeaux antique* (Bordeaux, 1962), pp. 235–64.

27. See the testimonia in the editions of Schenkl, Peiper, and Prete, and the new material added by R. P. H. Green, "Ausonius' Use of the Classical Latin Poets," *Classical Quarterly*, 27 (1977), 441–52.

28. M. D. Reeve, "Some MSS of Ausonius," *Prometheus*, 3 (1977), 112–20; R. P. H. Green, "Marius Maximus and Ausonius' Caesares," *Classical Quarterly*, 31 (1981), 226–36.

29. B. Baldwin, "Tacitus, the Panegyrici Latini, and the Historia Augusta," *Eranos*, 78 (1980), 175–78.

30. P. Wessner, *Berl. Phil. Woch.*, 49 (1929), 296–303, 328–35.

31. H. Hagendahl, *Latin Fathers and the Classics* (Göteborg, 1958), p. 284; for St. Augustine, see J. J. O'Donnell, "Augustine's Classical Readings," *Recherches augustiniennes,* 15 (1980), 159–61.

32. R. Kaster, "Macrobius and Servius," *Harvard Studies in Classical Philology,* 84 (1980), 257.

33. See, for example, G. Highet, *Juvenal the Satirist* (Oxford, 1954), 186–87; cf. Zetzel, p. 223.

34. W. Kroll, "De Q. Aur. Symmachi studiis graecis et latinis," *Bresl. Phil. Abhandlungen,* 6, 2 (1891).

35. Aem. Lübeck, *Hieronymus quos noverit scriptores* (Lipsiae, 1872), p. 105; cf. Hagendahl, pp. 269–76.

36. See the example I quote in J. W. Binns, ed., *Latin Literature of the Fourth Century* (1974), pp. 149–50.

37. C. S. Lewis, *The Allegory of Love* (Oxford, 1936), pp. 75–76.

38. G. D. Economou, *The Goddess Natura in Medieval Literature* (Cambridge, Mass., 1972), pp. 42–50.

Chapter 3. The Carolingian Renaissance

1. Opinions differ on the appropriateness of applying the term "renaissance" to this phenomenon. See Paul Lehmann, "Das Problem der karolingischen Renaissance"; Angelo Monteverdi, "Il problema del rinascimento carolino"; and François Louis Ganshof, "La discussione sul tema: Il problema del rinascimento carolino," all in *I problemi della civiltà carolingia,* Settimane di studio del Centro italiano di studi sull'alto medioevo 2 (Spoleto, 1954), pp. 309–77. See also John J. Contreni, "Inharmonious Harmony: Education in the Carolingian World," *Annals of Scholarship: Metastudies of the Humanities and Social Sciences,* 1 (1980), 81–96, esp. pp. 81–82. G. W. Trompf draws an explicit comparison with the Renaissance in his "The Concept of the Carolingian Renaissance," *Journal of the History of Ideas,* 34 (1973), 3–26.

2. Pierre Riché, *Education and Culture in the Barbarian West from the Sixth through the Eighth Century,* trans. John J. Contreni (Columbia, S.C., 1976), parts 1 and 2.

3. See Eugen Ewig, "Milo et eiusmodi similes," in *Sankt Bonifatius: Gedenkgabe zum 1200 Todestag* (Fulda, 1954), pp. 412–40. One could also point to the effect of the Danish raids on Anglo-Saxon cultural life. See also John Baldwin, *The Scholastic Culture of the Middle Ages, 1000–1300* (Lexington, Kentucky, 1971), p. 2.

4. Riché, *Education and Culture,* pp. 422–26.

5. See Pierre Riché, *Les Écoles et l'enseignement dans l'Occident*

de la fin du Vᵉ siècle au milieu du XIᵉ siècle (Paris, 1979), pp. 65–79, for the personal cultural activities of the Carolingian leaders.

6. Charles Homer Haskins, *The Renaissance of the Twelfth Century* (Cambridge, Mass., 1927); Robert S. Lopez, "Still Another Renaissance?" *American Historical Review*, 57 (1951), 1–21.

7. Kenneth Clark, *Civilisation: A Personal View* (New York, 1969), pp. 17–18. For other proponents of this view, see Lehmann; Joseph de Ghellinck, *Littérature latine du Moyen Age*, vol. 1 (Paris, 1939); Max Manitius, *Geschichte der lateinischen Literatur des Mittelalters*, vol. 1 (Munich, 1911); M. L. W. Laistner, *Thought and Letters in Western Europe, A.D. 500–900*, 2d ed. (Ithaca, 1957); Frederick B. Artz, *The Mind of the Middle Ages, A.D. 200–1500: An Historical Survey*, 3d rev. ed. (Chicago, 1980); R. R. Bolgar, *The Classical Heritage and Its Beneficiaries from the Carolingian Age to the End of the Renaissance* (London and New York, 1954).

8. In addition to Ganshof and to Riché, *Education and Culture*, the following scholars are representative of this approach to the Carolingian period: Pierre Courcelle, *Late Latin Writers and Their Greek Sources*, trans. Harry E. Wedeck (Cambridge, Mass., 1969); Jacques Fontaine, *Isidore de Séville et la culture classique dans l'Espagne wisigothique*, 2 vols. (Paris, 1959); Erna Patzelt, *Die karolingische Renaissance* (1924; reprint ed., Graz, 1965); Reto R. Bezzola, *Les Origines et la formation de la littérature courtoise en Occident (500–1200). Première partie: La Tradition impériale de la fin de l'Antiquité au XIᵉ siècle* (Paris, 1958); Heinrich Fichtenau, *The Carolingian Empire: The Age of Charlemagne*, trans. Peter Munz (Oxford, 1957).

9. See Gustav Schnürer, *Church and Culture in the Middle Ages*, vol. 1, trans. George J. Undreiner (Paterson, N.J., 1956); Joseph Fleckenstein, *Die Bildungsreform Karls des Grossen als Verwirklichung der Norma rectitudinis* (Bigge-Ruhr, 1953); Percy Schramm, "Die von Karl bewirkte 'Correctio' (nicht 'Renaissance')," in Percy Ernst Schramm, *Kaiser, Könige und Päpste*, vol. 1 (Stuttgart, 1968), pp. 336–39; Hans Liebeschütz, "Theodulf of Orleans and the Problem of the Carolingian Renaissance," in D. J. Gordon, ed., *Fritz Saxl, 1890–1948: A Volume of Memorial Essays from his Friends in England* (London, 1957), pp. 77–92; Walter Ullmann, *The Carolingian Renaissance and the Idea of Kingship: The Birkbeck Lectures, 1968–9* (London, 1969); Karl F. Morrison, "The Church, Reform, and Renaissance in the Early Middle Ages," in Robert S. Hoyt, ed., *Life and Thought in the Early Middle Ages* (Minneapolis, 1967), pp. 143–59; Claudio Leonardi, "Alcuino e la scuola palatina: Le ambizioni di una cultura unitaria," in *Nascità dell'Europa ed Europa carolingia: Un'equa-*

zione da verificare, 2 vols., Settimane di studio del Centro italiano di studi sull'alto medioevo 27 (Spoleto, 1981), 1, 461–96.

10. See, for example, Donald Bullough, *The Age of Charlemagne,* 2d ed. (London, 1973); J. Hubert, J. Porcher, and W. F. Volbach, *L'Empire carolingien* (Paris, 1968); Walter Horn and Ernst Born, *The Plan of St. Gall: A Study of the Architecture and Economy of and Life in a Paradigmatic Carolingian Monastery,* 3 vols. (Berkeley, 1979).

11. See Bullough, *The Age of Charlemagne,* pp. 17–18, 70, 75; Maurice Prou, *Catalogue des monnaies françaises de la Bibliothèque Nationale: Les Monnaies carolingiennes* (Paris, 1896); and Karl F. Morrison and H. Grunthal, *Carolingian Coinage,* Numismatic Notes and Monographs no. 158 (New York, 1967).

12. See Carol Heitz, *Recherches sur les rapports entre architecture et liturgie à l'époque carolingienne* (Paris, 1963); idem, "Nouvelles interprétations de l'art carolingienne," *Revue de l'Art,* 1 (1968), 104–13; and idem, *L'Architecture religieuse carolingienne: Les Formes et leurs fonctions* (Paris, 1980).

13. See Ullmann, pp. 39–41.

14. Cyrille Vogel, *La Réforme culturelle sous Pépin le Bref et sous Charlemagne (Deuxième moitié du VIIIe siècle et premier quart du IXe siècle)* (Graz, 1965); Cyrille Vogel, "La Réforme liturgique sous Charlemagne," in Wolfgang Braunfels et al., eds., *Karl der Grosse: Lebenswerk und Nachleben,* 5 vols. (Düsseldorf, 1965–68), II, 217–32.

15. See Bonifatius Fischer, "Bibeltext und Bibelreform unter Karl dem Grossen," in *Karl der Grosse,* II, 156–216; Laistner, pp. 308–14; and Rosamond McKitterick, *The Frankish Church and the Carolingian Reforms, 789–895,* Royal Historical Society Studies in History 2 (London, 1977), pp. 115–54. For the little-studied liturgical work of Helisachar, see Heinz Löwe, ed., *Wattenbach-Levison, Deutschlands Geschichtsquellen im Mittelalter: Vorzeit und Karolinger, III. Heft* (Weimar, 1957), pp. 305–6.

16. See McKitterick, pp. 80–114; Réginald Grégoire, *Les Homeliaires du Moyen Age: Inventaire et analyse des manuscrits* (Rome, 1966); and Henri Barré, *Les Homéliaires carolingiens de l'école d'Auxerre: Authenticité, inventaire, tableaux comparatifs,* Studi e Testi 225 (Vatican City, 1962).

17. See Raymond Étaix, "Un Manuel de pastorale de l'époque carolingienne (Clm 27152)," *Revue bénédictine,* 91 (1981), 105–30; John J. Contreni, *The Cathedral School of Laon from 850 to 930: Its Manuscripts and Masters,* Münchener Beiträge zur Mediävistik und Renaissance-Forschung 29 (Munich, 1978), pp. 130–34; and Susan Keefe, "Carolingian Baptismal Expositions: A Handlist of Tracts and Manu-

scripts," in Uta-Renate Blumenthal, ed., *Carolingian Essays* (Washington, D.C., 1983), pp. 169–237.

18. See *Monumenta Germaniae Historica (MGH), Legum sectio II: Capitularia regum Francorum,* I, A. Boretius, ed. (Hanover, 1883), pp. 52–62 (no. 22) and pp. 78–79 (no. 29). See also Riché, *Education and Culture,* pp. 497–98; and Luitpold Wallach, "Charlemagne's *De litteris colendis* and Alcuin," in his *Alcuin and Charlemagne: Studies in Carolingian History and Literature,* rev. ed. (New York and London, 1968), pp. 198–226.

19. For the palace school under Charlemagne, see Laistner, pp. 189–206; Richard E. Sullivan, *Aix-la-Chapelle in the Age of Charlemagne* (Norman, 1963), pp. 148–72; Franz Brunhölzl, "Der Bildungsauftrag der Hofschule," in *Karl der Grosse,* II, pp. 28–41. The lives and writings of the various masters who came to the court are conveniently catalogued by Max Manitius, *Geschichte der lateinischen Literatur des Mittelalters,* and by Franz Brunhölzl, *Geschichte der lateinischen Literatur des Mittelalters,* vol. 1 (Munich, 1975).

20. *MGH, Legum Sectio II: Capitularia regum Francorum,* I, pp. 326–27 (no. 163).

21. See *MGH, Concilia,* I-2, p. 581 (cap. 34), and J. D. Mansi, ed., *Sacrorum conciliorum nova et amplissima collectio,* 53 vols. (1759–98; reprint ed., Graz, 1960), XIV, p. 1008 (cap. 34). See also Riché, *Les Écoles et l'enseignement,* pp. 76–79, and Thomas F. X. Noble, "The Place in Papal History of the Roman Synod of 826," *Church History,* 45 (1976), 1–16, esp. p. 10, and p. 4 of the appendix.

22. See Pierre Riché, "Charles le Chauve et la culture de son temps," in René Roques, ed., *Jean Scot Erigène et l'histoire de la philosophie,* Colloques internationaux du Centre National de la Recherche Scientifique no. 561 (Paris, 1977), pp. 35–46; and Edouard Jeauneau, "Jean Scot Erigène et le grec," *Archivum Latinitatis Medii Aevi (Bulletin du Cange),* 41 (1979), 5–50, esp. pp. 12–26.

23. See McKitterick, pp. 45–79.

24. See Bonifatius Fischer, "Bibelausgaben des frühen Mittelalters," in *La Bibbia nell'alto Medioevo,* Settimane di studio del Centro italiano di studi sull'alto medioevo 10 (Spoleto, 1963), pp. 519–600; and John J. Contreni, "The Formation of Laon's Cathedral Library in the Ninth Century," *Studi Medievali,* ser. 3, 18 (1972), p. 933, for a note on the text of Martianus Capella's *De nuptiis.* Carolingian scholars produced at least four Martianus Capella commentaries. Lupus of Ferrières's editorial work is well known. See Charles H. Beeson, *Lupus of Ferrières as Scribe and Text Critic: A Study of His Autograph Copy of Cicero's "De oratore,"* Mediaeval Academy of

America publication 4 (Cambridge, Mass., 1930). See also Claudio Leonardi, "I commenti altomedievali ai classici pagani: Da Severino Boezio a Remigio d'Auxerre," in *La cultura antica nell'Occidente latino dal VII all'XI secolo*, 2 vols., Settimane di studio del Centro italiano di studi sull'alto medioevo 22 (Spoleto, 1975), 1, 459–504.

25. See Bernhard Bischoff, *Paläographie des römischen Altertums und des abendländischen Mittelalters*, Grundlagen der Germanistik 24 (Berlin, 1979), pp. 307–11, for a list of representative studies of Carolingian manuscript production. McKitterick, pp. 19–44, discusses the most productive copying centers.

26. There is no major study of Carolingian Latinity, but see Karl Strecker, *Introduction to Medieval Latin*, trans. Robert B. Palmer (Dublin, 1968), pp. 35–37; Pierre Riché, *Dhuoda: Manuel pour mon fils*, Sources chrétiennes 225 (Paris, 1975), pp. 38–45; and Riché, *Education and Culture*, p. 426.

27. See the examples gathered in John J. Contreni, "The Biblical Glosses of John Scottus Eriugena and Haimo of Auxerre," *Speculum*, 51 (1976), 411–34; and idem, "Carolingian Biblical Studies," in Uta-Renate Blumenthal, ed., *Carolingian Essays: Patristics and Early Medieval Thought*, pp. 71–98.

28. See Léopold Delisle, "Notice sur les manuscrits originaux d'Adémar de Chabannes," *Notices et extraits*, 35-1 (1896); 311–12.

29. For a convenient roster, see Riché, *Les Écoles et l'enseignement*, pp. 102–10.

30. For Einhard's *Vita Karoli magni*, see *Eginhard: Vie de Charlemagne*, ed. Louis Halphen (Paris, 1947) (also in *Einhard and Notker the Stammerer: Two Lives of Charlemagne*, trans. Lewis Thorpe [Harmondsworth, 1969]); Richer of Reims, *Histoire de la France (888–995)*, ed. and trans. Robert Latouche, 2 vols. (Paris, 1967); and John of Salisbury, *The Metalogicon of John of Salisbury*, trans. Daniel D. McGarry (Berkeley, 1955).

31. E. A. Lowe, ed., *Codices Latini Antiquiores*, 11 vols. with a Supplement (Oxford, 1934–71).

32. See Bischoff, *Paläographie*; and idem, "Über den Plan eines paläographischen Gesamtkatalogs der festländischen Handschriften des neunten Jahrhunderts," *Archivalische Zeitschrift*, 59 (1963); 166.

33. The best general treatment of Carolingian pedagogy is Riché, *Les Écoles et l'enseignement*, pp. 187–284 (part 3: "Moyens et méthodes de l'acquisition du savoir").

34. See Paul Oskar Kristeller, "The Humanist Movement," in *Renaissance Thought: The Classics, Scholastic, and Humanist Strains* (New York, 1961), pp. 3–23; Paul Oskar Kristeller, "Humanist Learning in the Italian Renaissance," *Centennial Review*, 4 (1960), 243–66;

Jean Jolivet, "L'Enjeu de la grammaire pour Godescalc," in René Roques, ed., *Jean Scot Erigène et l'histoire de la philosophie* (Paris, 1977), pp. 79–87; and Karl F. Morrison, "*Unum ex multis:* Hincmar of Rheims' Medical and Aesthetic Rationales for Unification," in *Nascità dell'Europa ed Europa carolingia,* 2 (1981), 583–712, esp. p. 70.

35. For various pedagogical approaches to the liberal arts, see John J. Contreni, "John Scottus, Martin Hiberniensis, the Liberal Arts, and Teaching," in Michael W. Herren, ed., *Insular Latin Studies: Papers on Latin Texts and Manuscripts of the British Isles, 550–1066,* Papers in Mediaeval Studies 1 (Toronto, 1981), esp. pp. 27, 39.

36. See note 34 for the example of Hincmar of Reims. Some of the letter prefaces to Carolingian biblical commentaries illustrate this point as well. See also Contreni, "Carolingian Biblical Studies." That the schools were breeding grounds for ecclesiastical leaders hardly needs documentation. See, nevertheless, the explicit statement attributed to Charles the Great by Notker of Saint Gall (Thorpe, trans., *Einhard and Notker the Stammerer,* p. 95).

37. See the comments of Donald Bullough, *The Age of Charlemagne,* p. 105.

38. See above, note 15; and Bonifatius Fischer, *Die Alkuin-Bibel,* Aus der Geschichte der lateinischen Bibel 1 (Freiburg-im-Breisgau, 1957).

39. James F. Kenney has collected the appropriate references. See his *The Sources for the Early History of Ireland: Ecclesiastical, An Introduction and Guide* (1929; reprint ed., New York, 1966), pp. 534–37. See also Bernhard Bischoff, "Theodulf und der Ire Cadac-Andreas," in *Mittelalterliche Studien: Ausgewählte Aufsätze zur Schriftkunde und Literaturgeschichte* (3 vols., Stuttgart, 1966–81), II, 19–25.

40. Heiric of Auxerre, *Vita sancti Germani episcopi Autissiodorensis, MGH, Poetae latini aevi carolini,* III, pp. 429, 24–26.

41. See Wilhelm Heil, "Der Adoptianismus, Alkuin und Spanien," *Karl der Grosse,* II, pp. 95–155; and Brunhölzl, *Geschichte der lateinischen Literatur,* I, pp. 277–79.

42. See Maieul Cappuyns, *Jean Scot Erigène: Sa Vie, son oeuvre, sa pensée* (1933; reprint ed., Brussels, 1964), pp. 102–27; and B. Lavaud, "La Controverse sur la prédestination au IXe siècle," *Dictionnaire de théologie catholique,* 12 (Paris, 1935), cols. 2901–35.

43. See Horst Fuhrmann, *Einfluss und Verbreitung der pseudo-isidorischen Fälschungen von ihrem Auftauchen bis in die neuere Zeit,* 3 vols. (Stuttgart, 1974). For other Carolingian controversies, see the brief overview in Laistner, pp. 286–98.

44. Morrison, *"Unum ex multis,"* pp. 675–76.

45. See Fischer, "Bibelausgaben," pp. 586–97, and note 38 above.

46. See Joseph-Claude Poulin, *L'Idéal de sainteté dans l'Aquitaine carolingienne d'après les sources hagiographiques (750–950)* (Quebec, 1975).

47. Barré, *Les Homéliaires.*

48. Jean Porcher, "La Peinture provinciale," in *Karl der Grosse,* III, pp. 54–73.

49. See Brunhölzl, *Geschichte der lateinischen Literatur,* and Manitius.

50. Marc Bloch, *Feudal Society,* trans. L. A. Manyon, 2 vols. (Chicago, 1964), I, pp. 75–78.

51. See Einhard, *Vita Karoli magni,* 29 (pp. 80–84 of Halphen's ed., pp. 81–82 of Thorpe's trans.); Werner Betz, "Karl der Grosse und die lingua theodisca," in *Karl der Grosse,* II, 300–306; and Bullough, *The Age of Charlemagne,* pp. 116–18.

52. See *The Song of Roland,* trans. Dorothy L. Sayers (Harmondsworth, 1957); and Ramón Menéndez Pidal, *La* Chanson de Roland *et la tradition épique chez les Francs,* 2d rev. ed., trans. I.-M. Cluzel (Paris, 1960).

53. See, for example, W. Scherer, "Eine lateinische Musterpredigt aus der Zeit Karls des Grossen," *Zeitschrift für deutsches Alterthum,* 12 (1865), 436–46; and Pierre Riché, *Daily Life in the World of Charlemagne,* trans. Jo Ann McNamara (Philadelphia, 1978), pp. 181–90.

54. See Günter Glauche, *Schullektüre im Mittelalter: Entstehung und Wandlungen des Lektürekanons bis 1200 nach den Quellen dargestellt,* Münchener Beiträge zur Mediävistik und Renaissance-Forschung 5 (Munich, 1970), esp. pp. 10–22 ("Karolingische Ansätze zur Kanonbildung"); and Bernhard Bischoff, "Die Bibliothek im Dienste der Schule," in *La scuola nell'Occidente latino dell'alto Medioevo,* 2 vols., Settimane di studio del Centro italiano di studi sull'alto medioevo 19 (Spoleto, 1972), I, 385–415 (also in *Mittelalterliche Studien,* III, 213–33).

55. Alcuin, *De grammatica,* Jacques-Paul Migne, *Patrologia latina* (*MPL*), 221 vols. (Paris, 1844–64), 101: 853; and John Scottus, *Iohannis Scoti Eriugenae Expositiones in Ierarchiam Coelestem,* ed. Jeanne Barbet, Corpus christianorum, Continuatio medievalis 31 (Turnhout, 1975), I, 540–61 (p. 16). See also Contreni, "John Scottus"; and Colin Chase, "Alcuin's Grammar Verse: Poetry and Truth in Carolingian Pedagogy," in Michael W. Herren, ed., *Insular Latin Studies* (Toronto, 1981), pp. 135–52.

56. See Beryl Smalley, *The Study of the Bible in the Middle Ages,*

2d ed. (New York, 1952), pp. 37–38; Laistner, pp. 298–306; and Notker of Saint Gall, *De illustribus viris qui ex intentione sacras scripturas exponebant,* in Ernst Dümmler, ed., *Das Formelbuch des Bischofs Salomo III von Konstanz aus dem neunten Jahrhundert* (Leipzig, 1857), pp. 64–78 (also *MPL,* 131, 993–1004).

57. See Jacques LeGoff, *Les Intellectuels au Moyen Age* (Paris, 1957). We need a study of the correspondence that passed among Carolingian masters. I use the phrase "fraternity of men" here deliberately; one of the effects of the Carolingian program was to block women from active participation in intellectual life. See Suzanne F. Wemple, *Women in Frankish Society: Marriage and the Cloister, 500 to 900* (Philadelphia, 1981), pp. 175–88.

58. See Carl I. Hammer, Jr., "Country Churches, Clerical Inventories and the Carolingian Renaissance in Bavaria," *Church History,* 49 (1980), 5–17.

59. See McKitterick, pp. 80–114.

60. Ibid., pp. 211–16; see also note 17 above.

61. See T. A. M. Bishop, *English Caroline Minuscule* (Oxford, 1971).

62. See Riché, *Les Écoles et l'enseignement,* pp. 125–31; Donald A. Bullough, "The Educational Tradition in England from Alfred to Aelfric: Teaching 'utriusque linguae'," *La scuola nell'Occidente latino dell'alto Medioevo,* 2 vols., Settimane di studio del Centro italiano di studi sull'alto medioevo 19 (Spoleto, 1972), II, 453–94; and Joel T. Rosenthal, "The Education of the Early Capetians," *Traditio,* 25 (1969), 366–76.

63. See G. Paré, A. Brunet, and P. Tremblay, *La Renaissance du XIIe siècle: Les Écoles et l'enseignement* (Paris and Ottawa, 1933); Riché, *Les Écoles et l'enseignement,* pp. 334–44; and Baldwin.

64. The contributions of Donald A. Bullough, "Roman Books and Carolingian 'Renovatio'," pp. 23–50, and of Janet L. Nelson, "On the Limits of the Carolingian Renaissance," pp. 51–69, to Derek Baker, ed., *Renaissance and Renewal in Christian History,* Studies in Church History 14 (Oxford, 1977), came to my attention after this essay went to press.

Chapter 4. The Macedonian Renaissance

1. Secular art and nonfigural religious art, however, were both permitted and produced under Iconoclasm; see A. Grabar, *L'Iconoclasme byzantin: Dossier archéologique* (Paris, 1957), and R. Cormack, "The Arts during the Age of Iconoclasm," in Anthony Bryer and Judith Herrin, eds., *Iconoclasm* (Birmingham, 1977), pp. 35–44.

2. On manuscripts copied at this time, see Paul Lemerle, *Le Premier Humanisme byzantin* (Paris, 1971), pp. 75–77.

3. On prophecies of the end of the world at this time, see C. Mango, *Byzantium: The Empire of New Rome* (London, 1980), pp. 205–11, and A. H. M. Jones, *The Later Roman Empire* (Norman, 1964), I, pp. 316–17.

4. Theophanes, *Chronographia,* ed. C. de Boor (Leipzig, 1880), p. 455.

5. The figures for the educated class are adapted from those for the bureaucracy in W. Treadgold, *The Byzantine State Finances in the Eighth and Ninth Centuries* (New York, 1982), pp. 41–47. Additional figures for churchmen and monks are drawn from the treatise of Philotheus, ed. and trans. N. Oikonomidès, *Les Listes de préséance byzantines des IXe et Xe siècles* (Paris, 1972), pp. 174–77 and 184–85. I accept the estimate made by D. Jacoby, "La Population de Constantinople à l'époque byzantine," *Byzantion,* 31 (1961), 81–109, that the city's maximum population before the plague of 541 was 375,000. I would therefore guess that its population was something like 100,000 at its low point in the eighth century.

6. For a survey of linguistic changes in Greek up to this time, see Robert Browning, *Medieval and Modern Greek* (London, 1969), pp. 11–72.

7. A more complete list, with references, appears in W. Treadgold, *The Nature of the 'Bibliotheca' of Photius* (Washington, D.C., 1980), pp. 6–7.

8. The source of this statement is the student himself, Ignatius the Deacon. See his *Vita Tarasii,* ed. I. A. Heikel, Acta Societatis Scientiarum Fennicae 17 (Helsingfors, 1899), p. 423.

9. Robert Browning, "Literacy in the Byzantine World," *Byzantine and Modern Greek Studies,* 4 (1978), 39–54.

10. On these libraries, see C. Mango, "The Availability of Books in the Byzantine Empire, A.D. 750–850," in *Byzantine Books and Bookmen* (Washington, D.C., 1975), pp. 31–35.

11. Note that about half the material in the books described in Photius's *Bibliotheca* is lost today (Treadgold, *Nature,* p. 9).

12. Giovanni Mansi, ed., *Sacrorum Conciliorum Nova et Amplissima Collectio,* XI (Paris, 1901), 973 (Canon 68).

13. W. Treadgold, "Photius on the Transmission of Texts," *Greek, Roman and Byzantine Studies,* 19 (1978), 171–75.

14. On Tarasius's rank as head of the chancery, see now W. Treadgold, "The Unpublished Saint's Life of the Empress Irene," *Byzantinische Forschungen,* 8 (1981), 238–41.

15. Mango, "Availability," pp. 29–31.

16. See Lemerle, pp. 109–28, for a recent and careful discussion.

17. Ihor Ševčenko cites four saints' lives in "Hagiography of the Iconoclast Period," in Bryer and Herrin, pp. 114–16.

18. On the vexed question of how much of the work is by George and how much by Theophanes, see Cyril Mango, "Who Wrote the Chronicle of Theophanes?" *Zbornik Radova Vizantinološkog Instituta*, 18 (1978), 9–17. Otherwise on George and Theophanes, see Herbert Hunger, *Die hochsprachliche profane Literatur der Byzantiner* (Munich, 1978), I, pp. 331–32 and 334–39.

19. See Paul Alexander, *The Patriarch Nicephorus of Constantinople* (Oxford, 1958), pp. 157–58, who suggests plausibly that Photius had already read Theophylact and Nicephorus in one manuscript before composing his *Bibliotheca* (which I believe was compiled in 845).

20. Mango, *Byzantium*, p. 244.

21. On Nicephorus's style, which he touched up some time after he first wrote, see now Ihor Ševčenko, "Levels of Style in Byzantine Prose," *Jahrbuch der Österreichischen Byzantinistik*, 31 (1981), 294–95. Otherwise on Nicephorus, see Hunger, *Die hochsprachliche profane Literatur*, I, pp. 344–47.

22. Theophanes, p. 405.

23. On John, see Lemerle, pp. 135–47; but on the date when he became Patriarch, see W. Treadgold, "The Chronological Accuracy of Symeon the Logothete for the Years 813–845," *Dumbarton Oaks Papers*, 33 (1979), 178–79.

24. Theophanes Continuatus, ed. I. Bekker (Bonn, 1838), p. 190. On the whole story, see Treadgold, "Chronological Accuracy," pp. 185–87.

25. V. Laurent, "Une Homélie inédite de l'archevêque de Thessalonique Léon le Philosophe sur l'Annonciation," *Mélanges Eugène Tisserant*, II (Vatican City, 1964), 281–302.

26. On Leo, see Lemerle, pp. 148–76.

27. On the history by Photius's father, see C. Mango, "The Liquidation of Iconoclasm and the Patriarch Photios," in Bryer and Herrin, pp. 135–39. There is only circumstantial evidence that this work was a continuation of Nicephorus. In the passage Mango cites from the *Bibliotheca*, Photius says that the continuous narrative of the history began in the reign of Constantine V (741–775), and it is reviewed in the *Bibliotheca* immediately after Nicephorus's work, which ends in the same reign. See Photius, *Bibliotheca*, ed. and French trans. R. Henry (Paris, 1959–77), I, 98–99.

28. Theophanes Continuatus, p. 192.

29. On Photius in general, see Lemerle, pp. 177–204.

30. See note 5 above.

31. Lemerle, pp. 255–57.

32. On Cassia, see Ilse Rochow, *Studien zu der Person, den Werken, und dem Nachleben der Dichterin Kassia* (Berlin, 1967). On the authenticity of her encounter with Theophilus, see W. Treadgold, "The Problem of the Marriage of the Emperor Theophilus," *Greek, Roman and Byzantine Studies,* 16 (1975), 325–41.

33. Photius, *Bibliotheca,* I, 105 and 108, and III, 124.

34. Photius, *Bibliotheca,* II, 32–33.

35. On Isocrates, see Photius, *Bibliotheca,* II, 121.

36. Photius, *Photiou Epistolai,* ed. I. Valettas (London, 1864), p. 545. The other epistolographers whom Photius praises are somewhat better known: Marcus Aurelius, Libanius, St. Basil, and Gregory of Nazianzus.

37. See Treadgold, *Nature,* pp. 177–80, for an index to the books described in the *Bibliotheca* (arranged by century of composition).

38. Leo the Mathematician, in *The Greek Anthology,* ed. and trans. W. R. Paton (London, 1916–18), III, 104–6, 110, and 322.

39. Mango, "Availability," pp. 35–36.

40. *Suidae Lexicon,* ed. Ada Adler (Leipzig, 1928–38), III, 524–31 (Homer); II, 620–25 (Jesus); III, 616–22 (Origen); and II, 106–9 (Dionysius).

41. See the lists in Lemerle, pp. 285–87.

42. Those commissioned by Constantine are Genesius and Theophanes Continuatus (of which Book V is purportedly Constantine's own work), and the chief minister is Symeon the Logothete. On these historians, see Hunger, *Die hochsprachliche profane Literatur,* I, 339–43 (Theophanes Continuatus); I, 351–57 (Genesius and Symeon the Logothete); and I, 361–67 (Constantine Porphyrogenitus).

43. For a general discussion of the encyclopedism of the period, see Lemerle, pp. 267–300.

44. J. B. Bury, *A History of the Eastern Roman Empire* (London, 1912), pp. 448–49.

45. Ihor Ševčenko, review of Lemerle, *American Historical Review,* 79 (1974), 1533, quoting Lemerle, p. 305.

46. Mango, *Byzantium,* p. 255.

47. See H.-G. Beck, *Geschichte der byzantinischen Volksliteratur* (Munich, 1971), pp. 63–97 (*Digenes Acrites*) and pp. 101–5 (poetry attributed to Prodromus). Also see Hunger, *Die hochsprachliche profane Literatur,* I, 372–82 (Psellus), I, 400–409 (Anna Comnena); and I, 429–41 (Nicetas Choniates).

48. J. B. Bury, "Roman Emperors from Basil II to Isaac Komnenos," *English Historical Review,* 4 (1889), 43–45.

49. Mango, *Byzantium,* pp. 245, 246, 253, and 254.

50. Ibid., p. 255.

Chapter 5. The Anglo-Saxon Monastic Revival

1. For a sociohistorical analysis of the contrasts between Christian monachism and Roman culture, see Peter Brown, *The World of Late Antiquity A.D.* 150–175 (New York, 1971), pp. 49–112. For a charming presentation of the paradoxical relationship between monastic education and pagan letters, see Dom Jean Leclercq, *The Love of Learning and the Desire for God* (New York, 1961).

2. See Dom David Knowles, *The Monastic Order in England,* 2d ed. (Cambridge, 1963), ch. 1, "The Rule of St. Benedict." See also Herbert Bloch, "Monte Cassino's Teachers and Library in the High Middle Ages," *La Scuola nell' Occidente latino dell'alto medioevo,* 2 vols., Settimane di studio del Centro italiano di studi sull'alto medioevo, 19 (Spoleto, 1972), II, 563–65.

3. "Saecularium prioratus" means "the overlordship by secular persons"; see the *Regularis Concordia,* ed. Dom Thomas Symons (London, 1953), Proem 10 (p. 7); see also p. x of the Introduction.

4. Venerable Bede, *Historia Ecclesiastica Gentis Anglorum,* IV, 19, and *Vita sanctorum Abbatum,* 5, in Bede, *Opera Historica,* ed. J. E. King (London and New York, 1930), II, 98–99, 404–5.

5. See the anonymous *Life of Ceolfrith* in Dorothy Whitelock, ed., *English Historical Documents* (London, 1968), para. 14 and note 1 (p. 701).

6. Bede, *Vita Abbatum,* ch. 11, in *Opera Historica,* II, 416–17.

7. This magnificent Bible is the *Codex Amiatinus* of which the Biblioteca Laurentiana in Florence is so justifiably proud. The dedicatory inscription is cited in the *Life of Ceolfrith,* ch. 37 (in Whitelock, I, 701).

8. See M. L. W. Laistner, "The Library of Venerable Bede," in A. Hamilton Thompson, ed., *Bede, His Life, Times and Writings* (1935; reprint ed., New York, 1966). Laistner probably underestimates the classical holdings in Bede's library. He records only those works explicitly cited in Bede's texts, and we know that Bede was reluctant to credit the pagan authors he drew on. For some appreciation of the contribution that Bede's monastery made to eighth-century letters, see the admirable study by M. B. Parkes, *The Scriptorium of Wearmouth–Jarrow* (Jarrow Lecture; Jarrow, 1982).

9. Preface to King Alfred's translation of Gregory's *Pastoral Care,*

in Whitelock, I, 818–19. See D. A. Bullough, "The Educational Tradition in England from Alfred to Aelfric: Teaching, *Utriusque Linguae," La Scuola nell'Occidente latino dell'alto Medioevo*, 2 vols., Settimane di studio del Centro italiano di studi sull'alto medioevo,19 (Spoleto, 1972), II, 453–94, which assesses Alfred's contributions to education, especially the initiation of a tradition of teaching both in Latin and English, that continued into the tenth-century revival, particularly through Aelfric.

10. The famous praise poem on the Battle of Brunanburh occurs in the C version (British Library MS. Cotton Tiberius B.i) of the *Anglo-Saxon Chronicle*, under the year 937: translated by Whitelock in Whitelock, I, 200–201. There is also an interesting translation by Alfred Lord Tennyson.

11. Knowles, p. 36.

12. Vita sancti Dunstani auctore B, in William Stubbs, ed., *Memorials of Saint Dunstan*, Rolls 63 (London, 1874; reprint ed., London, 1965), p. 11.

13. F. M. Stenton, *Anglo-Saxon England*, 3d ed. (Oxford, 1971), p. 447. Knowles, p. 65, concludes that Dunstan and Aethelwold "called the dead to life; they created a great and flourishing system upon vacant soil; and to Dunstan especially, as to Augustine of Canterbury before him, are due in a very real sense the titles of patron and father of the monks of medieval England." However, Eric John in "The King and the Monks in the Tenth-Century Reformation," *Orbis Brittaniae* (Bristol, 1966), p. 161, insists that "the elder statesman" Dunstan only "prepared the way for the experienced monks, Oswald and Aethelwold, who actually, I believe, effected the revival." In any case, Dunstan was the original instigator of the entire movement.

14. *Vita sancti Dunstani*, sec. 21 (in Stubbs, pp. 32–33). See Stenton, pp. 365–66. Dunstan's earliest biographer relates, no doubt with bias, the scandalous affair in which Eadwig, the newly anointed king, absented himself at his coronation feast to take pleasure with a noblewoman and her daughter. The hierarchy and councillors judged that such behavior constituted an insult to the whole English people, so Dunstan and his kinsman, the bishop of Lichfield, were sent to fetch Eadwig. The affronted monarch returned, but the ladies, who were to become the queen and mother-in-law of the king, had their vengeance.

15. Stenton, p. 452; Eric John, "Some Latin Charters of the Tenth-Century Reformation," *Orbis Brittaniae* (Bristol, 1966), pp. 185, 208–9.

16. *Regularis Concordia*, secs. 1, 9–10.

17. John, pp. 179–80.

18. See D. H. Farmer, "The Progress of the Monastic Revival," in David Parsons, ed., *Tenth-Century Studies* (Chichester, 1975), pp. 10–19.

19. Aelfric, *Aelfrics Grammatik und Glossar*, ed. J. Zupitza (Berlin, 1880), p. 3.

20. See, for instance, the sharp criticism of the monks' Latin by C. E. Hohler, "Some Service-Books of the Later Saxon Church," in Parsons, ed., *Tenth-Century Studies* (Chichester, 1975), pp. 71–74. In discussing the monks' endeavors, Hohler remarks acidly that "their best was often absurd" (p. 71) and suggests that some of the blunders can be attributed to the quantities of mead the writers consumed each day.

21. See Helmut Gneuss, "The Origin of Standard Old English and Aethelwold's School at Winchester," *Anglo-Saxon England*, 1 (1972), 63–84.

22. For a critique of Aelfric's and Wulfstan's literary merits, see C. L. Wrenn, "The Benedictine Renaissance and Sermon Literature," in *A Study of Old English Literature* (New York, 1967), esp. pp. 224–42.

23. See James Campbell, ed., *The Anglo-Saxons* (Oxford and Ithaca 1982), pp. 160, 170, 181–89.

Chapter 6. The Twelfth-Century Renaissance

1. Jean-Jacques Ampère, *Histoire littéraire de France avant le douzième siècle* (3 vols., Paris, 1839–40), III, pp. 33, 457. Jacob Burckhardt's *Die Kultur der Renaissance in Italien* was first published in Germany in 1860; the first English translation, by S. G. C. Middlemore, was issued in London in 1878.

2. Louis J. Paetow, *A Guide to the Study of Medieval History*, rev. ed. (New York, 1931), pp. 228, 292, 408, 411. Although it was not published until 1931, Paetow had largely completed the *Guide* before his death in 1928.

3. Charles Homer Haskins, *The Renaissance of the Twelfth Century* (Cambridge, Mass., 1927), pp. 3–29.

4. Gérard M. Paré, A. Brunet, and P. Tremblay, *La Renaissance du douzième siècle: Les Écoles et l'enseignement* (Paris and Ottawa, 1933), pp. 138–46, 206–9.

5. Erwin Panofsky, "Renaissance and Renascences," *Kenyon Review*, 6 (1944), 201–36; revised and reprinted in Panofsky's collection of essays, *Renaissance and Renascences in Western Art* (New York, 1969), pp. 42–103. Panofsky had earlier expressed his views of the twelfth-century renaissance in an article he wrote with Fritz Saxl,

"Classical Mythology in Medieval Art," *Metropolitan Museum Studies,* 4 (1933), 228–80.

6. William A. Nitze, "The So-Called Twelfth-Century Renaissance," *Speculum,* 23 (1948), 464–71.

7. Eva M. Sanford, "The Twelfth Century—Renaissance or Proto-Renaissance?" *Speculum,* 26 (1951), 635–42.

8. Urban T. Holmes, "The Idea of a Twelfth-Century Renaissance," *Speculum,* 26, (1951), 643–51.

9. This aggregating approach also characterized the international conference on the twelfth-century renaissance held in Cerisy-la-Salle, France, in 1965. The proceedings of the conference have been published by Maurice de Gandillac and Edouard Jeauneau, eds., *Entretiens sur la Renaissance du 12ᵉ siècle* (Paris, 1968). A more recent volume of interpretive essays on the twelfth century defines the renaissance simply as "all that was new and vital in the age"; see Robert L. Benson and Giles Constable, eds., *Renaissance and Renewal in the Twelfth Century* (Cambridge, Mass., 1982), p. xxix. This volume is the proceedings of a conference that convened in Cambridge, Massachusetts in 1977, on the fiftieth anniversary of the publication of Haskins's *The Renaissance of the Twelfth Century.* It was published after this essay was written. To have taken adequate account of the many relevant ideas the volume contains, I would have had to revise much of this paper. An especially valuable contribution to the definition of the twelfth-century renaissance is the essay of Gerhart B. Ladner, "Terms and Ideas of Renewal," pp. 1–33. I refer to other essays in the volume in several of the notes below.

10. Elizabeth A. R. Brown, "The Tyranny of a Construct: Feudalism and Historians of Medieval Europe," *American Historical Review,* 79 (1974), 1063–88.

11. Richard W. Southern, "Medieval Humanism," in *Medieval Humanism and Other Essays* (New York, 1970), p. 29.

12. Ibid., pp. 29–60.

13. Holmes, p. 650.

14. See Hans Liebeschütz, *Medieval Humanism in the Life and Writings of John of Salisbury* (London, 1950); Sidney Painter, "John of Salisbury and the Renaissance of the Twelfth Century," in G. Boas, ed., *The Greek Tradition* (Baltimore, 1939), pp. 77–89; R. R. Bolgar, *The Classical Heritage and Its Beneficiaries* (Cambridge, 1954), pp. 183–201; Frederick B. Artz, *The Mind of the Middle Ages,* 3d rev. ed. (New York, 1958), pp. 432–35; Winthrop Wetherbee, *Platonism and Poetry in the Twelfth Century: The Literary Influence of the School of Chartres* (Princeton, 1972); and Paul O. Kristeller, "The Medieval

Antecedents of Renaissance Humanism," in *Eight Philosophers of the Italian Renaissance* (Stanford, 1964), pp. 147–65. Cf. R. W. Southern, "Humanism and the School of Chartres," in *Medieval Humanism and Other Essays* (New York, 1970), pp. 61–85.

15. David Knowles, "The Humanism of the Twelfth Century," in *The Historian and Character* (Cambridge, 1963), p. 26.

16. Ibid., p. 17.

17. Southern, "Medieval Humanism," pp. 29–33. Jean Leclercq has recently made a similar claim for the humanism of the twelfth century in his essay "The Renewal of Theology," in Benson and Constable, eds., *Renaissance and Renewal in the Twelfth Century* (Cambridge, Mass., 1982), p. 84: "This confidence in man, this refinement of the sensibility, this quality of language: are these not so many tokens of a true humanism?"

18. Southern, "Medieval Humanism," p. 52.

19. The success and influence of this treatise is evident in the survival of nearly 500 manuscripts: see Michele Maccarrone, ed., *Lotharii Cardinalis (Innocentii III) De miseria humane conditions* (Lugano, 1955, pp. x–xx.

20. *De miseria* 1.1: Lotario dei Segni, *On the Misery of the Human Condition*, ed. Donald R. Howard and trans. Margaret M. Dietz (Indianapolis and New York, 1969), p. 6.

21. Colin Morris, *The Discovery of the Individual, 1050–1200* (New York, 1972), p. 10.

22. Ibid., pp. 1–19, 158–67.

23. Carolyn W. Bynum, "Did the Twelfth Century Discover the Individual?" *Journal of Ecclesiastical History*, 31 (1980), 1–17. See also John F. Benton, "Consciousness of Self and Perceptions of Individuality," in Benson and Constable, eds., *Renaissance and Renewal in the Twelfth Century* (Cambridge, Mass., 1982), pp. 263–95.

24. Bynum, p. 3.

25. Colin Morris, "Individualism in Twelfth-Century Religion: Some Further Reflections," *Journal of Ecclesiastical History*, 31 (1980), 195–206.

26. Morris, *Discovery*, p. 160.

27. Martin Stevens, "The Performing Self in Twelfth-Century Culture," *Viator*, 9 (1978), 193–212.

28. Charles H. McIlwain, "Medieval Institutions in the Modern World," *Speculum*, 16 (1941), 277.

29. Jacqueline Rambaud-Buhot, "Le Décret de Gratien. Legs du passé, avènement de l'âge classique," in Gandillac and Jeauneau, eds., *Entretiens sur la Renaissance du 12ᵉ siècle* (Paris, 1968), pp. 493–506.

30. I undertake this reexamination in my forthcoming book, *The Origins of the University: The Schools of Paris and Their Critics, 1100–1215.*

31. See, for example, Christopher Brooke, *The Twelfth-Century Renaissance* (London, 1969), p. 186: "Much was lost when the first rapture of walking or riding hundreds of miles to sit at Abelard's feet was converted into the formal structured course of thirteenth century Paris. A generation bred on syllabuses can hardly understand the inspiration of medieval schools in their prime." Others, like Panofsky (see note 5 above) and Bolgar, *Classical Heritage*, contrast humanism and Scholasticism in a way that also suggests that the expansion of the schools and the development of the university were detrimental to the cultural revival. Cf. Haskins, *Renaissance*, pp. 368–96, where he describes the beginnings of the university as an integral part of the renaissance.

32. Jacques LeGoff, *Les Intellectuels au moyen âge* (Paris, 1957), pp. 9–69.

33. Gaines Post, K. Giocarinis, and R. Kay, "The Medieval Heritage of a Humanistic Ideal: '*Scientia donum Dei est, unde vendi non potest,*'" *Traditio*, 11 (1955), 195–234.

34. On Frederick's decree, see H. Koeppler, "Frederick Barbarossa and the Schools of Bologna: Some Remarks on the *Authentica 'Habita,'*" *English Historical Review*, 54 (1939), 577–607; and, for its date, Winfried Stelzer, "Zum Scholarenprivileg Friedrich Barbarossas (Authentica 'Habita')," *Deutsches Archiv*, 34 (1978), 123–65.

35. See Marc Bloch, *Feudal Society*, trans. L. A. Manyon (Chicago, 1961), pp. 103–8.

36. Georges Duby, *The Early Growth of the European Economy: Warriors and Peasants from the Seventh to the Twelfth Century*, trans. H. B. Clarke (Ithaca, 1974), pp. 257–70.

37. Marie-Dominique Chenu, *La Théologie au douzième siècle* (Paris, 1966), p. 11. The title given to the English translation of nine of the same essays better indicates the wide scope of Chenu's scholarship: *Nature, Man and Society in the Twelfth Century: Essays on New Theological Perspectives in the West*, trans. Jerome Taylor and Lester K. Little (Chicago, 1968).

38. Chenu, *La Théologie*, pp. 11–12.

39. Chenu, *La Théologie*, p. 21; *Nature, Man and Society*, p. 4.

40. Chenu, *La Théologie*, p. 49; *Nature, Man and Society*, p. 45.

41. Chenu, *La Théologie*, pp. 257–63.

42. Chenu, *La Théologie*, p. 387.

43. Alexander Murray, *Reason and Society in the Middle Ages* (Oxford, 1978).

44. Paré, Brunet, and Tremblay, *La Renaissance*, p. 34.

45. Haskins, *Renaissance*, p. 12.

46. On these *juvenes*, see Georges Duby, "Youth in Aristocratic Society," in *The Chivalrous Society*, trans. C. Postan (Berkeley and Los Angeles, 1977), pp. 112–22.

47. On the use of the term *moderni* in this period, see M. T. Clanchy, "*Moderni* in Education and Government in England," *Speculum*, 50 (1975), 671–88.

48. On the use and meaning of this metaphor, see Edouard Jeauneau, "Nains et géants," in Gandillac and Jeauneau, eds., *Entretiens sur la renaissance du 12ᵉ siècle* (Paris, 1968), pp. 23–38.

49. John of Salisbury, *Metalogicon* 3.4, ed. C. C. W. Webb (Oxford, 1929), p. 136.

50. On this important group of theologians and their influence, see John W. Baldwin, *Masters, Princes and Merchants: The Social Views of Peter the Chanter and His Circle*, 2 vols. (Princeton, 1970).

51. The best-known proponent of the early date is Henri Pirenne, *Medieval Cities* (Princeton, 1952), p. 78. The Crusades have been frequently chosen as a starting point; see, e.g., S. Packard, *Twelfth-Century Europe: An Interpretive Essay* (Amherst, Mass., 1973).

52. Cf. John F. Benton's comments on the impact that the Gregorian Reform had on the spreading of cultural change: "Consciousness of Self and Perceptions of Individuality," in Benson and Constable, eds., *Renaissance and Renewal in the Twelfth Century*, p. 293.

53. Bolgar, *Classical Heritage*, p. 201.

54. On the interpretation of Ovid in the twelfth century see Jean Leclercq, *Monks and Love in Twelfth-Century France* (Oxford, 1979), pp. 62–85.

55. In their summary of the views collected in the volume of essays they edited, Robert Benson and Giles Constable (*Renaissance and Renewal in the Twelfth Century*, pp. xxvii–xxviii) come to a different conclusion about the significance of these new directions.

56. On the choice of 1215 for the end of the twelfth-century renaissance, I share the view of Chenu, *La Théologie*, p. 398.

Chapter 7. The Palaeologan Renaissance

Sources of illustrations on pp. 151–60. 1, 3, 4, 5: Courtesy of Dumbarton Oaks, Center for Byzantine Studies, Washington, D.C. 2: Photo Lykides. 6: From a postcard (Georgiadis Sparti). 7, 12: Photo Ihor Ševčenko. 8, 16: Courtesy of Cyril Mango. 9: From K. Weitzmann, "Eine Pariser-Psalter-Kopie des 13. Jahrhunderts auf dem Sinai," *Jahrbuch der Österreichischen byzantinischen Gesellschaft*, 6 (1957), fig 8. 10: From D. Talbot-Rice and M. Hirmer, *The Art of Byzantium* (London,

1959), fig. 87. 11: From a postcard (Jugoturist, Belgrade). 13: From V. N. Lazarev, *Feofan Grek i ego škola* (Moscow, 1961), fig. 99. 14: From H. Belting, "Le peintre Manuel Eugénikos de Constantinople, en Géorgie," *Cahiers Archéologiques*, 28 (1979), fig. 7. 15: From M. Aronberg Lavin, "Piero della Francesca's Fresco of Sigismondo Pandolfo Malatesta before St. Sigismund," *Art Bulletin*, 56 (1974), fig. 1a.

1. For maps illustrating shrinking of the Empire's territory between ca. 1330 and 1453, see, for example, A. Laiou, *Constantinople and the Latins* (Cambridge, 1972), after p. 285; *Cambridge Mediaeval History*, IV, 1 (1966), map 7, "The Ottoman Advance in the Fourteenth Century," after p. 368; and the two maps in A. Bakalopoulos, "Les limites de l'empire byzantin jusqu'à sa chute (1453)," *Byzantinische Zeitschrift*, 55 (1962), 64–65.

2. E. Panofsky, "Renaissance and Renascences," *Kenyon Review*, 6 (1944), 201–36; and idem, *Renaissance and Renascences in Western Art* (New York, 1969). See also P. O. Kristeller, *Renaissance Thought and Its Sources* (New York, 1979), pp. 17–18 and the first note on p. 261.

3. See I. Ševčenko, "Levels of Style in Byzantine Prose," *Jahrbuch der Österreichischen Byzantinistik*, 31 (1981), esp. 298–304. See also "Discussion" and my "Additional Remarks," *Jahrbuch der Österreichischen Byzantinistik*, 32 (1982), 211–38.

4. For a date ca. 963 see, most recently, Ch. Aggelidē, Ἡ χρονολόγηση καὶ ὁ συγγραφέας τοῦ διαλόγου Φιλόπατρις, *Hellenika*, 30 (1977–78), 34–50; for a date in the reign of Isaac Commenus, see R. Anastasi, ed., *Incerti auctoris* Φιλόπατρις ἢ διδασκόμενος (Messina, 1968), esp. pp. 23 et seq.

5. See P. L. M. Leone, ed., *Niceforo Gregora, Fiorenzo o intorno alla sapienza* (Naples, 1975).

6. See F. W. Lenz, *Aristeidesstudien* (Berlin, 1964), esp. pp. 256–71; also, idem, *Fünf Reden Thomas Magisters* (Leiden, 1963), pp. ix-xix.

7. For Planudes's hexameters, see J. Iriarte, *Regiae bibliothecae Matritensis codices Graeci mss.*, I (Madrid, 1769), 263 (47 hexameters on Ptolemy's *Geography*); C. F. A. Nobbe, *Cl. Ptolemaei Geographia*, I (1843), XXI (4 epigrams); M. Treu, *Maximi Planudis epistulae* (Breslau, 1890), p. 204 (27 hexameters on a Nomocanon); S. Kougéas, "Analekta Planudea," *Byzantinische Zeitschrift*, 18 (1909), esp. pp. 117–18; Sp. Lampros in Νέος Ἑλληνομνήμων, 13 (1916), 415–16, 419–20 (elegiac distichs); C. Wendel, "Planudes, Maximos," in Pauly-Wissowa, ed., *Real-Encyclopädie*, 20 (1950), cols. 2219–20, 2228–30; and F. M. Pontani, ed., *Maximi Planudis Idyllium* (Padua, 1973) (latest edition of 270 hexameters in Theocritean vein; in the wake of C. F.

von Holzinger [1893], the late Professor Pontani finds Planudes's verses to be quite weak).

8. On Metochites's poetry (much of it still unpublished), see now I. Ševčenko and J. Featherstone, *Two Poems by Theodore Metochites* (Brookline, Mass., 1981). This study first appeared in *The Greek Orthodox Theological Review*, 26 (1981), 1–46.

9. See, for example, A. Turyn, *Studies in the Manuscript Tradition of the Tragedies of Sophocles* (Urbana, Ill., 1952), esp. pp. 16, 18, 202.

10. For the rediscovery of Ptolemy's *Geography* and the confection of 27 new maps to it, see J. Iriarte, I, 263; Kougéas, pp. 115–18; A. Diller, "The Oldest Manuscript of Ptolemaic Maps," *Transactions and Proceedings of the American Philological Association*, 71 (1940), 62–67, esp. p. 66; L. Bagrow, "The Origin of Ptolemy's Geographia," *Geografiska Annaler*, 27 (1945), 363–65 (on Planudes as the author of 26 maps); and E. Polaschek, "Klaudios Ptolemaios," in Pauly-Wissowa, ed., *Real-Encyclopädie, Supplementband* 10 (1965), cols. 745–46. On Planudes's edition of Nonnos as the basis of our whole manuscript tradition, see Wendel, cols. 2222–23; and R. Keydell, ed., *Nonni Panopolitani Dionysiaca*, I (1959), 13*–25*. On Planudes's editions of Plutarch and his finding of eight books of the latter's *Moralia*, see Wendel, cols. 2223–26; K. Ziegler, "Plutarchos von Chaironeia," in Pauly-Wissowa, ed., *Real-Encyclopädie*, 21 (1951), cols. 951–53; and Ph. Hoffmann, "Deux témoins apparentés des *Vies* de Plutarque: les *Parisini Gr.* 1671 (A) et 1674 (D)," *Scriptorium*, 37 (1983), 259–64. On the Planudean Anthology (a shortened and bowdlerized edition, but alone to have preserved 388 epigrams), see, for example, Wendel, cols. 2236–39; and H. Beckby, ed., *Anthologia Graeca*, I (1957), 70–72. The loci classici (several of them coming from Planudes's correspondence) on the search for texts and commerce of books in the early Palaeologan period have been gathered by I. Ševčenko in Underwood, *The Kariye Djami*, IV (Princeton, 1975), pp. 22–23 and notes 24–27; to these, add the two letters (nos. 76[75] and 77[76]) of Nicephorus Choumnos to an emperor's niece and widow of the *protovestiarios* Theodore Mouzalon (d. 1294), ed. J.-Fr. Boissonade, *Anecdota Nova* (Paris, 1844), pp. 91–94 (= *Patmiacus Gr.* 127 [the best manuscript], fols. 324ʳ–325ᵛ). The first of these letters accompanied a copy of Aristotle's *Meteorologica* (with the Commentary by Alexander of Aphrodisias) that Choumnos was lending the learned *protovestiaria*; it contained apologies for the copy's deficient penmanship and textual errors. In the second letter, Choumnos regretted owning only a few books, while others (probably his enemy Metochites) had acquired fame on account of possessing vast book collections. Would the *protovestiaria* provide Choumnos with books? On Metochites's library, see I. Šev-

čenko, "Observations sur les recueils des *Discours* et des *Poèmes* de Th. Métochite et sur la bibliothèque de Chora à Constantinople," *Scriptorium*, 5 (1951), 279–88.

11. For access to the ample bibliography on Metochites, see Ševčenko and Featherstone, p. 2, n. 4; also now see I. Ševčenko, "Storia Letteraria," *La Civiltà bizantina dal XII al XV secolo, Aspetti e problemi* (Rome, 1982), pp. 138–169 (bibliography on pp. 138–39).

12. The standard work on Plethon is still F. Masai, *Pléthon et le Platonisme de Mistra* (Paris, 1956); see pp. 393–404 on surviving fragments of Plethon's *Laws*. On Scholarios, see now F. Tinnefeld "Gennadios Scholarios," *Theologische Realenzyklopädie*, 12, 3/4 (1983), 375–76 (bibliography).

13. See Ch. Diehl, "Les mosaïques de Kahrié-Djami," reprinted in idem, *Études byzantines* (Paris, 1905), pp. 392–431. See also Ch. Diehl, "La dernière Renaissance de l'art byzantin," first published in 1917 and reprinted in idem, *Choses et gens de Byzance* (Paris, 1926), pp. 143–170.

14. For these quantitative estimates, see I. Ševčenko, *Society and Intellectual Life in Late Byzantium* (London, 1981), item I, where I analyzed a sample of 91 intellectuals, i.e., writers, active in the fourteenth century, and postulated that the total of writers in that century exceeded that of those known to us by about one-third. More recently, A. P. Kazhdan enlarged my sample by a further 59 names: see his review of my *Society and Intellectual Life in Late Byzantium* in *The Greek Orthodox Theological Review*, 27 (1982), 83–97, esp. pp. 91–96.

15. Scholars have been aware of the Roman, rather than Greek, orientation of middlebrow and lowbrow Byzantine chronicles. See the incisive observations by C. Mango, "Discontinuity with the Classical Past in Byzantium," in M. Mullett and R. Scott, eds., *Byzantium and the Classical Tradition: University of Birmingham Thirteenth Spring Symposium of Byzantine Studies* (Birmingham, 1981), esp. pp. 52–55.

16. The late Byzantine use of "Hellene" to refer to a contemporary Greek-speaking Byzantine and the ambivalent Byzantine attitudes toward this use have been the subject of much attention. See, for example, S. Runciman, *The Last Byzantine Renaissance* (Cambridge, 1970), pp. 19–23; A. E. Laiou, "From 'Roman' to 'Hellene,' " *The Byzantine Fellowship Lectures*, 1 (no date); M. Angold, "Byzantine 'Nationalism' and the Nicaean Empire," *Byzantine and Modern Greek Studies*, 1 (1975), esp. pp. 51–53, 65; and I. Ševčenko, in Underwood, p. 46 and n. 203. The Nicaean Emperors John III Vatatzes and Theodore II Laskaris are often quoted as promoters of the new use: see, for example, A. E. Vakalopoulos, *Origins of the Greek Nation: The Byzantine Period* (New Brunswick, N.J., 1970), pp. 37 et seq. The earliest

instance known to me in which the words "Hellenic population" mean "Byzantine Greeks (of the sixth century)" is the autograph scholion written soon after 932 by Arethas of Caesarea; see, for example, I. Dujčev, *Cronaca di Monemvasia* (Palermo, 1976), p. 12. This piece of evidence, if admitted as valid, would antedate the two twelfth-century examples adduced as the earliest instances of the "new" meaning by R. Browning in *Journal of Hellenic Studies*, 91 (1971), 214 (review of S. Runciman). For a dim view of the importance of the use of the term "Hellene" in the "new" sense, see C. Mango, "Byzantinism and Romantic Hellenism," *Journal of the Warburg and Courtauld Institutes*, 28 (1965), 33 (this sense was adopted by a few intellectuals and its use had no influence on the people).

17. On Metochites's essay on Demosthenes and Aelius Aristides and on his dependence on Gregory of Nazianzus, see I. Ševčenko, "Theodore Metochites, the Chora, and the Intellectual Trends of His Time," in Underwood, pp. 38, 40–41, 47–48. On Lakapenos as editor and commentator of his own letters, see S. Lindstam, *Georgii Lacapeni at Andronici Zaridae epistulae XXXII cum epimerismis Lacapeni* (Göteborg, 1924); and F. Foerster-F. Richtsteig, *Libanii Opera*, IX (1927), 132–60. On Michael of Ephesus as Metochites's source, see, for example, H. J. Drossaart-Lulofs, ed., *Aristotelis De Somno et Vigilia liber, adiectis veteribus translationibus et Theodori Metochitae Commentario* (Leyden, 1943), esp. p. xxvii and Commentary pp. 23 et seq. On the (late?) thirteenth-century date of the *Vaticanus Pal. Gr.* 381, see K. Weitzmann, "Eine Pariser-Psalter-Kopie des 13. Jahrhunderts auf dem Sinai," *Jahrbuch der Österreichischen byzantinischen Gesellschaft*, 6 (1957), esp. pp. 138–40, now reprinted, with a few additions, as item II in idem, *Byzantine Liturgical Psalters and Gospels* (London, 1980).

18. The only fifteenth-century treatise known to me about the respective merits of Plato and Aristotle that was written in Byzantium proper and before its fall is Scholarios's attack of ca. 1443 on Plethon's *On the Differences*. The attack depended on Western thought. The latest edition of Plethon's *On the Differences* is by B. Lagarde, "Le 'De differentiis' de Pléthon d'après l'autographe de la Marcienne," *Byzantion*, 43 (1974), 312–43. Plethon is hard on Aristotle; still, he recommends reading his books because they contain useful material. Bessarion's *Adversus calumniatorem* was reprinted (with the Greek text *en face*) by L. Mohler, *Kardinal Bessarion als Theologe* (1927). Christian considerations do play a role in Bessarion's defense of Plato. An influential Byzantine champion of Artistotle in Italy (but still a friend of Bessarion) was Theodore Gaza (d. 1475). On him, see for example, D. I. Geanakoplos, "A Byzantine Scholar from Thessalonike,

Theodoros Gazes, in the Italian Renaissance," in Ἡ Θεσσαλονίκη με-
ταξὺ Ἀνατολῆς καὶ Δύσεως (Thessalonica, 1982), pp. 43–58. On the
Aristotelian George of Trebizond (Bessarion's enemy and *calumniator*
of Plato), see J. Monfasani, *George of Trebizond: A Biography and
Study of his Rhetoric and Logic* (Leiden, 1976).

19. On the admission that rhetorical techniques should be acquired through a "correct" imitation of the ancients, see the *Dialogue
on Dogmatic Theology* by Philotheos of Selymbria, *Patmiacus Gr.*
366, fol. 374ʳ. The passage mentions Demosthenes and cribs from
some version of Hermogenes's manual *On the Ideas.* Philotheos's *Dialogue* is soon to be published by Maria Paschou. On Athanasius I,
see A.-M. Maffry-Talbot, *The Correspondence of Athanasius I, Patriarch of Constantinople,* Corpus Fontium Historiae Byzantinae 7
(Washington, D.C., 1975). For the text of Akropolites's fulminations
against *Timarion,* see M. Treu, "Ein Kritiker des Timarion," *Byzantinische Zeitschrift,* 1 (1892), 361–65; and R. Romano, ed., *Pseudo-
Luciano, Timarione* (Naples, 1974), pp. 42–45. Akropolites's request
for a copy of George of Pisidia is in R. Romano, "Pisidiana," *Vichiana,*
n.s., 10 (1981), 200–201.

20. See *Patmiacus Gr.* 366, fol. 392ᵛ.

21. See St. Bezdeki, "Un projet de reforme du calendrier par Nicéphore Gregoras," in C. Marinescu, ed., *Mélanges d'histoire géné-
rale* (Cluj, 1927), pp. 68–74; J. Mogenet and A. Tihon, *Barlaam de
Seminara* (Louvain, 1977), pp. 150–51; and A. Tihon, "L'astronomie
byzantine (du Vᶜ au XVᶜ siècle)," *Byzantion,* 51 (1981), 613. Gregoras realized that the duration of the tropical year was less than the value given in Ptolemy, but underestimated the difference.

22. See I. Ševčenko, *Études sur la polémique entre Théodore Métochite et Nicéphore Choumnos* (Brussels, 1962), pp. 42–44, 92, 105,
109–17, 129, 280–86. Other champions of the Ptolemaic tradition in
our period were Barlaam of Calabria (d. 1350), Nicephorus Gregoras
(d. ca. 1360), and Isaac Argyros (d. soon after 1373).

23. On this point, see now the exemplary survey by A. Tihon
(cited in note 21). Byzantines started to use Islamic scientific astronomy as early as the eleventh century, but the high point of Islamic
influence falls into our period. It must be said to the credit of some
refined fourteenth- and fifteenth-century literati that they too put
classicism second to common sense and made use of Persian or Western tables based on Islamic astronomy: George Lapithes, Theodore
Meliteniotes, Demetrios Chrysoloras, and John Chortasmenos are
cases in point.

24. See W. O. Schmitt, "Lateinische Literatur in Byzanz: Die Über-
setzungen des Maximos Planudes und die moderne Forschung," *Jahr-*

buch der Österreichischen Byzantinischen Gesellschaft, 17 (1968), 127–47. See also M. Papathomopoulos, ed., Μαξίμου Πλανούδη μετάφρασις τῶν Ὀβιδίου ἐπιστολῶν (Ioannina, 1976); and E. A. Fisher, "Ovid's Metamorphoses, Planudes and Ausonians," *Arktouros: Hellenic Studies Presented to Bernard M. W. Knox* (New York, 1979), pp. 440–46.

25. On Demetrios Kydones's translations, see now F. Kianka, "Demetrius Cydones and Thomas Aquinas," *Byzantion,* 52 (1982), 264–86 (see pp. 284–86 for an English translation of Kydones's letter to Chrysoberges on the translation of Thomas). Somewhat later, Gennadios Scholarios epitomized or translated some of Thomas's writings. His translations seem to belong to his early period. See G. Podskalsky, "Die Rezeption der thomistischen Theologie bei Gennadios II. Scholarios (ca. 1403–1472)," *Theologie und Philosophie,* 49 (1974), 305–22, esp. pp. 306–8; and S. G. Papadopoulos, "Thomas in Byzanz," *Theologie und Philosophie,* 49 (1974), 274–304, esp. pp. 296–97 and pp. 303–4.

26. For the *War of Troy,* see, for example, E. M. Jeffreys, "The Later Greek Verse Romances: A Survey," *Byzantine Papers* (Canberra, 1981), pp. 116–27 (bibliography in notes 1 and 43). For *Belisarius,* see, for example, E. Follieri, "Il poema bizantino di Belisario," *Atti del Convegno Internazionale sul tema: La poesia epica e la sua formazione* (Rome, 1970), pp. 583–651; H.-G. Beck, *Geschichte der byzantinischen Volksliteratur* (Munich, 1971), pp. 150–53 (with references to Beck's other writings on *Belisarius*). For an interesting literary analysis of the late romances, see A. Aleksidze, *Mir grečeskogo rycarskogo romana XIII–XIV vv* (Tbilisi, 1979). (A French résumé is found on pp. 305–16.)

27. On paraphrases or "metaphrases," see my "Levels of Style," esp. pp. 309–12, and my "Additional Remarks," esp. pp. 23, 226–27, 238.

28. For proof that George Oinaiotes is the same man as the *Anonymus* of Florence, author of an elegant collection of letters, see St. I. Kourouses, Μανουὴλ Γαβαλᾶς . . . , I (1972), 105–9.

29. See E. M. Jeffreys, "Constantine Hermoniakos and Byzantine Education," *Dodone,* 4 (1975), 81–109.

30. Demetrios Kydones, *Speech to John V,* ed. R.-J. Loenerz, *Studi e Testi,* 186 (1956), 22, lines 9–10; and Kydones, *Letter* to Simon Atumanos, in Loenerz, 141, lines 65–66 and 76–79. The former is dated 1371; the latter, 1367–68.

31. In addition to Kydones's, the lives of Manuel Kalekas (d. 1410) and Maximos Chrysoberges (d. ca. 1430) followed this pattern.

32. On Argyropoulos, see, for example, E. Bigi, "Argiropulo,

Giovanni," in *Dizionario biografico degli Italiani*, 4 (1962), 129–31;
and D. Geanakoplos, "The Italian Renaissance and Byzantium: The
Career of the Greek Humanist—Professor John Argyropoulos in Florence and Rome (1415–1487)," *Conspectus of History*, I, 1 (1974), 12–
28. On Chrysoloras, see, for example, I. Thomson, "Manuel Chrysoloras and the Early Italian Renaissance," *Greek, Roman and Byzantine Studies*, 7 (1966), 63–82. See, in general, P. O. Kristeller, *Renaissance Thought*, pp. 137–50, 297–300; and from the Greek scholarly point of view, D. A. Zakythinos, Τὸ πρόβλημα τῆς Ἑλληνικῆς
συμβολῆς εἰς τὴν Ἀναγέννησιν, reprinted in idem, Μεταβυζαντινὰ
καὶ Νέα Ἑλληνικά (Athens, 1978), pp. 229–43 (see also pp. 130–228 of
this book).

33. See P. Miljković-Pepek, *Deloto na zografite Mihailo i Eutihij*
(Skopje, 1967). (A French résumé is found on pp. 245–63.)

34. On Theophanes the Greek, see V. N. Lazarev, *Feofan Grek i
ego škola* (Moscow, 1961); and M. V. Alpatov, *Feofan Grek* (Moscow,
1979). See also G. I. Vzdornov, *Iskusstvo knigi v Drevnej Rusi* (Moscow, 1980), pp. 103–5.

35. See H. Belting, "Le peintre Manuel Eugénikos de Constantinople, en Géorgie," *Cahiers Archéologiques*, 28 (1979), 103–14. See also
D. Mouriki, in *Jahrbuch der Österreichischen Byzantinistik*, 31/2
(1981), esp. pp. 749 et seq.

36. See my *Society and Intellectual Life*, item I, p. 92.

37. The twin inscriptions of the Tempio Malatestiano run as follows: "Sigismund Pandolfo Malatesta, son of Pandolfo, having victori-
ously overcome the exceedingly many and grave dangers in the course
of the Italic War, and obtained, in such a critical circumstance, what
he had prayed for, has raised up, for the sake of his accomplishments—so manly and so felicitous—this temple to the Immortal God
and to the City at a magnanimous expense, leaving behind a monu-
ment both famous and hallowed." See M. Aronberg Lavin, "Piero
della Francesca's Fresco of Sigismondo Pandolfo Malatesta before St.
Sigismund," *Art Bulletin*, 56 (1974), 345–74, esp. pp. 345–46 (translation, photograph, and transcription); and eadem, "The Antique
Source for the Tempio Malatestiano's Greek Inscriptions," *Art Bulletin*, 59 (1977), 421–22. The twin inscriptions date from the fifties of
the fifteenth century. Their remarkably regular lettering is eclectic,
but for the most part genuinely antique. The only instances of incon-
gruity are the undersized *omicrons*, reminding one of the omicrons in
the literary papyri of the second century A.D. and the *hederae*, or ivy
leaves (in Greek inscriptions, their use begins in the Roman period).
As for the formulae, "for the sake of" and "having obtained . . . what
he had prayed for" have a nonclassical sound: they occur with some

frequency in Christian inscriptions of the fifth and sixth centuries. See the examples I adduced in *Dumbarton Oaks Papers*, 17 (1963), 394–95.

38. The (by now unfortunately destroyed) inscription runs: "John Palaiologos, the faithful Emperor and Sole Ruler of the Romans in Christ the Lord; in the month of August of the 4th indiction of the year 6949 [1441]." See B. Meyer-Plath and A. M. Schneider, *Die Landmauer von Konstantinopel*, II (Berlin, 1943), 140. The only Byzantine inscription known to me that employs the antique forms of *sigma* and *omega* is that on the walls of Ankara. It dates from the reign of Michael III (murdered 867) and has a non-antique overall appearance.

Selected and Annotated Bibliography

Introduction: Renaissances and Dark Ages

Bolgar, R. R. *The Classical Heritage and Its Beneficiaries* (Cambridge, 1973). Covers the period of the present book plus the Renaissance, but is more concerned with the Classics and less concerned with Late Antiquity and the Middle Ages.

Bowen, James. *A History of Western Education,* vols. 1 and 2 (London, 1972–75). A readable general survey, extending from 2000 B.C. to A.D. 1600.

Curtius, Ernest R. *European Literature and the Latin Middle Ages,* trans. Willard R. Trask (New York, 1953). Analytic rather than chronological and somewhat idiosyncratic, but wide-ranging and perceptive.

Dawson, Christopher. *The Making of Europe: An Introduction to the History of European Unity* (New York, 1936). A general cultural history of both East and West from about 200 to 1000, sympathetic to medieval and particularly to Christian culture.

Ferguson, Wallace K. *The Renaissance in Historical Thought: Five Centuries of Interpretation* (Boston, 1948). A masterly work of intellectual history; includes many references to modern interpretations of pre-Renaissance times.

Geanakoplos, Deno J. *Interaction of the "Sibling" Byzantine and Western Cultures in the Middle Ages and Italian Renaissance (330–1600)* (New Haven, 1976). A collection of studies, most of which focus on Byzantine influence on the Italian Renaissance.

Ker, W. P. *The Dark Ages* (London, 1904). A literary history of the West from about 500 to 1000. Old but still a classic.

Mullet, M., and R. Scott, eds. *Byzantium and the Classical Tradition* (Birmingham, 1981). A collection of papers by different scholars.

Panofsky, Erwin. *Renaissance and Renascences in Western Art* (Stockholm, 1960). Explores the idea of a renaissance, but understandably has little to do with literature.

Reynolds, L. D., and N. Wilson. *Scribes and Scholars: A Guide to the Transmission of Greek and Latin Literature*, 2d ed. (Oxford, 1974). Reliable treatment of a subject closely related to cultural revivals.

Sandys, J. E. *A History of Classical Scholarship*, vol. 1: *From the Sixth Century B.C. to the End of the Middle Ages*, 3d ed. (Cambridge, 1921). Outdated but not superseded for the present purpose. Rudolf Pfeiffer's two volumes entitled *A History of Classical Scholarship* (Oxford, 1968–76), reflecting the limited interests of many traditionalists, simply skip the years from A.D. 1 to 1300.

Toynbee, Arnold. *A Study of History*, vol. 9: *Part X. Contacts Between Civilizations in Time (Renaissances)* (London, 1954), pp. 1–166. Includes a survey of "renaissances," which are seen primarily (and exaggeratedly) as Western rediscoveries of Greek culture.

Chapter 1. The Second Sophistic

Bowersock, G. W., *Greek Sophists in the Roman Empire* (Oxford, 1969). An examination of their social and political importance.

Bowersock, G. W., ed. *Approaches to the Second Sophistic* (University Park, Pa., 1974). Includes an extensive bibliography for the Second Sophistic. All the papers are useful.

Bowie, E. L. "Greeks and Their Past in the Second Sophistic," *Past and Present*, 46 (1970), 3–41. A detailed analysis of archaism in the literature of the period; central to the topic of the present paper.

———. "The Importance of Sophists," in J. J. Winkler and G. Williams, eds., *Later Greek Literature*, Yale Classical Studies 27 (New York and Cambridge, 1982), pp. 29–59. A response to Bowersock's *Greek Sophists*, modifying his conclusions.

Kennedy, G. A. *The Art of Rhetoric in the Roman World* (Princeton, 1972). Chapter 8, "The Age of the Sophists," is a comprehensive account of the movement and its main figures, as well as of contemporary Latin and Christian rhetoric. Chapter 9 gives an account of the theorists of rhetoric.

Lesky, A. *A History of Greek Literature*, trans. J. Willis and C. de Heer from German 2d ed., Bern 1963 (London, 1966), pp. 829–45. Among standard literary histories, this is the most up-to-date and authoritative for this period.

Perry, B. E. "Literature in the Second Century," *Classical Journal*, 50 (1955), 295–98. A brief characterization of the literature of the period. See also Perry, *The Ancient Romances: A Literary-Historical*

Account of Their Origins (Berkeley, 1967), Part I, for the relationship between academic literary tradition and romance.

Philostratus, *Lives of the Sophists*, ed. and trans. W. C. Wright (London, 1921; Loeb Classical Library). The basic ancient text on the Second Sophistic.

Reardon, B. P. *Courants littéraires grecs des IIe et IIIe siècles après J.-C.* (Paris, 1971). Fuller treatment of most major authors and associated topics.

Russell, D. A. *Greek Declamation* (Cambridge, 1983). An authoritative and thoughtful account.

Van Groningen, B. A. "Literary Tendencies in the Second Century A.D.," *Mnemosyne*, 18 (1965), 41–56. Another brief treatment.

Winkler, John J., and Gordon Williams, eds. *Later Greek Literature*, Yale Classical Studies 27 (New York and Cambridge, 1982). Relevant contributions are those by B. P. Reardon, E. L. Bowie, Graham Anderson, and John J. Winkler.

Chapter 2. The Latin Revival of the Fourth Century

Alföldi, A. *Die Kontorniaten: ein verkanntes Propagandamittel der stadtrömischen Aristokratie in ihrem Kampfe gegen das christliche Kaisertum* (Budapest, 1942–43). Highly influential explanation of cultural revival in terms of pagan propaganda.

Bloch, H. "A New Document of the Last Pagan Revival in the West, 393–394 A.D.," *Harvard Theological Review*, 38 (1945), 199–244.

Brown, P. *Augustine of Hippo: A biography* (Berkeley, 1967).

———. *Religion and Society in the Age of Saint Augustine* (London, 1972). Both of Brown's books offer provocative new insights on the intellectual world of the late fourth and fifth centuries.

Cameron, Alan. "The Date and Identity of Macrobius," *Journal of Roman Studies*, 56 (1966), 25–38.

———. *Claudian: Poetry and Propaganda at the Court of Honorius* (Oxford, 1970).

———. "Paganism and Literature in Late Fourth Century Rome," in M. Fuhrmann, ed., *Christianisme et formes littéraires de l'antiquité tardive* (*Entretiens sur l'antiquité classique* XXIII; Fondation Hardt, Geneva, 1977), pp. 1–40.

———. *The Last Pagans of Rome* (forthcoming). A comprehensive study of the themes treated in Chapter 2 of this volume.

Cavallo, G. "Libro e pubblico alla fine del mondo antico," in idem, ed., *Libri, editori e pubblico nel mondo antico*, 2d ed. (Laterza, 1977), pp. 83–132. The best study of books and manuscripts in Late Antiquity.

Courcelle, P. *Late Latin Writers and Their Greek Sources*, trans. H. E. Wedeck (Cambridge, Mass., 1969). The standard work on knowledge of Greek in the late fourth- to sixth-century West.

Fuhrmann, M. "Die lateinische Literatur in der Spätantike," *Antike und Abendland*, 13 (1967), 56–79. On the third-century break.

Kitzinger, E. *Byzantine Art in the Making* (Cambridge, Mass., 1977). A good account of the late fourth-century artistic "Renaissance."

Levine, P. "The Continuity and Preservation of the Latin Tradition," in Lynn White, Jr., ed., *The Transformation of the Roman World: Gibbon's Problem after Two Centuries* (Berkeley, 1966), pp. 206–31.

Liebeschuetz, J. H. W. G. *Continuity and Change in Roman Religion* (Oxford, 1979).

Lommatsch, E. "Litterarische Bewegungen in Rom im vierten und fünften Jhdt. n. Chr." *Zeitschrift für vergleichende Litteraturgeschichte*, 15 (1904), 177–92. Very influential exaggeration of the role of the senatorial aristocracy.

MacCormack, S. *Art and Ceremony in Late Antiquity* (Berkeley, 1981). On the revival of rhetoric and panegyric.

Marrou, H.-I. *S. Augustin et la fin du culture antique* (Paris, 1938). Should be read together with the same author's *Retractatio* (Paris, 1949), in which he modifies his brilliant picture of "un lettré de la decadence." Both works were reprinted in one volume in 1958.

Matthews, J. *Western Aristocracies and Imperial Court A.D. 364–425* (Oxford, 1975). An excellent analysis of the social and political background.

Momigliano, A., ed. *The Conflict Between Paganism and Christianity in the Fourth Century* (Oxford, 1963). The best introduction to the world of the fourth century.

Schanz, M. *Geschichte der römischen Literatur*, Vol. 4.1 (Munich, 1914) and vol. 4.2 (with C. Hosius and G. Krüger, Munich, 1920). The only comprehensive and detailed account of the Latin writers of Late Antiquity; still indispensable.

Syme, R. *Ammianus and the 'Historia Augusta'* (Oxford, 1968). An evocative picture of historical writing in the fourth century.

Zetzel, J. E. G. *Latin Textual Criticism in Antiquity* (New York, 1981). An up-to-date critical account of the editing of texts in Late Antiquity.

Chapter 3. The Carolingian Renaissance

Braunfels, Wolfgang et al., eds. *Karl der Grosse: Lebenswerk und Nachleben*, 5 vols. (Düsseldorf, 1965–68). Volume 2, *Das geistige*

Leben, edited by Bernhard Bischoff, focuses on the motives and products of the renaissance.

Brunhölzl, Franz. *Geschichte der lateinischen Literatur des Mittelalters*, vol. 1 (Munich, 1975). Brunhölzl not only brings Manitius (see below) up to date, he also casts a wider net and surveys all types of Latin writings.

Bullough, Donald A. *The Age of Charlemagne*, 2d ed. (London, 1973). An important interpretation of Carolingian history; accompanied by numerous, well-chosen illustrations.

——. "*Europae Pater*: Charlemagne and His Achievement in the Light of Recent Scholarship," *English Historical Review*, 75 (1975), 59–105. An important interpretive review of the 1965 *Karl der Grosse* volumes (see above), with references to additional research.

Gibson, Margaret, and Janet Nelson, eds. *Charles the Bald: Court and Kingdom*, British Archaeological Reports, International Series 101 (Oxford, 1981). An important collection of essays, many of which discuss aspects of the late ninth-century renaissance.

Halphen, Louis. *Charlemagne and the Carolingian Empire* (New York, 1978). This classic work, first published in France in 1947, provides a good introduction to Carolingian political history.

Hubert, Jean, Jean Porcher, and Wolfgang F. Volbach. *L'Empire carolingien* (Paris, 1968). An exquisite guide to Carolingian art forms with extensive illustrations, maps, indices, glossaries, and bibliography.

Laistner, M. L. W. *Thought and Letters in Western Europe, A.D. 500–900*, 2d ed. (Ithaca, 1957). First published in 1931, *Thought and Letters* remains a convenient introduction to Carolingian authors. It is based largely on Manitius's *Geschichte der lateinischen Literatur* (see below) and on Laistner's own soundings in Carolingian textual and intellectual history.

McKitterick, Rosamond. *The Frankish Church and the Carolingian Reforms, 789–895*, Royal Historical Society Studies in History 2 (London, 1977). This important volume traces the impact of the renaissance on the Christian people by examining the episcopal and monastic response to the Carolingian reform program.

——. *The Frankish Kingdoms under the Carolingians, 751–987* (New York, 1983). This learned book has excellent chapters on the foundations of the Carolingian renaissance and on scholarship, book production, and libraries in the Frankish kingdoms.

Manitius, Max. *Geschichte der lateinischen Literatur des Mittelalters*, vol. 1 (Munich, 1911). Manitius defined literature narrowly and excluded from his discussion theological and liturgical works. Nevertheless, his handbook treatment of Carolingian authors is still a useful guide to the older secondary literature, to editions, and, especially, to the manuscripts.

Medioevo latino: Bollettino bibliografico della cultura europea dal secolo VI al XIII. This new bibliographical guide, the first volume of which was published in Spoleto in 1980 by the Centro italiano di studi sull'alto medioevo, provides a convenient means to keep abreast of new work on Carolingian authors and texts.

Morrison, Karl F. *The Two Kingdoms: Ecclesiology in Carolingian Political Thought* (Princeton, 1964). An important exploration of change and conflict in Carolingian theories of government.

Nascità dell'Europa ed Europa carolingia: Un'equazione da verificare, 2 vols. Settimane di studio del Centro italiano di studi sull'alto medioevo 27 (Spoleto, 1981). Contains an important recent examination of Carolingian culture by leading specialists, many of whom address the question of unity and variety in Carolingian intellectual life.

I problemi comuni dell'Europa post-Carolingia. Settimane di studio del Centro italiano di studi sull'alto medioevo 2 (Spoleto, 1955). Focuses largely on the political and economic legacies of the Carolingians. Art and culture are considered as well.

I problemi della civiltà carolingia. Settimane di studio del Centro italiano di studi sull'alto medioevo 1 (Spoleto, 1954). This first fruit of the annual April meeting of leading specialists in early medieval studies contains an important discussion of the "problem" of the Carolingian renaissance.

Revue d'histoire ecclésiastique. This periodical, published in Leuven (Louvain), Belgium, contains an extensive bibliography, much of which is useful for keeping up on research in Carolingian studies.

Riché, Pierre. *Education and Culture in the Barbarian West from the Sixth through the Eighth Century,* trans. John J. Contreni (Columbia, S.C., 1976). A fundamental guide to the background of the Carolingian renaissance with an extensive bibliography.

———. *Daily Life in the World of Charlemagne,* trans. Jo Ann McNamara (Philadelphia, 1978). Although its bibliographical apparatus is not as full as in the two other titles listed here by Riché, who is the leading scholar of early medieval culture and education, this book provides a good introduction to themes rarely treated in general studies of the Carolingian period.

———. *Les Écoles et l'enseignement dans l'Occident de la fin du Ve siècle au milieu du IXe siècle* (Paris, 1979). A synthesis based on the results of Riché's own research and more than six hundred studies by other scholars.

La scuola nell'Occidente latino dell'alto medioevo, 2 vols. Settimane di studio del Centro italiano di studi sull'alto medioevo 19 (Spoleto, 1972). Important for the institutional history of culture, as well as for Carolingian schools.

Sullivan, Richard E. *Aix-la-Chapelle in the Age of Charlemagne* (Norman, 1963). An excellent guide to the nerve center of the renaissance, couched in a sensitive interpretation of the ideas and ideals that animated the Carolingians.

Ullmann, Walter. *The Carolingian Renaissance and the Idea of Kingship: The Birkbeck Lectures, 1968–69* (London, 1969). Links the renaissance to the Carolingian concern for society as a whole.

Chapter 4. The Macedonian Renaissance

Alexander, Paul. *The Patriarch Nicephorus of Constantinople* (Oxford, 1958). A study of the life, times, and writings of that scholar-Patriarch.

Beck, Hans-Georg. *Kirche und theologische Literatur im byzantinischen Reich* (Munich, 1959). The standard history of Byzantine religious literature.

———. *Geschichte der byzantinischen Volksliteratur* (Munich, 1971). The standard history of Byzantine literature in nonclassicizing Greek.

Bryer, Anthony, and Judith Herrin, eds. *Iconoclasm* (Birmingham, 1977). Studies, several related to literature and education, by various scholars.

Byzantine Books and Bookmen (Washington, D.C., 1975). Studies by different authors, largely dealing with the Macedonian period.

Hunger, Herbert. *Die hochsprachliche profane Literatur der Byzantiner* (Munich, 1978). The standard history of secular Byzantine literature in classicizing Greek.

Hussey, Joan. *Church and Learning in the Byzantine Empire, 867–1185* (London, 1937). Now mostly superseded by the French and German works listed here, but useful for those who want a study in English.

Lemerle, Paul. *Le Premier Humanisme byzantin* (Paris, 1971). The best and fullest survey of the Macedonian renaissance.

Mango, Cyril. *Byzantium: The Empire of New Rome* (London, 1980). A history of Byzantine civilization, largely concerned with the period of the Macedonian renaissance.

Speck, Paul. *Die kaiserliche Universität von Konstantinopel* (Munich, 1974). Generally persuasive refutation of earlier, poorly substantiated theories of an "imperial university" at Constantinople.

Toynbee, Arnold. *Constantine Poryphyrogenitus and His World* (Ox-

ford, 1973). Not always reliable, but contains much useful information, including a treatment of Constantine's activity as a scholar.

Treadgold, Warren. *The Nature of the 'Bibliotheca' of Photius* (Washington, D.C., 1980). An introduction to that work of Byzantine
scholarship.

Chapter 5. The Anglo-Saxon Monastic Revival

Aethelwold. Saint. *Regularis Concordia: The Monastic Agreement of
the Monks and Nuns of the English Nation*, ed. and trans. Dom
Thomas Symons (London, 1953). Dom Symons presents not only
the best edition and translation of the *Concordia* but also a splendid
introduction.

Campbell, James, ed. *The Anglo-Saxons* (Oxford and Ithaca, 1982). A
survey of Anglo-Saxon history with essays and copious illustrations. Eric John's "The Age of Edgar" discusses the government and
institutions of the tenth century.

Clemoes, Peter, ed. *Anglo-Saxon England*, 12 vols. to date (Cambridge, 1972–). An annual publication; usually contains at least one
major article about the tenth century.

Graham, R. "The Intellectual Influence of English Monasticism Between the Tenth and the Twelfth Centuries," *Transactions of the
Royal Historical Society*, n.s. 17 (1903), 23–65. Old but still valuable; a succinct, highly informative historical survey based mainly
on primary sources.

John, Eric. *Orbis Britanniae and Other Studies* (Bristol, 1966). The
latter part of this book contains some astute, challenging essays
about the tenth-century reform. John generally casts Dunstan as
the elder statesman and Aethelwold as the experienced reformer
and administrator of the reform (see, for instance, p. 161).

Knowles, Dom David. *The Monastic Order in England: A History of
Its Development from the Times of St. Dunstan to the Fourth
Lateran Council, 940–1216*, 2d ed. (Cambridge, 1963). The master
historian of English monasticism provides the most complete, if a
somewhat bland, account of the tenth-century reform.

Meyer, Marc Anthony. "Women and the Tenth Century English Monastic Reform," *Revue benedictine*, 87 (1977), 34–61. An interesting discussion of women's contributions to the success of the monastic reform.

Parsons, David, ed. *Tenth-Century Studies: Essays in Commemora-
tion of the Millennium of the Council of Winchester and 'Regularis
Concordia'* (Chichester, 1975). A mixed collection by various
scholars; Chapters 2, 3, 5, and 7 make important contributions.

Raine, James, ed. *The Historians of the Church of York and Its Arch-bishops*, 2 vols., Rolls 71 (London, 1879; reprint ed., London, 1965). A collection of the main sources for our knowledge of York and its archbishops, such as Oskytel and Oswald.

Robinson, J. Armitage. *The Times of Saint Dunstan* (1923; reprint ed., Oxford, 1969). Although some of its statements have been challenged, this study contains many salient details that are still valid and interesting.

Stenton, F. M. *Anglo-Saxon England*, 3d ed. (Oxford, 1971). The standard, unsurpassed scholarly history of Anglo-Saxon England, with important sections on the Benedictine reform (pp. 364–72, 433–62, esp. pp. 456–57, 460–62).

Stevenson, Joseph, ed. *Chronicon Monasterii de Abingdon*, vol. 1 (London, 1858). The second book (pp. 121ff.) contains the histories of Aethelwold and his associates and of the kings of Wessex during this period.

Stubbs, William, ed. *Memorials of Saint Dunstan, Edited from Various Manuscripts*, Rolls 63 (London, 1874; reprint ed., London, 1965). Contains the earliest and most reliable life of Saint Dunstan, by "B," as well as important documents, letters, and later lives.

Whitelock, Dorothy, ed., *English Historical Documents, c. 500–1042* (London, 1968). A comprehensive volume that contains, among other items pertinent to our study, a translation of the *Anglo-Saxon Chronicle*, charters and laws, and ecclesiastical sources.

William of Malmesbury. *De Gestis Pontificium Anglorum libri quinque*, ed. N. E. S. A. Hamilton, Rolls 52 (London, 1870). Although William of Malmesbury composed this history in the twelfth century, many of his sources were nearly contemporary and he is one of the "most trustworthy chroniclers" (p. vii). The deeds of Dunstan and his contemporaries are recounted in Book 1.

Chapter 6. The Twelfth-Century Renaissance

Baldwin, John W. *Masters, Princes and Merchants: The Social Views of Peter the Chanter and His Circle*, 2 vols. (Princeton, 1970). An important study of the efforts of a group of theologians who were active in Paris in the late twelfth century to address their learning to social issues.

————. *The Scholastic Culture of the Middle Ages, 1000–1300* (Lexington, Mass., 1971). A useful interpretive study of how education, thought, and art developed within the cities.

Benson, Robert L., and Giles Constable, eds. *Renaissance and Renewal in the Twelfth Century* (Cambridge, Mass., 1982). Twenty-six studies, originally written to commemorate the fiftieth anniversary of Haskins's *The Twelfth-Century Renaissance.* Topics include the thought, religion, literature, art, architecture, and social foundations of the renaissance.

Bloch, Marc. *Feudal Society,* 2 vols., trans. L. A. Manyon (Chicago, 1961). The classic study of feudalism as a social and political system; especially valuable for its analysis of the mental aspect of social changes.

Brooke, Christopher. *The Twelfth Century Renaissance* (London, 1969). A beautifully illustrated introductory essay that focuses on the achievements of several key figures of the period.

Chenu, Marie-Dominique. *La Théologie au douzième siècle,* 3d ed. (Paris, 1976). A landmark study; selected articles have been translated by Jerome Taylor and Lester K. Little in *Nature, Man, and Society in the Twelfth Century: Essays on New Theological Perspectives in the West* (Chicago, 1968).

Clagett, Marshall, Gaines Post, and Robert Reynolds, eds. *Twelfth-Century Europe and the Foundations of Modern Society* (Madison, 1966). A useful collection of essays about intellectual and social developments and about Eastern influences on twelfth-century culture.

de Gandillac, Maurice, and Edouard Jeauneau, eds. *Entretiens sur la renaissance du 12ᵉ siècle* (Paris, 1968). The proceedings of a 1965 conference; includes important studies of thought, literature, and art.

Duby, Georges, *The Early Growth of the European Economy: Warriors and Peasants from the Seventh to the Twelfth Century,* trans. H. B. Clarke (Ithaca, 1974). An essay on the social and economic changes that helped make the cultural advances of the twelfth century possible.

Grane, Leif. *Peter Abelard: Philosophy and Christianity in the Middle Ages,* trans. F. Crowley and C. Crowley (London, 1964). An excellent, brief introduction to the intellectual changes and controversies of the early twelfth century.

Haskins, Charles Homer. *The Renaissance of the Twelfth Century* (Cambridge, Mass., 1927). The pioneering work that established the idea of the twelfth-century renaissance.

———. *The Rise of the Universities* (Ithaca, 1957). Originally written as a series of lectures in 1923, this work remains the best short introduction to the origins of the university.

Hollister, C. Warren, ed. *The Twelfth-Century Renaissance* (New York, 1969). A useful collection of interpretive essays and sources.

Holmes, Urban T. *Daily Living in the Twelfth Century* (Madison, 1952). A mine of interesting information about the period based on the observations of Alexander Neckham.

Knowles, David. *The Evolution of Medieval Thought* (New York, 1962). The best general introduction to the subject.

Leclercq, Jean. *The Love of Learning and the Desire for God,* 2d ed., trans. C. Misrahi (New York, 1974). The essential study of monastic thought and culture.

LeGoff, Jacques. *Les Intellectuels au moyen âge* (Paris, 1957). A very important essay on medieval thought and education.

Mayer, Hans E. *The Crusades,* trans. John Gillingham (Oxford, 1972). A comprehensive and lucid study of this important subject.

Moore, John C. *Love in Twelfth-Century France* (Philadelphia, 1972). A pleasant study on a theme central both to the religious and secular literature of the period.

Morris, Colin. *The Discovery of the Individual, 1050–1200* (New York, 1972). A very learned and lucid book that makes a strong case in support of its provocative thesis.

Murray, Alexander. *Reason and Society in the Middle Ages* (Oxford, 1978). A difficult but important book that relates intellectual and cultural changes to the increased circulation and importance of money.

Panofsky, Erwin. *Renaissance and Renascences in Western Art* (New York, 1969). Critical studies of the concept of renaissance.

Paré, Gérard, A. Brunet, and P. Tremblay. *La Renaissance du douzième siècle: Les Écoles et l'enseignement* (Paris and Ottawa, 1933). The standard work on the schools and Scholasticism.

Pirenne, Henri. *Medieval Cities: The Origins and the Revival of Trade,* trans. F. D. Halsey (Princeton, 1952). The classic and still essential study of the rise and importance of cities.

Southern, Richard W. *The Making of the Middle Ages* (New Haven, 1953). A brilliant and beautifully written study of the achievements of the eleventh and twelfth centuries.

———. *Medieval Humanism and Other Essays* (New York, 1970). A collection of important studies of medieval thought and life, mostly on the twelfth century.

Tierney, Brian. *The Crisis of Church and State, 1050–1300* (Englewood Cliffs, N.J., 1964). A very useful collection of sources and of interpretation on the lengthy dispute between popes and kings that was so important to the political development of Europe.

von Simson, Otto. *The Gothic Cathedral: Origins of Gothic Architecture and the Medieval Concept of Order* (Princeton, 1962). An important study of the origins of Gothic form.

Chapter 7. The Palaeologan Renaissance

Art et société à Byzance sous les Paléologues (Venice, 1971). Proceedings of a colloquium held in Venice in September of 1968. Contributions pertaining to art history, sociology of art (patronage), intellectual history, and literature (by A. Grabar, D. A. Zakythinos, I. Ševčenko, H.-G. Beck, J. Meyendorff, A. C. Orlandos, A. Xyngopoulos, T. Velmans, H. Belting, and V. J. Djurić).

Beck, H.-G. *Theodoros Metochites, Die Krise des byzantinischen Weltbildes im 14. Jahrhundert* (Munich, 1952). Brilliant analysis of Metochites's outlook, based on his Essays.

————. *Kirche und theologische Literatur im byzantinischen Reich* (Munich, 1959). Standard reference volume on ecclesiastical authors and their works.

————. *Geschichte der byzantinischen Volksliteratur* (Munich, 1971). Standard work on popular literature. See Section III (pp. 117–53) on late-Byzantine romances.

Geanakoplos, D. *Greek Scholars in Venice* (Cambridge, Mass., 1962). Deals with Byzantines active as scholars, teachers, scribes, and printers after 1453. "Venice" in the title includes Venetian possessions in the Levant.

————. *Byzantine East and Latin West: Two Worlds of Christendom in Middle Ages and Renaissance* (New York and Evanston, 1966). See Part I, Chapter 3, on the Council of Florence; see Part II, Chapters 4–5, on Venice and Crete as transmitters of Byzantine culture to the west during the Renaissance and later.

————. *Interaction of the "Sibling" Byzantine and Western Cultures in the Middle Ages and Italian Renaissance (330–1660)* (New Haven, 1976), esp. Chapters 9–14, mostly devoted to the vicissitudes of Greek scholars (from Byzantium or Venetian possessions in the Levant) in the West.

————. "A Reevaluation of the Influences of Byzantine Scholars on the Development of the *Studia Humanitatis*, Metaphysics, Patristics, and Science in the Italian Renaissance (1361–c. 1521)," *Proceedings of the PMR Conference* [Annual Publication of the Patristic, Mediaeval, and Renaissance Conference, Augustinian Historical Institute, Villanova University], 3 (1978), 1–25. Up-to-date report on the contribution that Byzantine emigré scholars made to Renaissance thought and learning. Ample footnotes.

Gill, J. *The Council of Florence* (Cambridge, 1959 and 1961). Most dependable and thorough narrative history of the council.

Hunger, H. "Von Wissenschaft und Kunst der frühen Palaiologenzeit," *Jahrbuch der Österreichischen byzantinischen Gesellschaft,*

8 (1959), 123–55. Well-drawn general picture. Lists Palaeologan manuscripts that are the oldest or the best witnesses for their respective antique authors.

———. *Die hochsprachliche profane Literatur der Byzantiner*, 2 vols. (Munich, 1978). Standard reference volumes on Byzantine secular literature in high and middle styles.

Kristeller, P. O. *Renaissance Thought and Its Sources* (New York, 1979). See Part Three, "Renaissance Thought and Byzantine Learning," pp. 137–63, and important notes, pp. 297–306. Concise but masterly survey of Italian Humanism's indebtedness to Byzantium, in part resting on the evidence of manuscripts, manuscript catalogues, translations, and comings and goings of scholars.

Masai, F. *Pléthon et le Platonisme de Mistra* (Paris, 1956). Still the best treatment of Plethon, of his attitudes toward the Hellenic past and Orthodox religion, and of his various milieus.

Medvedev, I. P. *Vizantijskij gumanizm XIV–XV vv.* (Leningrad, 1976). On the intellectual world of Late Byzantine humanists. The author uses primary sources. Appendix I discusses Plethon's works and offers a Russian translation of parts of the *Laws*.

———. "Neue philosophische Ansätze im späten Byzanz," *Jahrbuch der Österreichischen Byzantinistik*, 31 (1981), 529–48. On original traits in the writings of late Byzantine philosophers and theologians. The author applies notions of semiotics when interpreting (and praising) the system of Plethon.

Meyendorff, J. *A Study of Gregory Palamas*, trans. A. Laurence (London, 1964). Somewhat shortened but updated version of the French original published in 1959. Still the most authoritative study.

———. *Byzantine Hesychasm: Historical, Theological, and Social Problems. Collected Studies* (London, 1974). Sixteen previously published articles; items 6 and 8 deal with intellectual history.

Nicol, D. M. *The Last Centuries of Byzantium, 1261–1453* (London, 1972). Reliable, thorough, and well-written narrative. Good bibliography.

———. *Chuch and Society in the Last Centuries of Byzantium* (Cambridge, 1979). These Birkbeck Lectures of 1977 represent the most up-to-date treatment of some basic intellectual trends in late Byzantium. The book contains ample bibliography.

Prosopographisches Lexikon der Palaiologenzeit (Vienna, 1976–). This computer-generated work (so far consisting of 15,236 entries to the end of L) gives up-to-date biographical and bibliographical information on all personalities of the period.

Runciman, S. *The Last Byzantine Renaissance* (Cambridge, 1970). In this short book (the Wiles Lectures for 1968), a great narrative historian gives a bird's-eye view of the topic of the present chapter.

―――. *Byzantium and the Renaissance* (Tucson, Arizona, 1970). A pleasant vignette of Byzantine intellectuals settling in the West, a "brain drain on . . . a distinguished scale."

Setton, K. M. "The Byzantine Background to the Italian Renaissance," *Proceedings of the American Philosophical Society,* 100 (1956), 1–76. Still the best treatment of the subject, offered against an ample background in space and time.

Ševčenko, I. "Intellectual Repercussions of the Council of Florence," *Church History,* 24 (1955), 291–323. Reprinted as item IX in the same author's *Ideology, Letters, and Culture in the Byzantine World* (London, 1982). On intellectual attitudes before, during, and after the Council, down to our century.

―――. "The Decline of Byzantium Seen Through the Eyes of Its Intellectuals," *Dumbarton Oaks Papers,* 15 (1961), 169–86. Reprinted as item II in the same author's *Society and Intellectual Life in Late Byzantium* (London, 1981). The views that intellectuals of the thirteenth through fifteenth centuries held of themselves, their state and its future, the Turks, and the West.

―――. "Society and Intellectual Life in the Fourteenth Century," *Actes du XIVe Congrès International des études byzantines,* 1 (1974), 69–92. Reprinted as item 1 in the same author's *Society and Intellectual Life in Late Byzantium.* A statistical study of numbers, social standing, attitudes, and views of Palaeologan intellectuals.

Underwood, P., ed. *The Kariye Djami,* IV: *Studies in the Art of the Kariye Djami and Its Intellectual Background* (Princeton, 1975). On the art of the Chora Monastery and on artistic, spiritual, and intellectual trends at the time of its reconstruction and decoration (essays by A. Grabar, I. Ševčenko, J. Meyendorff, O. Demus, J. Lafontaine-Dosogne, P. Underwood, and Sirarpie Der Nersessian).

Verpeaux, J. *Nicéphore Choumnos, homme d'état et humaniste byzantin* (Paris, 1959). A solid work, on the chief political and literary rival of Metochites.

Wilson, N. G. *Scholars of Byzantium* (Baltimore, Md., 1983). See Chapter 12, "The Palaeologan Revival," and Chapter 13, "The Epigoni." The best treatment of the philological aspect of our topic, both in terms of presentation and substance. The author is intimately acquainted with manuscripts reflecting the activity of Palaeologan scholars.

Index

All proper names appear in their Latin or English form except for some mentioned only in Chapter 7, which appear in their Greek form.